Small City on a Big Couch

Contemporary Psychoanalytic Studies
16

Contemporary Psychoanalytic Studies (*CPS*) is an international scholarly book series devoted to all aspects of psychoanalytic inquiry in theoretical, philosophical, applied, and clinical psychoanalysis. Its aims are broadly academic, interdisciplinary, and pluralistic, emphasizing secularism and tolerance across the psychoanalytic domain. CPS aims to promote open and inclusive dialogue among the humanities and the social-behavioral sciences including such disciplines as philosophy, anthropology, history, literature, religion, cultural studies, sociology, feminism, gender studies, political thought, moral psychology, art, drama, and film, biography, law, economics, biology, and cognitive-neuroscience.

Small City on a Big Couch

A Psychoanalysis of a Provincial Mexican City

Karen Rodríguez

Rodopi

Amsterdam - New York, NY 2012

Cover image: Ruiz Camacho, María Guadalupe; "El ritmo de mi cuerpo"
Oil on Canvas, 2011; 60 X 30 cm.

Cover Design: Studio Pollmann

The paper on which this book is printed meets the requirements of "ISO 9706:1994, Information and documentation - Paper for documents - Requirements for permanence".

ISBN: 978-90-420-3507-2
E-Book ISBN: 978-94-012-0783-6

Printed in the Netherlands

Contents

Foreword

In this inventive work Karen Rodriguez imagines the city as analysand on the psychoanalytic couch. She interrogates a key question around the way "the city" digests difference textually and asks readers to conceptualize a psychoanalytic critique of globalization and colonialism through consideration of concepts such as difference, subjectivity, and creativity. Treating the city as an object for analytic inquiry, she elaborates ways in which enigmatic objects may bring to light universal features of our psychic reality; its timelessness, wishful thinking, and exaggerated manifestations. The city performs an enigma that belongs to the psyche: Guanajuato is a city where independence from maternal and paternal Spain is both celebrated and disavowed. As an imagined analysand, the city initially seems to reside in the Lacanian hysterical or borderline positions, characterized by idealistic identification with Spain and with the image of purity, virginity, and femininity. Yet, at the same time, the city refuses to submit to such identifications and rebels against them. Guanajuato is conceptualized as a feminine subject because of its geographical 'curviness' and nonphallic - unruly, irregular and "quirky" – layout; but also, because, in the author's developed fantasy, the city refuses representation. As a patient, the city's narrative is caught in adolescent idealization and displays a passion for ignorance. The city is imagined as an analysand caught in a struggle, refusing abjection yet is inevitably abject. The city, through a phantasized analysis, is shown to leave the place of oscillation (moving towards and away from the Other) through a textual return to its roots that re-writes its history and re-defines its subjectivity. In a way, the city maintains its subjectivity by identifying with impossibility.

Rodriguez enlarges the clinic by treating cultural scenes as analytic objects. By drawing on the theories of Kristeva, Rodriguez posits a way to think about the tension created by a desire for difference and authority as it applies to individual, social, and cultural struggles. Her text calls upon the reader's aesthetic conflict through a style of writing that places the writer herself in an impossible position, as the analyst of a city and the narrator that reads and utters the city's speech. The reader too is invited to engage in reconciliation with impossibility, which leans upon imagination; elaborating the universal and singular ways in which impossibility, reconciliation, and imagination become grounds for transformation.

Oren Gozlan, Psy.D.
Contemporary Psychoanalytic Studies, Editorial Board

Acknowledgments

This book owes an intellectual debt to people in a wide range of places. In the United Kingdom, gratitude to Adrian and Mehri Holliday, Shane Blackman, and Steve Pile for provocative discussions, food, and friendship on both sides of the ocean. Without their critical insight, this work would not have evolved in the same way.

In the United States, gratitude to Clary Loisel at the University of Montana and Joanne Mulcahy at Lewis and Clark University for critical comments and enduring friendships. To Rubén Gallo at Princeton University for his kind reading at the end. To psychoanalyst Karol Marshall and psychotherapist Janice Abarbanel for insights into practice. To Julie Van Pelt for sharp editing offered with humor and goodwill. Gratitude to the Council on International Educational Exchange (CIEE) for financial support for this research. To the editors at the *Delaware Review of Latin American Studies* and *Reconstruction: Studies in Contemporary Culture* for permission to reprint a city description and a previous version of chapter 5, respectively.

In Mexico, gratitude to several anonymous psychologists whose perspectives contributed immensely to my research; to philosopher Dianne Romain, mentor extraordinaire; to my colleagues at the Universidad de Guanajuato, Luis Palacios, Benjamín Valdivia, Randy Walz, Ernesto Camarillo, and Flor Aguilera Navarrete for their local knowledge; and in particular to my two Kristeva-minded graduate students, Rodrigo Rojas Torres and Paola Rebollo Huitrón, who pushed my thinking about Kristeva during the final stages of writing. To Edgar Miranda at the Universidad Autónoma del Estado de México for the opportunity to give a seminar on Kristeva, and to Guadalupe Ruíz Camacho for permission to use a fragment of her beautiful artwork for the cover, and to both for their friendship. In Mexico City, to the curators of the Colección Jumex for permission to use several images from the "Sin techo está pelón" exhibit.

In other far-flung sites, thanks to Sheila Cavanaugh at York University in Toronto for a final critical read, and to Sheila, Bradley Rink at the University of Cape Town, and Christine Hentschel at Humboldt University in Berlin for critical intellectual stimulation, cross-cultural friendships and collaboration. And finally, to Eric van Broekhuizen at Rodopi in Amsterdam and Oren Gozlan in Toronto for their kind support during the publication process.

Most of all, gratitude to Lalo and Lalito. If love is the bottom line for psychic health, as Kristeva argues, they have been my unfailing source.

You see flowers, but after our underground voyage they may seem less external, less decorative.

Kristeva, *Hatred and Forgiveness*, p. 242

One

Small City on a Big Couch

My office in Guanajuato is always cool even on the warmest of days, thanks to the thick 200-year-old colonial walls that surround it. I am pulling a sweater around me when my new analysand comes in. I know her socially; she is familiar to me, but we are not intimates and have never spoken at length. I also know that she writes, but I have not read her work—yet. Although she has a rather striking beauty, her manner is classic provincial. Demure, reserved, composed. I wonder briefly if her writing is this contained, or if perhaps her words break away from such expected demeanor. As I pull my chair closer, she sits down politely on the edge of the couch looking unlikely to relax into it too quickly.

My analysand is a city, and she is poised on my hypothetical couch. In for analysis. An unusual case to say the least. How does one psychoanalyze a city, read her texts, study her language, and pay attention to her body? This will be a new endeavor, but here we are, four hours north of Mexico City, smack in the middle of this large country, together in my office. In the middle of the country and in the middle of our stories, which have apparently now overlapped. In this tiny place that seems to shelter so much otherness despite its tranquil appearance, will she reveal her complexities? Will she have something to say about her own subjectivity that goes beyond the rote patter of stereotypes assigned to provincial sites in Mexico? My city, my other, with whom I hope to forge a relationship of trust through this oddly embodied analytic process …

While there is ample literature about how the world's megacities find themselves making sense of cultural difference in the multiple spaces of daily life, very little is said about how small cities—equally enmeshed in constant contact with the Other—are working out their own encounters with difference. How does the small city negotiate subjectivity? How is otherness made sense of and articulated? How to listen? *Small City on a Big Couch* interrogates the position of the small city, employing the theory of psychoanalyst/cultural theorist Julia Kristeva to ask if the small provincial city of Guanajuato, Mexico, can indeed speak back. Constructed as female and other within Mexican intellectual discourse, can this city articulate her own disruptive ways of understanding self and other amid constant contact with difference? Could she disturb the status quo? What might we learn from her efforts? Could we find some sort of model that would help us to confront others in such a way that neither of us loses our subjectivity or destroys the other in the process?

I approach the city from the psychoanalytic perspective. Or better said, I take on the role of psychoanalyst and adopt her as my analysand—fictionalized, but what better way to understand her than to engage her as a subject and see if she is up to the task of exerting full subjectivity back? To do so, I follow Kristeva's psychoanalytic theory, which is daunting in its complexity, depth, and volume. A Bulgarian native living in Paris, Kristeva centers her own self/other positions in much of her writing, which makes her work an appropriate frame for this analysis. This appeals to me, since, like Kristeva, I am both resident and foreigner where I live, and I too write in different genres and in different languages. And like the city, I am also writing my way to partial understandings of self and other in a context of ongoing contact with difference. The whole analytical process thus functions like a contact zone (Pratt, 1991) in which foreign theory, national theory, local settings, exotic settings, texts, genres, and bodies all encounter and attempt to make sense of one another.

While the process of analysis takes an unexpected shape, ultimately this book argues that small cities might just constitute the perfect site from which to reassert locality and a sense of self in this age of high-speed, fragmented globalization.

THE SMALL CITY

The capital of the state of Guanajuato, the city of Guanajuato is located in the geographical center of Mexico about four hours north of Mexico City. Founded during the colonial period in the 16th century, the city retains a colonial air largely thanks to the fact that the baroque and churrigueresque architecture has been preserved. Guanajuato's main downtown area has held the distinction of being protected by the UNESCO World Heritage program since 1988, and it is considered one of the country's most beautiful sites. Guanajuato is also one of Mexico's most unusual cities due to an unwieldy topography that prevented development along the traditional colonial and/or Mesoamerican grid layout. The use of underground tunnels further marks the city as unique—Guanajuato is the only city in Mexico that boasts a tunnel system—and these tunnels serve as practical and UNESCO World Heritage–related means of dealing with ever-increasing and unsightly traffic. Guanajuato thus maintains a graceful and protected colonial façade, which is mirrored by a local culture that also attempts to be graceful and that is concerned with protecting a certain heritage "look." The city is frequently characterized as old-fashioned and preoccupied with her own appearance. Indeed, both locals and visitors tend to describe the city as traditional, tranquil, Catholic, set in her ways, even change-averse.

Despite these portrayals, Guanajuato is not a tiny village where change is slow to occur. The population is around 160,000, although estimates range enormously. Entering from the León highway, you find a sign that indicates approximately 74,000 inhabitants; however, if you come in from Dolores Hidalgo at the northern end, there is a sign claiming 154,000. Immediately, texts in the public eye open up questions and expose contradictions ... The city also draws in a range of cultural others on a daily basis, as it is home to a large state university and hosts a yearly arts festival that is international in terms of both the artists who participate and the spectators who attend. Furthermore, while out-migration is not heavy in the city itself, the state of Guanajuato is consistently included as one of the top three states that send the most migrants to the United States, which also creates links with difference (INEGI, 2000). Therefore, despite being nowhere near the border or an ocean, the city has been a contact zone for generations: a space "where cultures meet, clash, and grapple with each other, often in contexts of highly asymmetrical relations of power" (Pratt, 1991, p. 34). The city draws in domestic and foreign tourists, academics, artists, and others; and from this unusual mix of elements, complex questions of dealing with otherness emerge. The setting provides a small yet astonishingly rich site in which to study difference thanks to the concentration of others moving through the city at any time.

HOW THE CITY BECAME FEMALE

Geographical space, like the human body, has structure and mass or matter, and culture inscribes a space (making it place) in much the same way it inscribes the body, giving it gender, ethnicity, and so on. Not surprisingly, cities have been organized along idealized body principles since the ancient Greeks and Leonardo da Vinci, and the notion of the body politic has long informed academic understandings of the city (Ferrar, 2000; Sennett, 1994). In terms of development, cities are also frequently portrayed as attempting to reach bodily perfection, most specifically as developers try to create a healthy city, a clean city, a modern city. However, while the relationships between city spaces and human bodies have been studied (Foucault, 1977; Massey, 1994; Pile, 1996), there has not been work that quite considers the city *itself* as a subject with a body and a psyche. Furthermore, even as cities may be bodylike, they are more often than not ungendered, which hinders any attempt to understand their psyche, since so much of the psychoanalytic is tied up in sexuality. As Elizabeth Grosz comments,

> if there is a morphological correspondence or parallelism between the artificial commonwealth (the "Leviathan") and the human body

> *in this pervasive metaphor of the body-politic, the body is rarely attributed a sex* [emphasis added]. (1998, p. 46)

I do not mean to gender the city too strictly; space will surely retain both masculine and feminine aspects. However, cities are quickly gendered within national and global contexts in a complicated process that relates geography, economics, language, and culture. The phrase "feminization of the third world" is commonly used to evoke the third world's lower status, higher poverty, and general dependence upon the first world, envisioned as male, white, and powerful. *Provincia* (the provincial regions), as I will discuss below, is similarly feminized in Mexico (and in Latin America in general). Seeing cities as gendered is not a creative gesture, therefore, but a way to fill in a missing and crucial piece in our understandings.

Lucas Alamán, a 19th-century historian born to Spanish parents made wealthy from the local mines, famously referred to Guanajuato as "*un papel arrugado*" (a wrinkled paper). Already a text ... The city's irregular and quirky layout makes for a complex body that I posit as undeniably female. Both the topography and the architecture tend to be curvy, soft-angled, colorful, penetrable, and porous. The city's bowl shape also conjures up receptive images of womb, pelvis, cupped hands, containers—indeed, there is nothing phallic in the architectural style or natural landscape. Yet there exist other nuances beyond the facile equation of shapes with gender.

While both the traditional Mesoamerican model and the traditional Spanish-colonial model for cities coincided in a grid layout, with power radiating out from a concentrating center, Guanajuato never took on this expected shape. Its *centro*, or center of town, thus does not extend out neatly into grids (colonial and indigenous style) or in concentric circles (early European, Middle Ages style). And it is not built around a central square, or *zócalo*, flanked by the largest or most ornate church, the main government buildings, and the wealthiest businesses and homes. This model, which underwrote the planning of other colonial cities in Mexico and the rest of Latin America, was considered the ideal. Colonial cities were typically planned and drawn, mapped and measured, and carefully edited before they were constructed. Ángel Rama writes, "Over the framework provided by linguistic discourse, the planners stretched the canvas of graphic design" (1996, p. 7). It was thus decreed that cities in the colonies would be constructed to look exactly alike "except where the nature of the ground prevents" (p. 9). In Guanajuato, the "nature of the ground" decidedly prevented such controlled construction. Had it not been for the rich mining resources, it is unlikely that this hilly city would have been created at all. Efforts from early settlement to the present have centered around trying to impose the correct hierarchal order onto the space and inhabitants and, more recently, around trying to preserve a colonial *fachada* (façade) that communicates certain information about the past to today's tourist, upon whom the city places increasing economic dependence. The city's unruly body will disrupt this attempt to impose order again and again, as the female body tends to do.

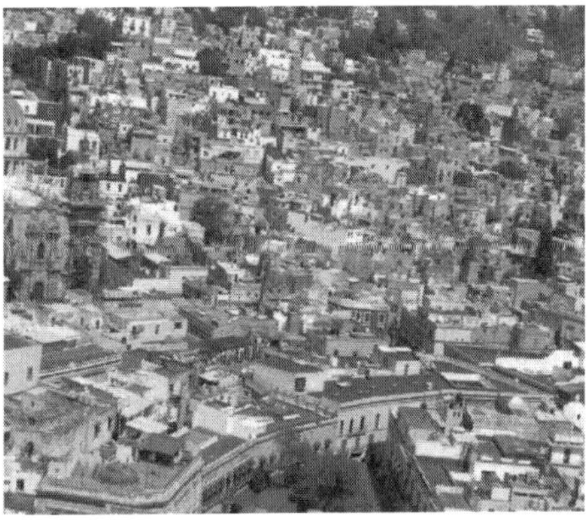
The disorderly city

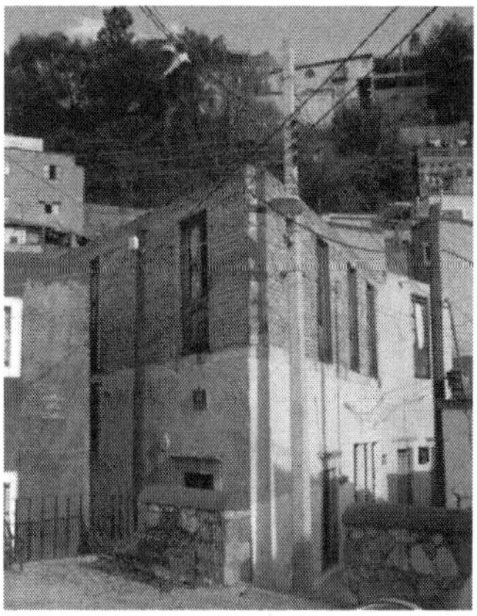
No right angles, chaos

While receptivity can be seen as welcoming, in the case of Guanajuato it is also protective. The city's bowl shape is not one smooth hollow like a traditional valley; rather, there are multiple folds that close off parts. Traditional colonial cities' square grid forms protect the middle plaza and its key powerful institutions; the farther a neighborhood lies from the main plaza, the more economically powerless, sexually deviant, and physically dangerous it is, not to mention open to incursions from others. The city's warped plazas-in-the-middle repeat this protective pattern, albeit in a less geometrically perfect style thanks to the topography. Like women, the city is a "being of folds, a catastrophe of being that the dialectics of the trinity and its supplements would be unable to subsume" (Kristeva, 1987, p. 256).

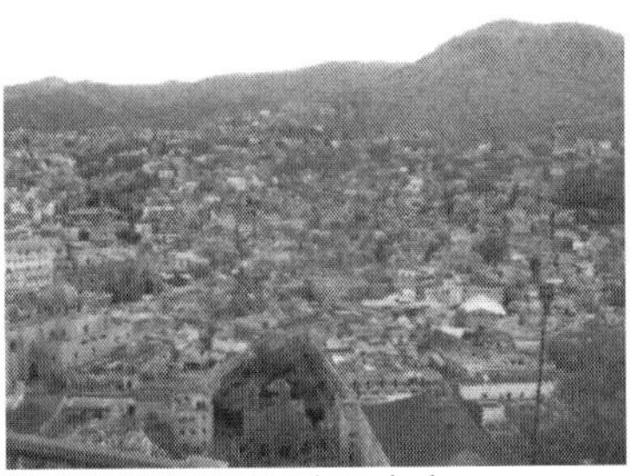
Protective bowl shape

Protected as the city's insides might be, the main area of the city is, nevertheless, overwhelmingly penetrable. The picturesque alleyways (*callejones*) form tiny and infinite labyrinths that interrupt these interior spaces and deregulate the separation of classes, inside and outside, and so on. Domestic residences quite commonly have three or four different entrances and, in between the packed houses, irregularly shaped outdoor plazas provide other openings on the landscape that are entered through the thin *callejones*. Below ground, the tunnels echo the female body with their sensual curves and layered entry, and they again interrupt the space. The entire geography downtown opens and closes, narrows and widens. The interplay between protected-closed elements and penetrable-open elements is everywhere. Thus the topography has made it impossible to completely enforce a traditional Spanish-Moorish architecture of hierarchy that protects and regulates.

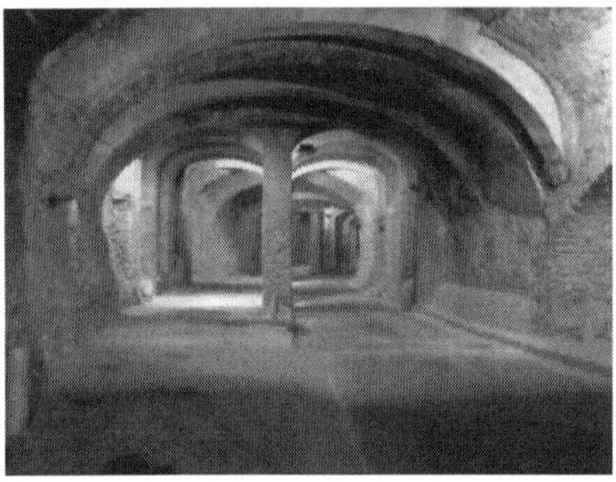

Main tunnel beneath the city *centro*

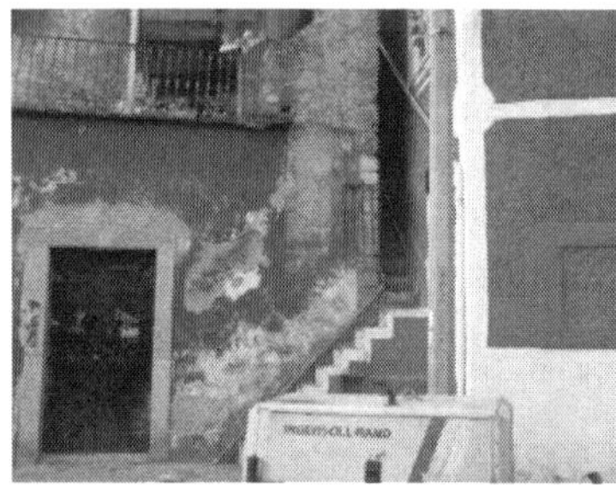

Another point of penetration—ubiquitous tiny *callejones* (alleyways)

Further contributing to the city's potential femininity is the provincial aspect. As a body, *provincia* has also always signified the nostalgic sensual, held in contrast to the degradation of Mexico's urban industrial centers, which novels such as Luis Zapata's *El vampiro de la colonia Roma* (1979) and Eduardo Antonio Parra's *Nostalgia de la sombra* (2002) have described as a dark underworld of prostitution and sexual deviance, drug trafficking, and violence. In sharp contrast and by way of example, the protagonists of two other contemporary novels, Rosa Nissán's *Viajes de mi cuerpo* (2003) and Sara Sefchovich's *Demasiado amor* (1990), have been able to find love and sexual fulfillment only in *provincia*, and the novels both use a geographical *recorrido* (tour) of Mexico's small towns and rural landscapes as the means and site in which the female body is recovered. Both novels emphasize the abundant, sensual character of everything in *provincia*—the landscapes, the food, the people, the crafts—all of which they portray (not necessarily correctly) as absent in Mexico City.

Emily Hind's (2004) study of portrayals of *provincia* in recent Mexican film echoes this opposition. She finds that *provincia* represents an idyllic "promised land" for urban escapees (p. 27). In the many films she cites, *provincia* never speaks for itself; it is always constructed as the object of urban desire. Earlier films of the 20th century modeled *provincia* as a site of stability where the status quo was never challenged, but Hind finds that contemporary films portray *provincia* as, ironically, a site of freedom from urban confinements. Strikingly, Hind notes, the provincial sites in many films are not named; they are invented, generic *provincias* visited by outsiders. Yet another compelling argument that *provincia* does not speak for herself ... Hind concludes that *provincia* is converted into "a symbol instead of a more authentically depicted reality" (p. 38). It becomes "a soundstage for a national metaphor largely directed at the Mexico City–based audience without more careful detailing of a specific, grounded *provincia* and its unique customs" (p. 43). Derived of its own voice and desire, lacking singularity, *provincia* can again be seen as the feminine geographic, and Guanajuato is easily situated within these constructions.

HOW THE CITY BECAME AN ANALYSAND

Cities tend to be considered as geographical objects of study, not psychoanalytical subjects, and I did not initially set out to study the city as an analysand. Rather, I began my research with an interest in the rampant textual production noticeable in the city's downtown area. If one looks between the colored, oddly angled façades, there is a staggering quantity of texts stuck on walls, tacked onto public bulletin boards, and handed out on the main streets of the small downtown. Even more notable, many of these texts are ephemeral and last one night, several days or a month at most, before they are removed or, more frequently, covered by new texts. Others, in contrast, are permanent, cemented into the colonial buildings, but they are no less provocative—it is not uncommon to find competing street names, a former and a newer, plastered into old buildings within centimeters of each other. Texts thus have multiple physicalities, some quick and others lasting, and their material presence is one of layers, a presence that echoes the city's own layered topography of high hills, nested houses, underground tunnels, and mining veins. Between these levels and layers of texts drive a slow slew of cars and trucks painted with their own messages about products and services, from soda suppliers to mariachi groups, from construction work to graphic design. Why so much writing? Why such a preponderance of written words in the public sphere? The city is not a literary center, and although literacy is high, there are only several small and rather poor bookstores, and one or two libraries, so it is hardly a reading center either.[1]

[1] In 2000, the literacy rate for the entire urban locality was 95.8 percent (INEGI, 2000).

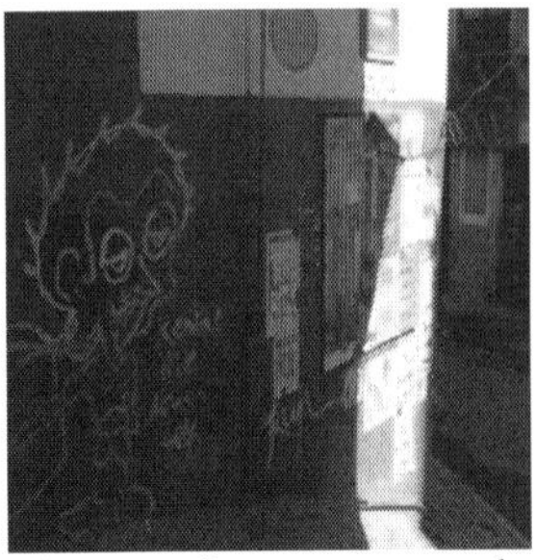

Range of permanent and ephemeral texts

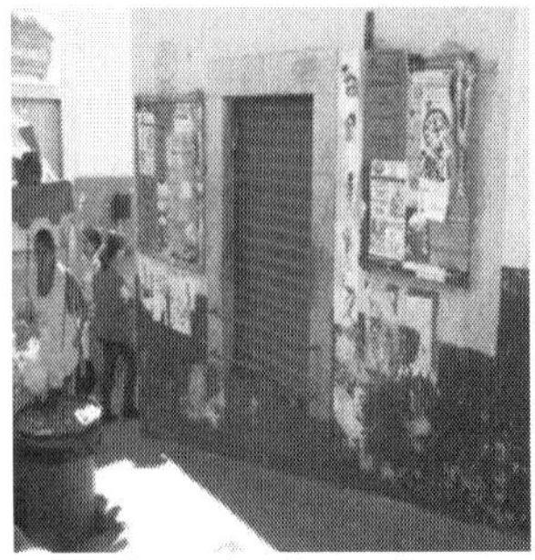

Texts in the main downtown

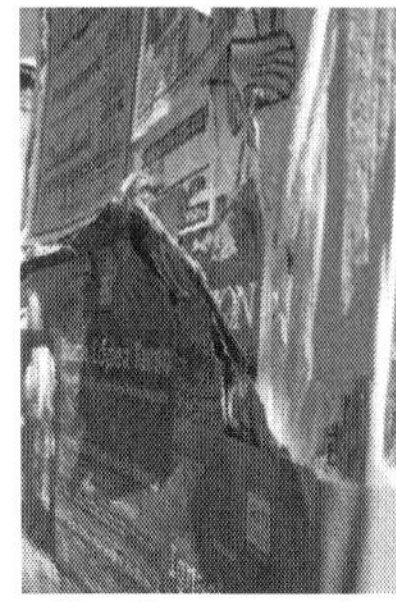

Peeling away in the sun

The messages communicated in the city's papered, tiled, and moving texts run the gamut, informing readers about meetings, menus, courses, festivals, film showings, bar events, health campaigns, and the like. In these messages, we find a rich heteroglossia (different social languages within one national language and different national languages within one social space) that complicates any easy reading and speaks to both class differences and the presence of foreigners, among other things.

I began to perceive that through all this wordiness, Guanajuato was writing her subjectivity, a subjectivity that involves managing the multiple others that come through town (whether physically or through the media). Writing seemed to be one way of coming to partial and ongoing understandings of both self and other. The more I delved into the texts, the more I began to perceive the city herself as a sort of overarching author of all of this work and to see the textual abundance as constituting an oeuvre. While psychoanalyzing a city is unusual, psychoanalyzing an author and her work constitutes a fairly everyday endeavor in the academic world.

At the national level, country psyches have been analyzed (see, e.g., Stein, 2003, on multiple American issues; Cancelmo, 2003, and Coates, Rosenthal, & Schechter, 2003, on the United States working through 9/11; or Davis, 2003, Jucovy, 1992, and LaCapra, 1994, on the Shoah in Germany, to name only a few). Kristeva herself has analyzed France and the European subject throughout her work. Mexico, to be discussed below, has a history of self-psychoanalyzing as well. It follows that within each national psyche, or within each national family, individual cities will have their own identities and roles, their own unique experiences of both the national past and contemporary moment that conscribe their particular processes of desire and loss. Kristeva writes, "What is a subject? That which in man or woman remains open to a search for meaning and sharing" (2011, p. 32). Certainly there is also much in a city that remains open to this search for meaning and sharing since cities are, as much or more so than their human counterparts, multiple, dynamic, and contested. Meaning is always in flux and always shared by many, even if there is no consensus.

THE BIG COUCH

The potential couch of psychoanalytical theory and practice on which to sit the city is both deep and wide. While psychoanalysis has European roots that date back to Freud's pioneering work at the end of the 19th and early 20th centuries, there is also a significant genealogy of psychoanalytical work in Latin America. In Mexico, psychoanalysis as an analytical paradigm appeared in the early 1920s, and it deeply affected intellectual work in many disciplines.[2] Faced with an unresolved history of Spanish conquest and colonialism (15th–19th centuries), a still recent memory of the French invasion (19th century), and U.S. cultural and economic encroachment (20th century), Mexico's search for a national self became a key focus of the State and the obsession of intellectuals, many of whom turned to psychoanalyzing the nation in an effort to provide some understanding of the much-discussed identity question.[3] As Manuel Gamío (1916) termed it, the nation's intellectuals were "*forjando patria*," creating a sense of the nation.

In 1934, Samuel Ramos wrote the first true analysis of the Mexican psyche in his *Perfil del hombre y la cultura en México*, opening up this theme and influencing other writers for several decades to come. In this seminal work (a best seller in its day and printed three times), he claimed that Mexico suffered from an inferiority complex, drawing on the theory of Alfred Adler in Europe. Much of this Ramos captures in the character of the *pelado*, the urban migrant of the 20th century who is consumed by his own frustrated sense of inferiority, which he expresses through violent means. In the works that followed, Emilio Uranga's *Análisis del ser mexicano* (1952) described a melancholy nation and saw the *indigenista* (pro-Indian) movement as a projection of the *mestizo* role onto the Indian. Uranga also spoke out in favor of analyzing local circumstances and against using external models. Santiago Ramírez, in *El mexicano, psicología de sus motivaciones* (1957/1977), attributed México's problems to the fact that its citizens confronted an excess of the maternal element and a corresponding absence of the paternal influence. All of these writers, many of whom were members of the Grupo Hiperión, must have been well aware that only a small segment of the population was

---

[2] See Rubén Gallo's *Freud's Mexico* (2010) for an in-depth consideration of how Mexico's literati, artists, and intellectuals were inspired by Freud's work and of how Freud himself may have imagined Mexico through his own readings and experiences from afar.

[3] It should be stressed, however, that national character has always been taken as that of central Mexico, or the *altiplano* region (Maccoby, 1967, p, 246). This region is not representative of the rest of the country and should rightly be criticized as biased; the realities of northern Mexico are inextricably tied to border issues with the United States, and southern Mexico experiences different constructions of poverty related to its more rural nature as well as ethnic-based marginalization related to a larger indigenous presence. Guanajuato, however, does lie at the edge of the central region covered by the bulk of the literature and, given the history of Spanish dominance, fits generally into these characterizations.

undergoing psychoanalysis; however, they tended to make sweeping generalizations about national identity, and, given the absence of personal reflection in the texts, one wonders if they saw these national complexes as reflective of their own lives as well.

In 1950, Octavio Paz published his canonical *Labyrinth of Solitude* on the Mexican character. He couched Mexico's separation from Spain in terms of a wound, proclaiming that "the Mexican and his Mexicanism must be defined as separation and negation" (1961, p. 88.) While he claimed that "the Mexican does not want to be either an Indian or a Spaniard. Nor does he want to be descended from them" (p. 87), he also asserted that the nation was obsessed with seeking its origins as a way out of its profound sense of being alone. Frey (2001, p. 252) affirms that it is also Paz who established La Malinche, Cortés's indigenous lover and translator, as the object of Spain's desire and the violated woman who symbolizes the entire Mesoamerican culture violated by the Spanish conquistadores. With Cortés, La Malinche produced a mixed-race, *mestizo* son and became considered at once the mother of the eventual Mexican nation, a traitor to her people, a passive victim, and an Eve-like figure of uncontrolled sexuality, the consequences of which will be grave for Mexican women, who Paz links in bulk to her image.[4] Of course, La Malinche's own account is missing in the historical record (Messinger Cyprus, 1991).

Reflecting upon this early work, Leopoldo Zea, perhaps Mexico's most eminent philosopher of the last century, is quoted as calling the Mexican historian a "cultural psychoanalyst" because historians (along with philosophers, social scientists, etc.) were helping the nation carve out a cultural identity after political autonomy was gained in the Revolution (Leddy Phelan, 1956, p. 314). It is worth noting that the work on the national character that emerged in the first half of the century assumed an essential, fixed Mexican self (for the nation at any rate), one that was eminently knowable. Although there was a strong commitment to observing the local context and the specifics of Mexico's past, these scholars were not constructivists by any means.

At the border of philosophical and clinical writing, exiled German-born analyst (and member of the Frankfurt School) Erich Fromm moved from the United States to Mexico in 1950. After teaching at the national university (UNAM) for several years, he founded the Mexican Institute of Psychoanalysis in Mexico City, which he directed until 1976. His most known work on Mexico is *Social Character in a Mexican Village* (written with

---

[4] La Malinche is also referred to as La Chingada, the violated one, since she was first sent to the Spaniards as a slave against her will (according to most accounts). This word has given rise to a rich lexicon of vulgar words in Mexican Spanish. See Paz's chapter titled "Hijos de La Malinche" in *Labyrinth of Solitude* for a discussion of the word's etymology, uses, and cultural location within the conquest. He contrasts Spain's insult of *hijo de puta* (son of a whore) in some depth with Mexico's *hijo de la Chingada* (son of the violated one)—here we find even less female subjectivity or active will.

psychoanalyst Michael Maccoby in 1970), in which they studied campesinos' affective experiences of industrialization and rapid change.[5]

In 1987, Roger Bartra responded to the existing studies of the Mexican character with *Cage of Melancholy*, a stunning critique of early 20th-century images and understandings. In this work, he argues that political culture and national identity have been constructed around ideologically embedded myths about "the Mexican," and he undertakes a complicated analysis of how the Mexican national subject is produced within circular paths of logic that block any real challenge to the status quo. While his work moves away from the psychoanalytic toward a more political-literary stance, it is significant as a critique of earlier writing on the national subject.

Both within and alongside this effort to conceptualize the nation's identity in the early to mid-20th century, Mexico became defined as masculine, a bundle of characteristics symbolized and embodied most clearly by Mexico City. Matthew Gutmann, in *The Meanings of Macho: Being a Man in Mexico City* (1996), writes that this has had an impact at both the academic and everyday level:

> An equation of machismo with Mexican culture as a whole has occurred well beyond the confines of mere social science; it has also been common in the stories Mexicans tell about themselves, both in daily discussions among Mexicans and in the grand proclamations of the scholarly elite. Stereotypes about machismo are critical ingredients in the symbolic capital used by ordinary Mexicans. Even if verbally denigrated by many, machismo is widely regarded in Mexico as constituting part of the national patrimony in much the same way as the country's oil deposits are considered a source of national if not necessarily individual identity. (p. 27)

Within the masculine national, *provincia*, understood in Mexico as anything not the capital, was constructed as female. Accordingly, Mexico City was linked to the *mestizo* (the "new" Mexican subject of mixed blood), positioned as male, urban, violently aggressive, the center, future-looking. *Provincia*, female, was associated with the Indian, the rural, the passive, the peripheral, and the past. Mexico's overriding psychoanalytical issues that emerged in this literature included an inferiority complex, cycles of violence, tremendous tensions between men and women, and narcissism. Reading through it, one quickly concludes that Mexico City is where national identity,

---

[5] While Fromm was influential in creating a Mexican clinical psychoanalytic presence, after the 1976 coup in Argentina many prominent Argentine psychoanalysts were exiled to Mexico City, including the Viennese-born Marie Langer, Marcelo Pasternac, Néstor Braunstein, Juan Carlos Plá, and Gilberta Royer, to name just several. They too brought diverse experiences and ideas to Mexico's clinical practice. From its inception, therefore, psychoanalysis in Mexico was open to a high degree of intercultural dialogue.

with its positive and negative aspects, is located. Yet this disproportionately populous, resource-heavy city from which the bulk of cultural productions of identity have always emanated depends on its provincial other to create its self. The feminized other of *provincia* is left playing a rather mute but essential supporting role.

Literature about Mexico's (human) female side has tended to be damning. The most well-known indictment of Mexican womanhood, although there are many, comes from Paz's *Labyrinth of Solitude*. He constructs women as sexually repressed and characterizes them as suffering objects of violence, obsessed with motherhood to the extent that it impedes their full development as adults. Furthermore, he claims that national identity, represented by men, depends on this dialectic to maintain its own subjectivity. Paz envisions woman as simply "a reflection of masculine will and desire" (1961, p. 35). He argues that "womanhood, unlike manhood, is never an end in itself" (p. 36) and that women are incapable of having personal and private desires (p. 37). Paz would seem to be a Lacanian here, finding woman to be purely other with no self whatsoever and no other of their own! Worse still, he states, "She is an answer rather than a question" (p. 37). She has no control over her own sexuality and only responds when provoked. This implies that women cannot initiate communication, let alone raise revolutionary questions, because nothing semiotic can emerge from her body. For Paz, she is much like the frozen religious icon, an idol (p. 37). From this reading, one would extrapolate that the female provincial city would also be a passive receptacle of the metropolis's desire, a frozen piece of the past incapable of her own desire. The question that emerged from these readings was the following: If *provincia* is constructed as female, can she speak? And if so, can she speak in ways that break away from and challenge these constructions?

This debate is not unique to the Mexican setting, of course, and it throws us immediately into the heart of the discussion over the role of women in psychoanalysis. Rooted in work of Sigmund Freud, psychoanalysis has traditionally been interpreted as having a phallocentric orientation that relegates women to secondary status. The question of whether women can truly be speaking subjects within the patriarchal system and whether they can challenge this system via language has been hotly debated among feminists, psychoanalysts, and others for decades, perhaps most sharply in the confrontation between Jacques Lacan and Luce Irigaray.[6] Julia Kristeva has also probed deeply into these issues and contributed vital insights into the relationship between woman-body-language-patriarchy, at times garnering feminist support (e.g., from Oliver, Rose, and Jardine) and at others incurring feminist criticism (from Fraser, Butler, and Spivak, to name just a few). This has sparked intense debate, and many misreadings, over what Kristeva's own

[6] Luce Irigaray was dismissed from Lacan's Seminar and thrown out of the École Freudienne because of her critiques of Freud and Lacan himself. She was particularly incensed by Lacan's refusal to acknowledge women as subjects.

understandings and intentions are, especially with respect to women, language, and the revolutionary potential she roots therein.

THE KRISTEVAN COUCH

Across decades, disciplines, and genres, Julia Kristeva has created a vast oeuvre around the question of how we approach difference and what happens to our subjectivity in the process. In particular, she is concerned with how language and the body enter into these efforts to work out subjectivity. Kristeva is a multidisciplinarian par excellence, drawing examples from politics (*Strangers to Ourselves*, *Nations without Nationalism*), from literature (studying Marguerite Duras, Romeo and Juliet, Céline, Colette), and from art (e.g., Bellini, Giotto, Georgia O'Keefe), and even from mathematical models in her earlier work (*Desire in Language*). Perhaps the only area she has not explored has been the ethnographic one! Her most essential preoccupations include abjection, melancholia, and love; sexuality and motherhood; sublimation, creativity, and "the feminine genius"; as well as the personal and social possibilities of psychoanalysis. Yet despite the astounding breadth of interests Kristeva weaves through her oeuvre, which currently includes around 30 books and numerous articles, she remains committed to the question of difference. As Kelly Oliver asserts, "Alterity, otherness, and the stranger are always at the center of her texts" (1993a, p. 12). Kristeva's writing addresses the question of how the self attempts to understand the other at the linguistic and bodily margins where they meet. She questions the processes through which strangers (strange people, strange texts, strange languages) are understood, invited in, made part of the self and excluded. How might it be possible to live together without erasing difference?

Surprisingly, despite Kristeva's prolific output, there is no existing how-to book for undertaking a Kristevan analysis. Clinical guides to Lacanian analysis exist (see, e.g., Fink, 1997, 2007; Harari & Moncayo, 1997; and Hill, 2002), and there is ample literature about how to apply Klein (Hinshelwood, 1994; Segal, 1981) and Winnicott (Fromm & Smith, 1989; Grolnick, 1993), yet Kristeva's methodology has not been fully articulated, and the information we have is somewhat scant. Her methods have generally been linked to her Russian Formalist roots and to dialectical approaches, particularly those associated with Hegel. When Kristeva joined the avant-garde Tel Quel group in 1965, Freudian considerations and the theme of sexuality in general were gaining prominence, and she added these elements to her Formalist base (Guberman, 1996, p. 6). She therefore continued to examine the inner workings of a text, enriching this approach with a concern for politics and the psychoanalytical (Mastrangelo Bové, 1984). In his introduction to the translation of *Desire in Language*, Leon Roudiez observes that Kristeva fits the concepts she uses to the object of study at hand, "not 'applying' a theory, but allowing practice to test theory, letting the two enter into a dialectical relationship" (1980, p. 1).

While these guidelines provide some windows into Kristeva's methods, they do not establish a detailed way of proceeding that could easily be brought into a clinical situation (albeit a semifictional one in the case of my city). If one could be trained at a (thus far mythical) Kristevan Institute, what would an analysis look like? While that question alone could be the subject of another study, this book attempts to imagine one answer, contextualized where possible to accommodate the unusual case of the city-analysand.

A Few Points of Departure

A Kristevan analysis assumes as its point of departure a speaking subject or *parlêtre*, a subject who comes into subjectivity when she separates from the maternal and enters language, becoming both the subject *of* and subject *to* language and other symbolic systems. The speaking subject is heterogeneous in nature, comprised of the conscious and the unconscious and composed of two dispositions, the *semiotic* and the *symbolic*, which will get discharged into language. Kristeva defines the semiotic as the translinguistic rhythm, musicality, and unrepresentable excess from the drives and affects that cannot be fully accommodated in language even as it enters in. Signs of this poetic aspect of language emerge in things such as alliteration and onomatopoeia. The symbolic, on the other hand, she uses to refer to the coherent, nonpsychotic, and communicable part of language. This aspect situates language within the realm of the Law, the symbolic order, and grammatical and social codes that must be obeyed (or transgressed). Purely semiotic language would be unintelligible and even psychotic—delirious noise that no one beyond the subject herself understands—but purely symbolic language would be dead, closed to challenge and creativity, and unable to confront difference. Therefore, the two dispositions are necessarily linked in permanent tension.

Because of this, Kristeva's speaking subject of heterogeneity is constantly *en procès*, which is translated as both "in process" and "on trial." Subjectivity is never fully attained or resolved, just as a system is never firmly closed. The semiotic continually emerges to challenge and enliven the subject and language, to push the boundaries of both. Therefore, the subject confronting otherness, just as the system confronting otherness, will be put on trial and will struggle to reassert its collapsed borders, sometimes expanding to accept the other, sometimes rejecting him. Within a Kristevan schema, these crises often revolve around abjection, melancholy, and crises of primary narcissism and love. We will see that the city is constantly reconstituting her own subjectivity, which is put into crisis again and again by the others with whom she interacts. She must ask herself on a daily basis: How to salvage tradition while becoming modern? How to be Mexican yet retain something of Spain and accept something of the United States? How to approach globalized cultural goods, other ideas and ways of life? These concerns keep the city fluttering between possibilities as she attempts to create and sustain a subjectivity, no matter how fluid or ephemeral. She is also split between her conscious and unconscious desires that manifest themselves in different ways during these efforts. While my anthropomorphizing of the city may appear to reify her because she does have a bodily unity that is visually observable, I take her borders to be porous and her subjectivity to be unequivocally divided, multiple, and in process.

One tends to imagine the analysand enclosed in a small consulting office sequestered from exterior happenings; however, Kristeva understands the individual psyche as deeply connected to the larger world and its trauma. Kristeva identifies a broadly defined contemporary Western crisis based on her studies of the psychic effects of Guy Debord's *Society of the Spectacle* (1967). Bombarded by images signifying other images, and having lost religion as one provider of meaning, analysands lose their footing and become eerily silent when it comes to expressing themselves and giving voice to their desire.[7] She finds the numbed contemporary subject adrift in images that think for him and that anesthetize him to the point where he is unable to revolt, question, or create. This also means that subject can no longer articulate (symbolize, represent) what torments him. Increasingly isolated, the contemporary subject loses his ability to connect with others. In Kristeva's view, the Western analysand can no longer represent the border between self and other or even fathom the relationship between separation and connection (Beardsworth, 2004, pp. 56–59).

For the female subject in particular, this disconnection is inscribed over an existing schism maintained throughout the centuries in Christianity's patriarchal ideology: the Virgin, a woman who is deprived of joy, pain, sex, and death, stands in as a symbol of women's less than full existence within the symbolic system.[8] Women are thus even further distanced from ways to articulate the connection between language and the body. For men or women, however, psychic life is endangered within the current crises. The resulting "new maladies of the soul," as Kristeva (1995) has termed these everyday issues, include anxiety, depression, anorexia, missed creativity and unfulfilled sexuality, among other problems.

Kristeva argues that these larger Western contexts affect individual psyches in broadly similar manners; at this juncture, however, she stresses her commitment to considering each individual as singular and unique. She asserts, "We must try to be as concrete—I would even say microscopic—as we can be" (Guberman, 1996, p. 42). To this end, each treatment becomes "an idiolect, a work of art, a new theoretical creation within the Freudian world"

[7] Kristeva does not advocate a return to religion; rather, she sees religion as having provided a way for society to elaborate the semiotic within the symbolic, to symbolize the border where the subject begins to emerge (Beardsworth, 2004, p. 123).

[8] An atheist with an abiding interest in religion, Kristeva was raised between her family's Eastern Orthodox faith and schooling with French Catholic nuns. She refers in general to "Christianity" in her work, most likely to be able to bridge both Eastern Orthodox and Roman Catholic traditions. I refer simply to Catholicism, Mexico's dominant religion, because in Mexico the word "Christian" is signified as the opposite of Catholic, that is, Protestant faiths in which the Virgin Mary does not play a role, and, as we shall see, the Virgin is a fundamental symbol in Kristeva's work.

(Kristeva, 1995, p. 36). Following this understanding, which does hint at the ethnographic, I attend to the city's singularity by focusing on her particular body and her particular spatial gestures. I also examine her unique texts, the bulk of which circulates only locally. I focus on the particularities of her role in Mexican history and in contemporary national life as well. In this sense, without denying that there exist many other colonial cities in Mexico that share similar histories, architectural styles (bodies), and everyday lifestyles, such as Zacatecas, Morelia, Querétaro, Cuernavaca, Puebla, and Mérida, among others, I hone in on the local specifics of Guanajuato's historical and contemporary realities. Finally, while other cities produce text, I underline the unique contours of this city's local oeuvre as it interacts with this particular local space.

What does the crisis-ridden subject need to do in order to heal herself? For Kristeva, the speaking subject must reconnect the semiotic and symbolic, body and language. The subject needs to return to psychic space (the realm of the imagination, the maternal and preverbal, the bodily drives) to retrieve that which is missing from contemporary life and then exit this space to communicate with others in the social world. This process can be enacted along several paths, which include entering the psychoanalytic process, engaging in sublimatory creative processes (such as writing, making art or music, and so on), passing through mystic experiences of religion, or becoming a mother. From what she labels as the "somewhat narrow though not socially irrelevant paths of private life, psychological life, art and literature," Kristeva examines how the subject can return to a point of questioning, to care enough to imagine new alternatives and to reach out to others (2000a, p. 7). "Twenty-five years of analytic practice have convinced me that listening to the unconscious reveals the vulnerability of the speaking being at the borders of biology and meaning, a permanent imbalance, a source of anxiety but also creativity" (Kristeva, 2011, p. 41). The imagination, she argues, is our greatest defense against the spectacle.

While the city will use the creative process as a way back to psychic life, she is also in analysis, of course. Within the analytic process, Kristeva emphasizes Freud's "evenly hovering" style of listening, which permits the analyst to attach and detach as the subject attempts to speak her trauma. She therefore places a tremendous importance upon transference and countertransference relationships that are catalyzed within the analytic process. When these relationships are catalyzed, the analysand's past crises are effectively reopened; he or she returns to the past through the present. This opens up the existing trauma to new signification and meaning, new interpretations that will hopefully liberate the analysand from the troubles that hold him back. In Kristeva's way of proceeding, when the speaking subject runs of out words, the analyst steps in to suggest interpretations, to provide her own associations as they emerge in the transferences. These interpretations are then offered like a gift to the analysand in hopes of bringing him closer to symbolization. Presented with a potential interpretation, the troubled analysand suffering from an incapacity to symbolize his pain, might be able to respond, saying "no, that's not quite it" or "yes, that sounds like how I feel." The analyst thus eases the subject back to symbolic expression by offering him the freedom to choose new interpretations. In the process, the analysand also experiences forgiveness: not in the confessionary sense where someone of more stature grants it; rather, it comes through the gift of the analyst's interpretation, "a pardon whose ambition, through the refinement of its models and formulations, is to make psychic rebirth possible" (Kristeva, 2011, pp. 193–194).

The overarching goal of analysis for a Kristevan therapist is thus the restoration of psychic life. Analysis will not rid one of desire, make authority disappear, or alleviate suffering permanently; however, it can bring an analysand to a greater ability to express her desire and to live with others who are equally desirous and equally subjected to authority. Because the other is fundamental in this process, Kristeva focuses on those sites where the self and other meet, where they put each other into crisis, and where meaning (signification) takes place. She locates these junctures at the borders, margins, boundaries, or what Gruzinski names "these indistinct regions" between binary oppositions set up in language and carried out through practice (2002, p. 24). In these no-man's-lands where the individual meets language and a social life with others, Kristeva finds not only crises of signification (Who am I? What does this word/text mean? Who are you?) but also the rather delicious possibilities of transgression, revolution, jouissance. This fits Mary Louise Pratt's contact zone, which is nothing if not a place of infinite, porous borders where languages, bodies, and subjectivities find themselves in constant contact. Contact demands a rethinking of the self, whether to refortify, transform, or transgress. Accordingly, my analytical work with the city hones in on these meeting points as I ask how she confronts and makes sense of difference, knowing that a fuller expressive life will require an ability to encounter the other in a way that neither denies his difference nor erases the self (Kristeva, 1991). A successful analytical path, therefore, will require the city to recognize her own and others' desires, to accept both, and to be able to articulate it in her texts. This is my understanding of the goal of analysis within a Kristevan framework and in the context of my city-analysand.

Two caveats are necessary. First, cities are not humans, of course, which means that one must enter into the imaginary aspects of this construction to read this book, but certain methodological accommodations to the city's "city-ness" have also been made. Although I read and psychoanalyze the city's text without including an oral voice, in the same way one might read and psychoanalyze a deceased/distanced human author's texts, I also incorporate comments and opinions from local psychologists interviewed during the process, even posing one psychologist as an analytic supervisor when the city's case gets complicated (see Chapter 5). During the research I also immersed myself in the city's more elite side of social life, attending a range of charity, political, and social events beyond my own daily contexts. At these events, I questioned attendees about their perceptions of things occurring in the city at the time. Although this is not a traditional ethnography, the interviews, observations, and participant observations greatly contributed to my textual/spatial interpretations and constitute a less literary and less strictly psychoanalytic form of proceeding that was important to the analytic process as well.[9]

Second, my portrayal tends heavily toward the dominant aspect of the city's nature as parochial, traditional, and repressed. I study the middle/upper-class representations and "issues" from which these dominant aspects emerge. A lower-class emphasis or a study of student life at the university would certainly illuminate different experiences within, around, and despite this context. Therefore it is important to underline that, while the city suffers from certain problems that stem from the dominant ways of being and that bring her in for analysis, she is not "just" this struggle, just as an anorexic patient is not only her illness, a sad person not only his depression, or a literary author not only her nature-based symbolism or her use of a certain trope. Where possible, I try to note the presence of other emotions beneath the more visible nature of the city to keep this complexity acknowledged. This relates back to the larger context as well. As Guberman aptly observes, "What is provisional now are the moments of status quo" (1996, p. 37). Like other contemporary individuals and places, the city is in crisis, and her efforts to write viable positions for self and other occur in a context of flux. Everything is permanently open to change.

POSITIONING THE RESEARCHER-ANALYST

To write about a place is to create a representation and, consciously or unconsciously, to write oneself into it. This immediately calls up a host of desires, fantasies, and fears about what kind of place to write and how to carve out one's niche within this portrayal. If it is a human need to want to create a certain place for oneself in the local social text, beyond this admitted desire lurked another deeper one. From the moment I began reading about Kristeva's

---

[9] The overlaps between ethnography and psychoanalysis are multiple. Psychoanalytic ethnographies study the psychic dimensions of life in a given site, while an ethnographic psychoanalysis would attempt to analyze the individual (city, in my case) within wider sociocultural or political contexts. Obviously the costs and logistics an actual analyst would have to employ to study each analysand ethnographically make this proposition less feasible, but this does not mean that analysts ignore or discount the external contexts within which each analysand is located. For a particularly strong perspective on this, see Kima Cargill's article "Off the Couch and onto the Streets: Toward an Ethnographic Psychoanalysis" (2006). For an actual psychoanalysis of a community (undertaken to identify ways through traumatic experiences), see the works of anthropologist Ricardo Ainslie (2004) and Ainslie and Kalina Brabeck (2003), which explore a Texas community's struggle to make sense of a murder. For perhaps the best point of departure on the intersections between anthropology and psychoanalysis, see the work of anthropologist/psychoanalyst Anthony Molino (2004), in which he interviews Katherine Ewing, Wesley Shumar, Marc Augé, and Vicent Crapanzo, among others, about these relationships and about research practice.

understandings of the semiotic, I knew that I needed a large dose of it. I have long been plagued by the stifling intimacy that small city life exudes and have been needled by the wish to transcend the routine of everyday life. By taking on this analysis, I wanted to seek out the imaginative, creative, and transgressive elements of the local community, and I wanted, through writing about it, to uncover something stimulating.

My sense of being somewhat marooned in a small city makes me realize that in some ways and on some days I subscribe to the common depictions of *provincia* in Mexico that portray areas like Guanajuato as stagnant peripheries. I find myself longing for a larger city with major libraries, endless museums, more diversity, and intellectual and creative anonymity. Other days, I shamelessly yearn for the exotic, a place less reserved, a place that flaunts its abundant, colorful nature, its sounds, smells, foods, bodies—in short, every stereotype assigned to Mexico and Latin America in general that seems to be lacking in this slow, stately place. As much as one tries to escape cultural constructions (on both sides of the border), they are still there and occasionally surface in our desires. While I find myself attracted to the resistant experimental writings of literary authors who write strange and wild ways to new worlds, full of semiotic experimenting, it is Kristeva's work that most speaks to me because she searches for radical possibilities within the system and within a world of others. In *New Maladies of the Soul* (1995), Kristeva asserts that this dulled sense we all feel is a result of having gone too far into the "soulless symbolic" of language, and that a turn back to the semiotic would cure our postmodern crises and allow us to find new ways to live with others. I attempt to enter into both Kristeva's and the city's lyrical semiotic as a way to confront our shared concerns about finding a way to do just this.

A MAP OF THE BOOK

This book is somewhat nonlinear, like the city. Each part inscribes what comes next and often it redoubles back on its earlier ideas. However, a basic storyline of the city psyche emerges.

Chapter 2, "The Presenting Problem: Digestive Issues in the Contact Zone," examines the problem that brings the city in for analysis, namely her sense of feeling overwhelmed by others. The constant pressure to accommodate so many cultural others within her small space produces psychosomatic symptoms of nausea and indigestion. A particularly other, external text throws her into abjection, forcing her to confront aspects of her (grotesque) body that she prefers not to acknowledge. While she creates her own textual reply and reasserts her boundaries, this experience reveals that her strategies for confronting otherness, while somewhat functional, leave her strained and stressed. The tourism spectacle weighs upon these efforts heavily. Like many speaking subjects, the city is anxious to find ways to relate to the other, and I identify a certain readiness for analysis in her text. The fact that she is drafting tentative responses is a positive sign.

The next chapter, "Deeper Desires: The Perfect Colonial Present, a Don Quijote Fetish, and Maternal Issues," probes further, taking on the recurring image of Don Quijote in the city's texts. How is it possible that Guanajuato, sloganed as the "birthplace of the Independence War," chooses a Spanish text (Cervantes's *Don Quixote de la Mancha*) to represent herself? How is it that the "right" tourist look is Spanish? The dynamics around the Don Quijote icon's institutionalization into the city's sense of self reveals a city in want of love, as Kristeva says. Through the Don Quijote texts, the city attempts, without success, to both have and be the lost maternal by attempting to preserve a colonial look. Like Narcissus, an enduring reference for Kristeva, the city is left melancholy, guilty, and wounded after Independence. While the city plays a maternal role to the nation (which theoretically could permit a reworking of a depressed female sexuality), she reproduces the usual (Catholic, patriarchal) discourse of maternity. As Kristeva has consistently argued, there is a need for a more functional discourse of maternity that includes women's creativity and sexuality. Clearly, the city has maternal issues related to separation, which explain the unhealthy degree of self-surveillance and repression taking place. She is trying too hard to present the perfect Spanish colonial façade; she is editing beyond what is tenable.

In Chapter 4, "*Calladita, te ves más bonita*: Analyzing Silences and Erasures," I pause to consider several topics that the city chooses *not* to write about, examining a racy novel whose message seems to have been missed, the city's management of Diego Rivera and his art, and the figure of the abject miner who rarely appears on the city's surface. What emerges from the previous examination of the Spanish maternal and these newer examples is a strong theme of abandonment. The void that the city attempts to fill with so much text is put into relief. A final text, this time public, signals that the return to the feminine is urgent indeed. The pressure that the city self-imposes to keep up an idealized appearance is pushing her to the limit. Is she not deleting herself? We seem to be on the verge of something, and I am led now to the body.

Chapter 5, "Releases and Returns: Or, Sex and the (Provincial) City," takes up the theme of sexuality, critical to any psychoanalysis. One might expect to find here an obvious opening for transgression in a city filled with tourists and university students. In these sessions, we discuss the city's turn to writing in other languages as a strategy to attempt to escape such repression/self-regulation. What emerges in the series of her texts we examine is a specific spatialization of desire via the use of foreign language, space, and time, all of which locate desire "elsewhere." While these strategies create a brief opening for transgression, they also mark a failed process of projective identification. Her slight deviance is followed by a return to the norms (textual, spatial, moral) that prohibit any real disruption and change. I realize that these strategies are ephemeral and controlled by the same pressures to fit the ideal image that I identified in the previous chapters. These were not results that I expected or had hoped for.

What follows is an interlude in which I delve into my own crisis about my reactions to what appeared to be emerging in the analytic process. In Chapter 6, "Transferences: Of Cities and Analysts," I analyze a poster text that crystallized my dissatisfaction with where the analysis seemed to be heading. Working through the personal and intellectual desires that I projected onto the analysis, I discuss in depth the notions of transference/countertransference. This leads me to wander through issues of splitting and projections onto place, and here I examine both my own case with the city and Kristeva's East-West divisions, particularly in her portrayals of Byzantium and the fictional Santa Varvara in her novels. This illuminates several essential points about possible paths out of the city's dilemmas, not the least of which is writing. After a consideration of my own case notes, I am ready to disconnect from the transferences, to give the city what she needs: a way out of the frozen representations in which she is mired, a new interpretation.

In Chapter 7, *Revolt, They Said*: Two Virgins, One Indian Princess, and the T-shirt Girl," I craft an interpretation that is more hopeful. We turn back to identify key symbols/icons/myths from which the city could launch a revolt, a quietly radical disruption of the spectacle that has so confined her. Specifically, I refer the city to a related set of her texts about two locally celebrated Virgins, a legend about the city's origins, and a more contemporary T-shirt text. This discussion again relates to space and the city body, moving from a mountain cave to the altar of the main church, to street displays of piety. Through this resignification of the texts in question, I identify a strong base for a disruptive female potential intimately related to the city body. *Revolt*, say these images, as spaces and times are reopened. Everything is positioned at the limits of self and other, semiotic and symbolic. Will the city succeed?

In the final chapter, "Tales of Love and Life After Analysis: Of Art, Opera, and Halloween," I consider the ambivalences of ending the analytic process and ask if the city has been able to resignify her stories and if her psychic life has indeed been restored. Referencing Kristeva's psychosexual model set out in *Colette* and her recent reflections in *Hatred and Forgiveness*, I show how the city is enacting the new discourse of maternity-femininity that Kristeva has been formulating. Through art, music, and a final set of texts related to Day of the Dead and Halloween, the city models a new way of opening up to others based on a deep connection with her bodily self. We see a small city poised to meet the other, with her psychic life renewed. While subjectivity processes are never finished, we will find ourselves, for the moment, at a good stopping place.

A FEW CAUTIONS

Cultural studies researchers maintain that one interpretation is never the only interpretation and that our understandings are situated within our intellectual commitments. This certainly holds for this book. The psychoanalytic perspective is not the only way to understand a city, nor is a textual approach the only route that could have been taken toward a study of the city psyche. Furthermore, the quantity of written words produced locally extends far beyond what one book could reasonably cover. A look at less public genres of expression, verbal or otherwise, would also be fascinating. However, I chose to study the public texts and their less public psychic underpinnings, as they exist in the blurry overlap between the local and national context. And much like anyone studying a prolific literary author, I examined those texts that seemed to speak both to me and to each other, which means that other researchers could easily have chosen other texts to study.

Consequently, I do not claim that the texts I examine represent the city's one, authentic, and "true" voice, nor, more importantly, that the city has one identifiable voice. Because I see the city as embodying multiple subjectivities, she too may speak differently through different types of texts not considered in this book, just as many of us speak in different languages and in different registers of language as we move between our own multiple subjectivities and subcultural memberships. Additionally, what the city writes will evolve and change over time, as do our own articulations of self. To assert that any person or place has a single fixed subjectivity would be to go against all the theory used in this book and would effectively deny us all multiple facets and the possibility of growth. This study of local texts unveils the city's partial understandings and partial processes of attempting to understand self and other at this particular moment.

Are the findings generalizable? I am convinced that texts in other small cities would have something to say about their own contexts, desires, and understandings of difference; however, I remain equally sure that the quantity and particular arrangement of texts in this site are unique. At the end of the book I argue for further psychoanalyzing of cities without advocating an approach that would necessarily include public text. A study that looks at other samples of local language might be more suitable in sites less inundated with paper, and this would certainly not detract from the depth of analysis one could achieve.

Literary critic Norman Holland, in *The Mind and the Book: A Long Look at Psychoanalytic Literary Criticism* (1998), responds to the question "Why engage in psychoanalysis?" by suggesting that the question itself connects with the issue of why we read a text in the first place. We read, he says, following Horace, for delight, and literary criticism provides us with ways to maximize this pleasure. In much the same way, living in cities provides pleasure, and a psychoanalysis of place can thus enhance our awareness and enjoyment of a site in which we find ourselves. Holland argues that the critic's contribution is to tell us to notice this, watch how that works, and so on, sensitizing us to the details and delights within a text. He argues that critique thus offers "another way of entering the imaginative world" of a text, a way that is deeply connected to empathy. What he means by this is that only by listening to/reading carefully our other can we develop empathic understandings. My own study thus aims to take on the city-subject, saying "notice that," "watch this," as Holland advocates. Indeed, this book could be subtitled “A Cultural Theorist’s Guide to the City.” It reflects a path into imagining the world of the city from an empathic standpoint that travels beyond the stereotypes so prevalent in my mind at the beginning of the research. I thus invite the reader into this journey of reading and listening to Guanajuato and offer the following book as my interpretation of this process.

Two

The Presenting Problem
Digestive Issues in the Contact Zone

We begin. I pull out an empty leather notebook. The white pages waiting for text reach out to me as always, eliciting curiosity and faith that what is unknown will start to take some decipherable shape, and—why not be honest—summoning up a sheer desire to know. The links between desire and intellectual curiosity have long been recognized, and even though I've skipped the required step of self-analysis that true psychoanalysts must go through, I am aware of this element on my own. I intensely want to know what the city is all about.

Happily, this morning my desire to know coincides with the city's desire to tell me. While we are both a bit hesitant and nervous about getting started, there is also a palpable energy in the office. After some perfunctory greetings, we get down to work. She is complaining of minor digestive problems that she feels may be related to her sense of being rather overwhelmed by others.

I feel nauseous all the time, very heavy, she says, *weighted down by all this contact.*

The term *presenting problem* refers to the initial concern that brings a patient in for psychoanalysis, although, in research terms, we find an easy parallel with our initial intellectual curiosities that bring us to our research questions and our field site. The presenting problem (like all research problems) quickly softens to unveil increasingly complex questions, uncovering deeper issues not suspected at the onset of the process. In the city's case, she comes in with nausea and a queasy sense of unease. Too many tourists, she says, too much of a good thing, too much to digest at once.

Tourists are one of the city's key others, perhaps the most significant other, as they provide both economic and cultural nourishment. However, like many foodstuffs, tourists simultaneously nourish and defile. What is external may at times fascinate and feed (in the form of cultural ideas and cash); but, at other times, the external corrupts and denigrates (in the form of less traditional ideas, unacceptable values and practices). Because the tourist is double, he must be carefully handled. He must, like a foodstuff, be broken down in a digestive process that separates out nutrients from toxins. With her underground tunnels (which expel waste, such as excess floodwater, trash, traffic), the city boasts a tremendous digestive system working to process an even greater flow of difference. But she can only handle so much.

While the city consumes tourists on a daily basis in varying ways, the main organ through which tourists are brought in and digested is the Festival Internacional Cervantino, or the FIC, as it is called locally. The FIC began in the 1970s, when cultural performances from elsewhere were combined with existing university performances of Cervantes's *entremeses cervantinos*, which had been taking place for about two decades, and staged together as an arts festival. Gradually, more performances were added, and the FIC currently draws Mexico's finest national talent as well as renowned international performance groups; without exaggeration, it constitutes one of Latin America's most prestigious artistic festivals. Each year one national state and one foreign country are featured as guests of honor, a structure that mirrors Mexico's recipe for tourist success—the message that one can be or have true Mexican-ness while concurrently being/having international-level quality and flair (Berger, 2006; Saragoza, 2001). However, this same success has also made the FIC somewhat other to the city, even as it has become a symbol of city identity and provides an enormous source of income.

How is this possible? Unlike many festivals, the FIC did not develop organically from uniquely local traditions or popular celebrations even while it has this local originating point. The use of Cervantes's texts roots the festival in the university, and the original performances were undertaken in public plazas, but there is nothing ultimately popular about this event. Over the last three decades, the festival has gotten increasingly international and high-end. Ricard and Robinson (2006) assert that contemporary festivals have become spectacles for outsider consumption. Indisputably, the FIC situates the city within the spectacle, as images are produced to market the festival and as many images and performances are increasingly distanced from the local urban body, moved indoors, and made elite. Compounding this, a major part of ticket sales have gone online and are now sold months in advance, which is not the way city residents tend to plan or purchase. On more than one occasion, blocks of seats for key events have also been reserved for outsider groups who have not shown up to use them. The disproportionate enjoyment of the festival by outsiders is thus rising. During the FIC weekends, over 30,000 tourists can pour into the city at once, which greatly strains her abilities to house them, feed them, and dispose of the waste they leave in their wake. Most of this digesting of the tourist other takes place in the tiny downtown, a contact zone of small proportions relative to the demand it faces. It is no wonder that the FIC can produce regular bouts of nausea and indigestion.

The city's opening complaint is quite clear and quite understandable. It permits an entrée into her psyche from a point of departure she has identified as speakable—something she is both willing and able to articulate. We begin here.

AN EXTERNAL TEXT: THE ABJECT POSTER

The first text we discuss during this session is not one written by the city herself, but, rather, an external one that prompted her to write back in response. Every year, a promotional poster is chosen through a formal contest to represent the festival. These promotional posters are hung all over town and linger on years after their original selection. One observes posters dating back to the 1970s in photocopy shops, school-supply stores, and other everyday locales, and it does not take long to realize that most of them display the same basic content. The majority of the posters depict the stacked-up architecture of Guanajuato in varying styles; notably, they tend to lack people, cars, street dogs, vendors, and any other sign of city life, which creates an odd timelessness across this poster genre. Recently the tendency has veered more toward abstract computer-generated designs, which are even more devoid of human aspects. However, in 2004, of the 435 posters submitted for the annual competition to choose the festival poster, the following poster, which radically challenged the traditional mold, was chosen. The poster was created by Luis and Lourdes Almeida, Mexico-city-based designers.

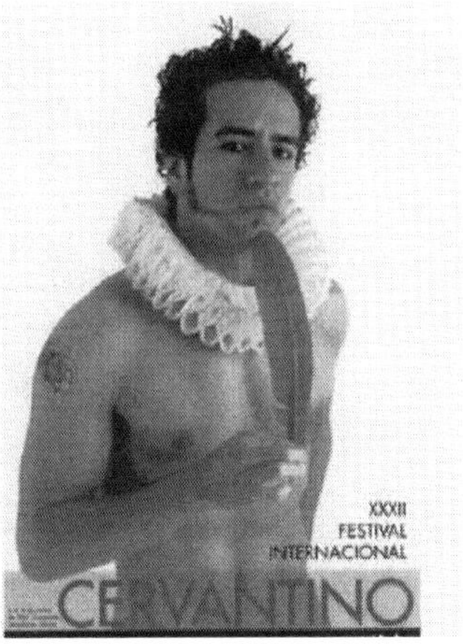

Recalled FIC poster

Approved by an organizing committee in Mexico City, the poster caused the city to react with horror. It was subsequently dis-approved by the local government and taken down. Why was this poster perceived as so threatening that it had to be expelled from the city body? If the city is nourished financially and culturally by this festival, the poster would seem to *attract* the visitors she needs and desires, not repel them. Indeed, a positive reading of the poster produces the message that Cervantes (represented by the collar and feather) and high culture in general are cool, hip, and youthful. They say that the FIC is to be enjoyed not only by middle-aged city dwellers and retired expat Americans but also by local and visiting youth, symbolized not only by the age of the model but also by his hairstyle, funky sideburns, and tattoo, not to mention seminudity. The poster would seem to communicate that the traditional and the modern can coexist without contradiction. Is this sort of combination of elements not the essence of the creativity supposedly embodied by the FIC, which has always featured such hybrid combinations as indigenous opera, Nigerian theater, and Dutch painting in a single festival? Does it not invite the local body (dominated by the city's large student population) to participate in this event and claim it as part of the self? The poster would, at the level of our first innocent reading, seem to invite young populations to attend the high-culture festival events along with or even instead of the more popular street performances (or random drinking and carousing) enacted at the margins of the festival.

The city did not read the poster in such a positive light. In the view of the local government leaders and many local residents, this poster reinforced the shameful fact that recent FICs had become increasingly denigrated at the public, popular level. Both officials and local residents alike were grumbling that during the Cervantino the city turned into *una cantina andando* (a walking cantina) with drunks all over the streets at all hours. The incoming visitor population had grown to include more rural youth, hippies, and Mexico City students, all with no spending money—no nutrients to bring! Individuals from these groups were sleeping in the quaint plazas, engaging in sexual encounters in the *callejones*, and eating, peeing, defecating, and vomiting indiscriminately in the tunnels and other public areas. In short, the city during FIC time became an open body, unrecognizable and incoherent with her usual presentation of self. All of her orifices—the many plazas and tunnels—were being literally flooded with the bodily processes usually hidden away from view in this well-heeled town where no one wears shorts in the *centro* or goes to the grocery store without makeup.

In the context of these concerns, the poster edged up too close to the issues of nudity and sex, and it connoted all of the lower bodily functions that had become too public, something underlined by the fact that the model is not wearing pants. One might also wonder if stereotype-soaked officials found this male body to be homoerotic given the sensitive expression, the suggestive long, red feather under his lips, the implied love of the theater … Homosexuality certainly exists in town, but it is not overtly (or politically) displayed in public. Another possible problem occurs if the poster is read as intending to appeal to female sexuality and voyeuristic desire. This too threatens traditional gender norms that call for the suppression or at least masking of female desire. (It is hard not to wonder, though, what would have happened if the model had been female, wearing the same collar and feather and little else …) As a final problem in the eyes of the city, the unkempt hair, tattoo, and piercings link the model to the hippie population, a group that the city actively tries to keep at its margins all year round.

The poster thus threw the city subject into crisis by provoking the question of whether this was "me or not-me," rubbing too close to her insecurities. It was perceived as degenerate and defiling, which Kristeva chides us to see as having less to do with the object itself and more to do with how it threatens a boundary (1982, p. 69). If the poster touched a nerve, it is because there was doubt present in the city's sense of self. It illuminated the fragility of the symbolic order by bringing the grotesque body into view. It dismantled the idea that the social reality at hand is fixed and sealed, which forced the city to restore the balance.

What the poster did was to throw the city into abjection. Kristeva works out her theory of abjection in *Powers of Horror* (1982), defining abjection as a moment or process in which the subject's borders are challenged, brought into question, or dissolved, which provokes a crisis. This happens at birth as the not-yet-subject struggles to separate from the mother, to make her into an object, which calls up the contradictory desires to remain in idyllic unity with her, on the one hand, and to emerge into the world of language and take up a subject position, on the other. This process repeats in later symbolic life when the subject is forced again to reassert the boundaries that others put into doubt. The abject, therefore, is that which puts one's borders into crisis, transgresses, disturbs, interrupts. That which is dirty, repulsive, violent, traitorous. The taboo. And most importantly, perhaps, it is "something rejected from which one does not part," which means that unlike the Freudian repressed, the Kristeva abject is always hovering (1982, p. 4). It can be excluded, but not denied. As a consequence, both the individual (city) subject and cultures in general enact purifying rituals to keep the abject at bay. At least temporarily …

The FIC poster became what Greaney brilliantly terms (in reference to Proust, one of Kristeva's core references across her own oeuvre), an "anti-madeleine, the trigger of involuntary memories of horror and disgust" (2008, p. 299). It provoked a collapse of meaning and unleashed a horrifying ambiguity that forced the city to question the boundary between her *me/not-me*. The poster brought up the grotesque and physical aspects of her body that she tries to control and hide. She panicked in front of this defilement because it threatened her definition of self as that which is pure, as a lovely colonial city of cultured performances. The poster thus compelled the city to contemplate her grotesque, lower body functions that did not fit into her self-image.

It is difficult, not to mention somewhat disloyal, to think of this colorful and quaint city in terms of a grotesque lexicon that usually speaks of defilement, abnormality, and the freakish. Kristeva's formulation of the abject owes much to Mikhail Bakhtin's (1984) understanding of the grotesque in *Rabelais and His World*. Bakhtin defines the grotesque body as one that is

> not separated from the rest of the world. It is not a closed, completed unit; it is unfinished, outgrows itself, transgresses it own limits. The stress is laid on those parts of the body that are open to the outside world, that is, the parts through which the world enters

> the body or emerges from it, or through which the body itself goes out to meet the world. This means that the emphasis is on the apertures or the convexities, or on various ramifications and offshoots; the open mouth, the genital organs, the breasts, the phallus, the potbelly, the nose. (p. 26)

What he most emphasizes is that the grotesque body neither respects margins nor closes off its openings. In the modern era, society attempts to close off the body from the natural world, thus censuring and hiding its functions, disguising its smells, masking its illness, making private its functions. Like human bodies, contemporary city bodies from Haussmann's Paris forward have found themselves under similar pressure to close off their cavities and to properly regulate their bodily functions (Farrar, 2000; Gandy, 1999).

Here, our city becomes grotesque precisely because she is full of Bakhtin's "parts through which the world enters the body." The city is multiply penetrable through her tunnels, alleyways, and open plazas. During the FIC, these open parts are frequently filled with trash and also serve as sites for both criminal and sexual activities. Worse, the tunnel walls regularly drip with sewage leaks and black runoff water, thus failing to completely fulfill their function as transporter of waste to sites outside the body. In contrast to these open sites, the city's statues and sharply angled hills provide the protrusions or "offshoots" that Bakhtin might read as equally gross. Smooth surfaces are not the city's characteristic look! Furthermore, the city overflows her boundaries as urban development no longer "fits" within her bowl shape. Cars clog up both the surface-level streets and the tunnels. During the FIC, the city practically hemorrhages tourists, as there is literally no space left on the public streets nor in hotels, and tourists (in this quantity) quickly exhaust the city's restaurant supplies, trash-collection abilities, and the like. Some newer FIC events are even being pushed out into the neighboring areas and the city of León because they no longer fit in the city's immediate space.

As if this were not enough, the city boasts one of the more grotesque features of the nation. Within the city body, one finds the infamous Museo de las Momias (Mummy Museum), a site that is both disgusting and uncanny. As the story goes, in the mid-19th century, space in the overcrowded local cemetery was tight. Some bodies belonging to families who did not pay the cemetery tax were dug up to make room for paying clients. Much to everyone's surprise, preserved by the rich minerals in the earth, these bodies had not decayed or disintegrated, but rather they had become mummies. The bodies, along with later bodies recovered from mining accidents, were put on display in a local museum where they remain today, faces often frozen in expressions of horror. Tourists trek through this building and observe the bodies of the city's past inhabitants—bodies of men, women, and even babies. Here is a grotesque example where the city literally consumes her own inhabitants only to spit them back out for tourists to reconsume in the Museo de las Momias. Although these dead bodies interest me less than those marked as other for different reasons, they provide an example of abjection at its most exaggerated. Corpses, writes Kristeva, bring us directly to the edge of what we can tolerate:

> The corpse, the most sickening of wastes, is a border that has encroached upon everything. It is no longer I who expel, "I" is expelled. The border has become an object. How can I be without border? (1982, p. 3-4)

Conceiving of the city as a grotesque body overflowing her boundaries and rife with protrusions and rarities, allows us to envision the city more completely. It permits us to consider not only her surface upper areas where the foreign and exotic come in but also the lower body parts of digestive processes, where these same elements become threats that must be managed. Given the tiny physical area of the city and the overwhelming pressures upon her bodily parts and services, it is not difficult to imagine that so many others provoke both anxiety and a degree of nausea and indigestion. While this can happen year-round, it is at high tourist times, when the city body is most strained, that the nausea increases.

For Bakhtin, there is no repulsion associated with the body that transgresses its own boundaries, but the abject Kristevan body causes the city tremendous angst because it is precisely at the city's grotesque sites (public areas that cannot be closed off or controlled) that the other is encountered, that the other penetrates the city *centro*. The FIC poster therefore drew attention to this ongoing problem and catalyzed the abjection process. It was *unheimliche*: "that which ought to have remained hidden, but has come to light" (Schelling cited in Freud, 1919, p. 347). The *unheimliche*, or "uncanny strangeness" as it is usually translated, is that which is both strange and familiar at once. As Bakhtin reminds us, "In the new official culture, there prevails a tendency toward the stability and completion of being. ... The ambivalence of the grotesque can no longer be admitted" (1984, p. 101). He is almost alluding, long before Debord of course, to the spectacle society that also refuses ambivalence and challenges to its own discourse. Concerned as the city was to put forth a clean and attractive image for tourists, this unveiling of her grotesque aspects was not acceptable.

The abject, whether a poster or a dead body, must be expelled and excluded. This is accomplished through ritual purification and law. While religion traditionally offered a mediating force that regulated the clean/unclean, defined what was sinful, and established food and sex prohibitions, in *Powers of Horror*, Kristeva emphasizes the ways in which art and literature in particular now serve this function. These written or visual texts provide the subject-in-crisis with a means through which to elaborate and symbolize what is desirable, painful, or outright horrific. Abject literature, such as the poster, offers us a way "to code our crises" (1982, p. 206), to achieve a necessary catharsis, and to redraw the boundaries of self in the process of writing/reading it. Furthermore, as philosopher Sara Beardsworth observes, for Kristeva, abject literature offers a "site of confrontation" between what bourgeois ideology represses and the semiotic (2004, p. 41). It thus reveals the fragility within the system, making the system (and language itself) face up to this underside. Another important function of the abject is that it provides a space into which the drives can be discharged, and it permits an organization of violence. As reader of the text, the city confronts the unthinkable, unfathomable abject, places herself into it, and then displaces it into words and images. This process purifies and provides an alternative to discharging actual violence against the offending poster, its supporters, or the populations it might represent.

The poster, through its visual language and the discussion it provoked, complies with all these abject literature functions. It catalyzed the abjection process, which threw the city into crisis and subsequently forced her to reconstitute her "clean and proper," redrawing the line between "who she is" and "who she is not." While one can read the abjection of the poster as elitist and probably homophobic, these acts are always acts of self-protection in the eyes of those who enact them. And like all processes of abjection, the abject Thing is never fully banished; the poster continues to hover around the city. It is still posted here and there in cafés, reminding the city that the subject is permanently *en procès*, and the social order is not as sealed as she might wish.

A TEXT OF SELF: "CITY OF ROMANCE"

As the city abjected the poster, she also created a text now more of the self. Ironically, her text will include many of those rejected elements, but she offers a now purified version. In 2005, the government's official tourist agencies produced a marketing campaign designed to draw in more tourism all year round, with the slogan "*Guanajuato, Ciudad Romance*" (Guanajuato, City of Romance). The images chosen for this campaign targeted the exact areas, albeit in different ways, that local officials were trying to scrub from the FIC—sex, nudity, and drinking. These images have been disseminated in tourist brochures as well as in large posters and billboards that are posted as far away as Querétaro, and the campaign is still current as of this writing.

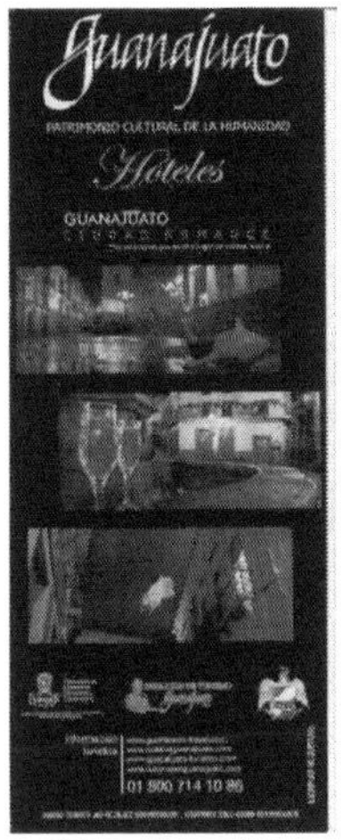

"City of Romance" brochure

The panels in the brochure depict a deserted nighttime city bathed in the warm light of the new colonial-style streetlamps. This is immediately recognizable by locals as an impossibly tranquil scene—the main streets of the city are rarely deserted at night, no matter how late the hour. Yet this image promotes an image of pristine-ness—no cars, no people, no drunks, no trash. A clean city body washed with rain, with nothing threatening her integrity. The first image features the colonial architecture and, next to a shiny puddle gleaming in the street, a lone shoe—red, high-heeled, silk—lying on its side. The intended message appears to be that the rush toward a romantic encounter made the shoe fall off and that the owner was more interested in other things than recuperating her lost shoe. While a high-heeled shoe could certainly get caught up in the cobblestone streets, this shoe is perfectly intact, which marks it as new (or new to Guanajuato, since the heel has not been mangled). Its overall elegance is highly exaggerated for the jeans-wearing bar crowd, which tells us about the staged nature of this scene and about who is being marketed to (i.e., neither the students nor the younger tourists, and certainly not the hippies).

The second image portrays the same empty, nocturnal street and displays two glasses of white wine or even champagne sitting on a fountain. The city is not known as a connoisseur of either of these drinks, nor would one necessarily be drinking something so elegant in the bars of the *centro* area pictured here, much less on the street. But alcohol is nonetheless linked to romance, and the two glasses are presumably to be shared by a (heterosexual) couple while on a romantic weekend in the city. The fact that most couples out at the bar scene are not married but younger and uncommitted is conveniently absent.

It is the final panel that is most telling and confusing, however. It is shot from below: our gaze is directed up at a second-story colonial window with a small balcony. A white, semitransparent camisole or similar sort of lingerie has been flung out the window and glides through the night air. The brochure reads, "*Hay emociones que en otro lugar no vivirás, aquí sí*" (There are emotions you could not experience in other places, but here yes). What does this aspect of the brochure tell the viewer? That a sexual encounter still framed by romantic elements is only possible in this city? That there is something more pure to be had here? Locals surely cannot fling their undergarments around the main plaza as this photo suggests! Following Barthes and Baudrillard, Casella (1999) sees brochures as sites in which myths are produced.[10] Focusing in particular on the juxtaposition of images and the resulting sequence read by viewers, she argues that tourism brochures constitute "mini tours" that teach viewers how to engage an experience in a particular site. However, such a text can only be successful if readers are equipped with

> the popular and historical knowledge required to fill in the gaps, to know for example what colorful means in a broad and symbolic sense and to add those meanings to their readings of brochures. (p. 205)

While Casella refers to the predominance of "local color" as a trope in Latin American tourism advertising, the same would apply for the area of romance. Readers of this text necessarily bring to it knowledge about what to expect in *provincia*. The brochure's images of clean-pristine, romantic and old-fashioned feed into ongoing understandings about *provincia* as a site of history and bucolic escape from the more negative associations of modern urban life elsewhere. While this brochure fits perfectly into the larger context that would draw out the urban/provincial binary, what does it mean locally? How is it that sex and alcohol were discouraged in the FIC poster case and yet openly promoted in this brochure?

Comparing the brochure and the FIC poster, it appears that the city wants to attract the tourism needed for her own bodily survival—edible resources in this small city must come from without. Foreign tourists arrive seeking romance, the Latin lover, "local color," and colonial charm. Domestic tourists arrive seeking the nostalgic romance of an older, pristine Mexican identity no longer available in the nation's urban centers. The city accepts her own hunger and engages in dialogue with her others in order to constitute herself as a speaking subject. She also responds to these *addressees*, as Bakhtin calls our interlocutors, by regulating her intake of their desires. These

---

[10] Similarly, Raymond Williams in "Advertising: The Magic System," *Advertising and Society*, 1, 1 (2000), underlines the "magic" process such signs and posters use to sell, not the object (or here locale) in question, but the quality or affective aspect the viewer desires. John Urry, in his most recent edition of *The Tourist Gaze* (2002) also emphasizes the mediated aspect of (post)modern tourism, as the media defines destinations and instructs tourists where and how to look, even though he allows for some variation in their gazes.

processes reinforce a sense of self, upholding who the city is and what she needs. This is the healthy, nutrient part that transforms the tourist other into something that "sits well," something "*tragable*" in slang Spanish, that which is acceptable and "swallowable." Together, the two texts and their myriad connotations thus simultaneously allowed the city to expand and contract her margins. Romance, not sex; female-sexual-object/male desire and not male-object/female desire; heterosexual vs. homosexual; hidden indoor bodies, not exposed or displayed bodies; two moderate and elegant glasses of champagne, not large bottles of alcohol being poured into bar-hoppers' open mouths on the dance floor. Because the FIC poster opened up too many questions and spaces and exposed socially unsanctioned desires, it had to be expelled. Because the romance brochure contained the city's images of self and other, it could be permitted.

None of this is black and white, of course. I make two readings here of this first city text. First, the healthy aspect: in major tourist sites such as Cancún, Acapulco, and Puerto Vallarta, Mexico has been force-fed tourist desires and tourist values, which the nation has arguably digested to the detriment of its own health (loss of indigenous languages, the modification of traditional foods and crafts, commoditization of cultural objects, increased problems with prostitution, environmental devastation, etc.). Images of spring break in Cancun and Puerto Vallarta that include nudity, students drinking from liter bottles of tequila, and so forth are regularly seen on cable TV and widely acknowledged (and disparaged) in the city. My city-analysand might be tempted to qualify other tourist cities as prostitute-like in their acquiescence to tourist desires at the expense of their own tastes, opinions, and needs, leaving them drained of any authentic identity or subjectivity. Accordingly, one reading of the city's admittedly repressive poster process and turn to more official representations is that this constitutes a healthy act of self-preservation.

Another necessary reading, however, is that this reveals the ways in which the city is buying into spectacle pressures as she attempts to become another category of tourist desire: idyllic *provincia*. Here, we see her denying her own bodily self in order to comply with these external fantasies. Her own semiotic was not discharged into the FIC discourse; instead she created the romance campaign which plays by the rules of the spectacle and reproduces existing imagery and understandings. This text of an idealized self that meets tourist desires simultaneously situates her within branding trends and distances her from the sexual body. The body cannot subsist on romantic idealizations and empty images. Clearly, the city is strained in her abilities to digest as much otherness as she is being presenting with.

READY FOR ANALYSIS

Let us take another look at the "City of Romance" brochure. If the items featured on the brochure say much about the city's desired identity, can they tell me something more? While the tourist reading has more to do with alcohol and sex, seen in the photographed frames as progressing from drinking with a potential partner, rushing to a room, and taking off clothing, perhaps there is more going here at the unconscious, symbolic level. As a text figuring into my interpretation of the city's presenting problem, it is also possible to read the brochure as a sign that the city is ready to undertake analysis.

The drinks pictured have not been imbibed, suggesting a moment about to occur and a pleasure/desire not yet acted upon (the pleasure of therapy and the possibility of an increased happiness waiting to be seized). Alcohol (the merging of the opposites of fire and water in alchemy) can also symbolize the release of the unconscious and lifting of prohibitions. One could thus interpret this as a sign that the city is ready to allow some of her unconscious desires and fears to rise to the surface. Furthermore, the transparency of the glasses matches the overall shininess and cleanliness of the photos, which is echoed by the multiple reflecting surfaces as well as an open sky in the final shot. This intimates that what is interior is about to be exposed, and perhaps signals the presence of the analyst who will reflect back to the city by providing a necessary addressee. The theme of exposure is echoed again by the clothing coming off: the discarded shoe, which impedes moving forward on the cobblestone, is no longer a problem; and the lingerie piece, which connotes sexual modesty/bodily esteem, has also been discarded. In sum, the city as read through the brochure photos can be understood as getting herself ready for psychoanalysis. Even the original two glasses in the first frame can now be seen as signaling a relationship, not a romantic one with an amorous other, but an analytic one (still steeped in love, as Kristeva understands it). The two glasses illustrate a dialogue being established, since they are identical and equally full, all of which lightly suggests the transference/countertransference dynamic that runs through the therapeutic relationship.

Most importantly, the city is still symbolizing for others. She is drafting tentative responses and communicating, trying to work through her anxieties in words and images instead of retreating to a closed, psychotic state. This is clearly a positive sign, and working through abjection is a normal part of subjectivity, and certainly, a normal part of writing. The city is analyzable, and she is ready to dig deeper. We are reminded of the incredible human need to narrate our stories for others. As Kristeva emphasizes, "The recounting of affects is an unbeatable antidepressant" (2011, p. 277).

What I will attempt to do is lead the city back to a reconnection between her texts and her sensory, desirous, drive-based body. In order to question the tourist spectacle, she must regain authorship over this perfect provincial identity of romance. As Kristeva argues in *Intimate Revolt*, the antidote to the spectacle is nothing less than the imagination. The city must find ways to write herself into the unstable space of the contact zone in a way that preserves her subjectivity while opening up to others at the same time. How to know if what we write interrupts or only reproduces the spectacle? This is a doubt that plagues us all, but Kristeva would exhort the analyst to pay attention to the specific and the singular, to help the city reconnect with the bodily, sensory self as the site from which original, creative, and questioning work will emerge. In the analytic process ahead, we will need to watch where this drafting takes the city in her writing, how bodily space is utilized to respond to the other, and what other psychoanalytical issues underwrite these processes and act upon her psychic space.

Three

Deeper Desires

The Colonial Present, a Don Quijote Fetish, and Maternal Issues

`As our sessions progress and the city speaks more about herself, I start to piece together some of the driving desires behind her composed façade. We begin to unearth unresolved issues rooted in her past, her equivalent to the early childhood stage so essential in psychoanalysis. I am deeply surprised to discover that Spain still matters in all this. While there are fairly rote descriptions about the separation from Spain that seem tired and out-of-date in the 21st century, this colonial history affects the city's current relationships more than I suspected. We also touch upon the deep repressions that the city imposes upon herself, which I believe are significant to her maintenance of self and which underwrite all of her relations with others. I begin to perceive a tension between her desired self-image of colonial tranquility and her truer conflicted state. The "real" problem appears to be emerging.`

Many (if not all) cities have some ideal that they attempt to embody. That Guanajuato aspires to a specific, well-bred, and well-heeled ideal can be witnessed not only in the "City of Romance" campaign but also in the many public texts posted downtown that invite city dwellers to performances, workshops, community- or state-sponsored contests, university seminars, and so on. Posters and flyers within this genre support certain sanctioned performances of local identity. They call "everyone to the theater," ask children to "draw your community," and exhort residents to participate in workshops on popular music, traditional toys, or traditional sweets, themes that connote the idyllic past and revive a certain type of collective memory, some of which is based more on fantasy than reality. These texts thus ask local residents to participate in the city's desired self-presentation, and one does not find in here invitations to consider alternative interpretations, to protest, or anything of the sort. However, to pull off the ideal identity, Gee reminds us,

> It is not enough to get just the words "right," though that is crucial. It is necessary, as well, to get one's body, clothes, gestures, actions, interactions, ways with things, symbols, ... beliefs, and emotions "right," as well, and at all the "right" places and times. (1999, p. 7)

Getting the body right, as our previous session made clear, involves working with both local perceptions and tourist/outsider constructions at once. To meet these desires, the city strives to be clean and orderly, controlled and groomed. Ironically, in the case of Mexico's heritage sites, this order must be enacted within or imposed upon a historical "look." For Guanajuato, the correct look is colonial (17th and 18th century), which is a gloss for *Spanish*, whether this is articulated or not, because the word *colonial* in Mexico is never a signifier for indigenous.

Literary scholar René Prieto writes, "Traveling forward, authors seek to fulfill fantasies in imaginary scenarios where their innermost wishes are acted out by traveling backward to infantile sources for those very wishes" (2000, p. 4). What he means is that authors create something new by turning back to childhood desires, even if unconsciously. As Freud noted in his 1907 essay "Creative Writers and Day-Dreaming," our creations have a "ready-made" aspect about them; we either build upon or reject our origins when we create (Gay, 1989, p. 442). The city, trying to move forward to create a new/better "look" is also pulling from "childhood" traumas and desires, her original separation from Spain: in short, in the moves noted here, she attempts to materialize a fantasy of colonial-era Spain.

This aligns with what Chang observes in Singapore and elsewhere: "Places become signifiers of themes rather than living embodiments on their own" (2000, p. 36). Chang talks about the "superficial but alluring aesthetics" that break actual links with real history and that match up appearances with the ideology of elites and authorities (p. 37). One local resident said something that supports the unreal aspect of these efforts. After observing the refurbishing of an 18th-century plaza, he said, "I do not recognize myself in this space," which one can read as yet another deconnecting of the body from the sign. The improved-upon city does not reflect the actual childhood of her current inhabitants; rather, it reflects the city's semifictional memories of her own Spanish origin.

The possibility that the city's lost other is Spain produces some ambivalence, both for the city in terms of historical events (to be discussed below) and for myself as her analyst. It would be absurd to suggest that in their daily life in Guanajuato city dwellers wake up worrying about whether they have Spanish or indigenous roots, or are somehow preoccupied with Spain at all. Most Guanajuato inhabitants (and most Mexicans) would probably be more likely to label the United States, not Spain, as the current most significant (and often threatening) other and would point northward to debates about cultural emulation, imposition, or rejection rather than across the ocean and back in time toward Spain.[11] But the city has a specific history with Spain. The city is the state capital, and the State of Guanajuato has the official slogan of "The Cradle of Independence," the birthplace of the War of Independence from Spain (1810–1821). The state and the city therefore embody and symbolize the Mexican self that separated from the Spanish other, at least in theory. Consequently, the last thing one would expect in Guanajuato is to see positive associations and identifications with Spain. But rather surprisingly to me, in terms of city history and tourist desires, Spain reemerged as a ghost in the background, lurking as an uneasy presence in current constructions of the "ideal city" identity.

One of the most prevalent symbols of the city is the figure of Don Quijote, hero of Miguel de Cervantes Saavedra's 17th-century Spanish text.[12] The figure of Don Quijote, often accompanied by his sidekick Sancho Panza, maintains an unexpected and ubiquitous presence in Guanajuato. The two appear cast as statues; their names are echoed in plaza names; and Don Quijote's face graces the side of public busses, where he is pictured, rather incongruously, in front of the Guanajuato skyline. He is also featured on the 2011 FIC poster, again in front of the local landscape. Enshrining this image, however, is the local Museo Iconográfico de Quijote, the "Iconographic Museum of Quijote," whose collections consist solely of representations of different aspects of Cervantes's novel. The connection between the novel and the city are recognized outside of the city as well: The 2009 film *El Estudiante*, shot in town but written elsewhere, featured an older Quijote-like and Quijote-quoting main character who returns to college (at the University of Guanajuato) to inspire the younger students with his quirky wisdom.

One is compelled to ask, why would the very site where Mexico was "born" as a nation willingly choose a Spanish icon to represent itself? Why is the city image not an indigenous or, at the very least, a *mestizo* symbol? While the city shares a colonial history with the rest of the nation, two details that make Guanajuato unique must be noted. First, the city was founded by the Spaniards when silver was discovered, and it never had a sedentary indigenous population. The local indigenous groups were fierce and nomadic, and they were never fully brought into Spanish control, which allows the city to maintain that she has a European bloodline and that indigenous people were simply absent. The city thus took on a Spanish "look" immediately as silver money began to flow, and she is considered one of Mexico's most beautiful

---

[11] This is my own opinion; others do insist that the much-talked-about inferiority complex with relation to Spain still persists. One of the psychologists that I interviewed about the city personality and psyche immediately brought up Spain and the shame of being indigenous (5 July 2007). Our different readings of this surprised both of us—probably, it would be more accurate to say that the roots of self-other troubles are embedded in the conquest history, however they are being replayed in current ways in the context of United States–Mexico versus Spain-Mexico.

[12] I employ the local spelling of Quijote with a "j" as it appears on the ticket and at the museum, rather than the "x" used by Cervantes, Foucault, and others.

destinations. Second, as noted above, the city is also the site in which the most significant moves to break from Spain in the early 19th century took place. Officially, this is where the split occurred and where the new nation was born in 1821 when the war ended. These two details thus set up a complex context in which allegiance to and rupture from Spain were both experienced profoundly in a very small space and in a relatively brief period of time. These two historical events thus create a contradiction that the city must work through.

The traditional reading of the conquest posits Spain as father and indigenous Mesoamerica as mother to the Mexican nation that would eventually result. Within common constructions, Spain is also depicted as the male figure that raped the indigenous mother. Despite this paternal identification, which is generally upheld throughout Latin America, Spain is referred to as the *madrepatria*, the mother-fatherland, a term that should lead us to consider *both* aspects of Spain's parental function. A Kristevan analysis places considerable weight upon maternal authority, maternal love, and maternal identifications. And given the fact that the female city-analysand shares the body of Spain (or aspires, in her desires, to look Spanish), this maternal identification seems worth pursuing. Therefore, in order to explore the city's maternal issues, I construct Spain as the maternal, or more precisely, focus in on her maternal aspect, without intending this to be a critique of the existing construction of indigenous mother/Spanish father. I believe that, as the *madrepatria*, Spain may very well embody both of the parental functions, but that an examination of the maternal side may have more explanatory power for this particular city and analysis.

The multiple and ever-growing number of Quijote texts produced by the city are embedded in three stories: (1) the story written by Cervantes; (2) the story of how Cervantes's book became a symbol of the city; and (3) the story of how the Iconographic Museum itself came to be. The texts of course emerge from *El ingenioso hidalgo Don Quixote de la Mancha*, first published in Spain in 1605 by Miguel de Cervantes Saavedra. Episodic in structure, the novel parodies the chivalrous romance style of the day through the recounting of the misadventures of the idealistic knight-errant Quijote and his more earthy, practical partner, Sancho Panza. While the story unfolds in Spain, scholars have documented evidence of Cervantes's awareness of the colonies, pointing out his various references to the slave trade, cacao, gold, and human sacrifice (de Armas Wilson, 2000). The novel itself arrived in the New World within a year of its publication; 72 copies of the first edition were shipped from Seville to Peru between 1605 and 1606 (Leonard, 1992).

While the novel appeared in Mexico in the 17th century, the story of Guanajuato's relationship with Don Quijote unfolds much later. It begins in 1952 when the University of Guanajuato began performing the *entremeses cervantinos*, Cervantes's short satirical works that combined humor with a characteristic mix of the real and the fantastic (see, e.g., his 1615 *Ocho comedias y ocho entremeses*), along with other works from Spain's Siglo de Oro literature. The *entremeses* were performed in the public plaza of San

Roque and continued until 1972, when they were formalized into the FIC (the Cervantino festival discussed in the previous chapter). The first FIC was organized by the federal Department of Tourism, the Instituto Nacional de Bellas Artes, and, notably, the Secretaría de Relaciones Exteriores. To date, it is symbolized by Don Quijote, which has meant that to see an image of Cervantes in Mexico is to think of the Cervantino Festival is to think of Guanajuato.

The final story brings us to the Iconographic Museum, a space quite distinct from the open-air plaza. In 1987, 15 years after the creation of the FIC, the museum was inaugurated for the sole purpose of housing images of Don Quijote and promoting knowledge about the novel. The initial collection of icons and images, and the impetus for the project, hailed from the private collection of an exiled Spaniard, Eulalio Ferrer Rodríguez. Spanish-born Ferrer had a personal history with Cervantes's novel. During the Spanish Civil War, he had been sent to a concentration camp in France for his ideological convictions. There, he met a Frenchman also imprisoned for political beliefs and, in exchange for several packs of cigarettes, the Frenchman gave Ferrer a copy of Cervantes's *Don Quixote de la Mancha*. Ferrer would later claim that the book saved his life—a testament to our need to read, to our need for intellectual stimulation, and concurrently, to the sense of identification or solidarity one finds through reading, especially when it is lacking in daily life.

Once liberated from prison, Ferrer migrated to Mexico City and eventually amassed a notable fortune working in advertising at the onset of the television era. In his private life, he developed a collection of Don Quijote–related icons, deepening his passion for the book. Years later, he came to Guanajuato for the FIC. Impressed by the local honoring of his favorite author and work, he offered to donate his collection of icons to the city if certain conditions were met. These included a suitably notable house and careful attention to the collection, with the provision that if any of these things lapsed, he could reclaim the works. A colonial house with the proper credentials was found, and the Iconographic Museum was born.[13] The museum, a building constructed in the late 17th century, currently houses over 800 works of Quijote-related art, including paintings, sculptures, etchings, and the like, in bronze, acrylic, oil, plaster, and other mediums.

While the city writes myriad Don Quijote texts that are both contained within and spread beyond the museum, I choose a particular Don Quijote text as the focus of my discussion with the city. The text (pictured

---

[13] The house is situated on land that is now downtown but was originally part of a larger hacienda where raw materials from the mines were processed and refined. Its illustrious and varied history includes the French emperor Maximiliano having spent a night there and an existence as a Catholic girls' school, sanatorium, student guest house, as well as home to an American mining engineer, whose descendants form part of the upper echelons of local society. Ferrer, *Museo Iconográfico del Quijote*, <http://museoiconografico.guanajuato.gob.mx>(2 Feb. 2007).

below) is a ticket for entrance to the museum. Abandoned as trash on a dusty pedestrian street, it caught my eye because of its bright color and playful style.

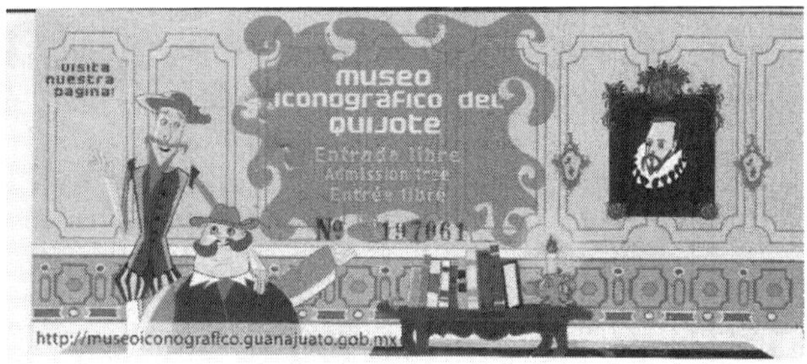

Quijote museum ticket

In hues of blue, purple, orange, and red, the images and text portray what is presumably a room inside the museum. Don Quijote and Sancho Panza stand at the forefront of the image. Behind them is a table, on top of which is a row of books, although the only one with a title is the red-spined *Don Quixote de la Mancha*. Also on the table is an old-fashioned candle, and behind the tables filling up the entire backdrop of the scene is an elegant colonial-style wall adorned with the museum name and, to the right, a framed portrait of Cervantes. Images are brightly colored, and the entire text looks like something that might have been produced by Cartoon Network. The lanky Don Quijote and squat Sancho Panza recall Shaggy and Scooby Doo, and one almost expects to see the ghost/monster/mummy peeking through the eyes of the painting of Cervantes. Furthermore, Don Quijote and Sancho look quite jolly, and this haunted-house-like setting is friendly and colorful, even while containing the requisite connotations of the past, such as ornate woodwork, the candle that suggests pre-electricity times, and the fancy antique décor. Probably what most contributes to the haunted-house effect is the ghostly miasma that frames the museum's name. But Don Quijote and Sancho Panza are not concerned. They are smiling at each other. Cervantes, on the other hand—disembodied and framed on the wall—looks more serious, and his gaze is directed toward the pair in front.

There is only one direct address to the reader, a reader who ideally would have been the one who purchased the ticket and thus accepted an invitation to visit the museum. It asks the reader to visit the webpage. The website opens the door for more action (the only verb on the text is the command *visita*, or "visit"), albeit in the disembodied realm of cyberspace. But otherwise, there is no direct form of address; the ticket is a marker of invitation accepted, a souvenir, a material reminder of a visit now in the past. The only other writing beyond the museum name is "admission free," written in Spanish, English, and then French, the Spanish text being in a slightly larger font.

Through the setting of the scene portrayed on the ticket, Guanajuato is drawn into the past and into fiction (given that the whole museum is predicated upon a novel), as well as into a strange mix of the real and the fantastic, as Don Quijote and Sancho Panza appear to be visiting a museum about their author, Cervantes. They are poised to read representations not only of themselves but more notably of *him*. Subject and object, author and subject, are suddenly reversed. What is going on here?

DON QUIJOTE IS DERADICALIZED, MADE INTO A WOMAN

Don Quijote is a dangerous figure for a city concerned with keeping up romantic, colonial appearances. She likes to keep self and other separate, her signs clean and manicured. Quijote, on the other hand, has always symbolized the semiotic and carnivalesque. Foucault writes that Quijote

> is the disordered player of the Same and the Other. He takes things for what they are not, and people one for another; he cuts his friends and recognizes complete strangers; he thinks he is unmasking when, in fact, he is putting on a mask. (2002, p. 51)

Eulalio Ferrer certainly understood the character and the novel in general as rebellious; his diary, quoted on the museum website (at the time of this writing), testifies that he viewed the text as ideologically in line with his own radical position with respect to the Spanish government:

> Cervantes is a writer of the people. And his work is a song to liberty, a denouncing of social injustices. There is no yours, no mine, but an ours. To be a gentleman, one doesn't have to be a rich man. … Cervantes created them [the characters] to be immortal. Oh what a relief to read Quijote![14]

Ferrer posits reading as a "relief," as a life-giving activity and a source of radical inspiration. The novel's carnivalesque and transgressive nature fits Kristeva's semiotic, poetic language that achieves the life-restoring function that she fears may get squelched in the increasingly closed symbolic world (Kristeva, 1995). Texts guide subjects through what she sees as a dissolution process—they provoke desire and dialogue, which then brings the reader to articulate a new version of self (Kristeva, 1980, p. 165). The episodic structure of Don Quijote may avoid some of the death-drive closure of a more traditional narrative, and its carnivalesque nature can be taken as Kristeva's semiotic. It is not surprising therefore, that Ferrer finds solace and solidarity in this character who disturbs the symbolic order. But in the city, something quite different will happen as she interprets Don Quijote. The city systematically deradicalizes Don Quijote through textual and spatial moves that domesticate

---

[14] All translations from Spanish to English are mine.

and purify any dangerous elements. Both the ticket text and Don Quijote's "museumification" illuminate these processes.

Let us begin with the text. With Cervantes reduced to a head, framed and hung on the wall, his characters are out of his hands. This scene recalls a defining moment in Guanajuato's history, creating a psychic echo of earlier trauma. The instigators of the Independence movement (Hidalgo, Aldama, Allende, and Jiménez), while they achieved their political goal, were not immediately glorified when they died. Considered insurgents by the still-undefeated Spanish, they were beheaded, and the heads were hung from the Alhóndiga building until the end of the war in 1821. The heroes' heads were displayed for the public, the very (national) subjects they authored and birthed, to contemplate. In his essay "The Medusa's Head," Freud (1922) claims quite directly that to decapitate is to castrate; one could easily read this as Spain cutting off the phallus (i.e., power) of the emerging nation (just as the narcos' tendency to behead can be taken as a castration of the contemporary state). The almost-Mexican citizens looked back upon their beheaded creators just as Don Quijote and Sancho Panza find themselves in front of their author's head in the ticket.

Once the war was over, the heads were taken down and the heroes duly glorified. But the act remained—the semiotic, rebellious bodies of the authors were done away with, buried or hidden, and only the heads were kept. The resulting subjects, birthed into being by their beheaded intellectual authors, moved forward to participate in the symbolic of the new Mexican state. Notably, while the Independence heroes are now revered in Guanajuato, they are honored for their creation of the nation—the symbolic, the law—not lauded as role models of dissent and nonconformity. The museum ticket therefore reminds the city of an early castration and speaks to a traumatic move into the new national symbolic.[15]

This same quieting of would-be rebels repeats elsewhere on the city body, most notably in the case of the Pípila statue. Looming over this otherwise tranquil town towers an enormous statue of the Pípila, a local miner who burned down the door of the Alhóndiga, the Spaniards' granary and storage facility for gold, and officially set off the Independence War. The text inscribed on the base of this statue, now a de rigueur tourist site, reads menacingly, "There are still more Alhóndigas to burn," as if to signal that this will always be a place where rebellion will be initiated and subjectivity reaffirmed through violent separations from the status quo. Yet since the Independence era, the city has been firmly conservative. To date, protests are small-scale and viewed with distaste because they disrupt the image of tranquility that people seek in the city. University strikes are rare, which is unusual in a national context of frequent student or faculty strikes. In 2006, when Andrés López Obrador insisted for months that he, not Felipe Calderón, won the presidential elections, none of the ambivalence and insecurity that

---

[15] Kristeva's *The Severed Head: Capital Visions* will appear in English at the end of 2011; however, she also uses the image of beheading in *Possessions* (1998).

rocked nearby areas touched this city. Despite the tone of the text on the Pípila statue, therefore, it does not seem that the tourist's idyllic/apolitical status quo is what the city hopes to burn (at least within the official view). Should the framed head of Cervantes on the ticket text be understood as a warning against rebellion, protest, and speaking out?

If Cervantes's novel is quieted in the city's ticket text, space is also used to transform Don Quijote into a transgression-free symbol. Like all museums, the Iconographic Museum transforms objects that are exotically or disturbingly other into something readable, palatable, and yet at the same time eerily untouchable and bloodless. (Even the Mummy Museum attempts something similar with the dead.[16]) Within the Iconographic Museum, we find hundreds of representations of Cervantes's novel created by an enormous range of artists. Yet as varied as the works of art are, they are simply objets d'art, inert objects. There is nothing playful or movement-oriented about them, nor do they seem to be contextualized in any intentional or collective way with the city.

Psychoanalysis offers a significant history of interpretation of museums, viewing collectionism as obsessive behavior that represents a perverse or overzealous substitution of the desired object with some other stand-in object. This stand-in, be it a charm, fetish, idol, or everyday object onto which or into which desire is displaced, serves as a symbol of something repressed. Freud claims that the fetish is a replacement for the mother's missing phallus (which the boy child reads as the threat of castration), serving as "a token of triumph and safeguard against it" (1927, p. 154). As a substitute for genitals, writes Freud (an avid collector himself), the collected item permits the collector's sexual gratification, deals with "the horror" of the female sex, and relates to the trauma of birth and separation. In the literature, collectors/fetishists are overwhelmingly male, and the city is female ... If cities are polymorphously perverse, a Don Quijote fetish could simply stem more from her masculine side. However, Kristeva often refers to the concept of the fetish without specifying gender, linking fetishes to separation anxieties in a more inclusive sense, rather than narrowly to the male fear of castration; she even goes as far as labeling language a fetish, since language compensates for, even denies, the loss of the maternal:

> It is perhaps unavoidable that, when a subject confronts the factitiousness of object relation, when he stands at the place of the want that founds it, the fetish becomes a life preserver, temporary

---

[16] By museumifying the mummies, of course, death is also excluded from the city body even as it put on display. Several years ago the museum was "made over," and its surreally elegant inauguration represented the mummies back to the city in a newer, more hygienic form. In the context of the current news images of mass graves in the north, it must be an uncanny experience for the urban tourist who has certainly seen the news images of these victims of narco-violence. Is the mummy museum not another mass grave, albeit a sponsored and touristic one?

> and slippery, but nonetheless indispensable. But is not exactly language our ultimate and inseparable fetish? (1982, p. 37)

She continues, "Fetishism appears as a solution to depression and its denial of the signifier" (1989, p. 45). The tendency to fetishize could thus be taken as less exclusively male from this perspective.

Let us briefly consider both possibilities. If Don Quijote is a fetish, Jeremy Braddock (2004) reminds us that fetishism can reveal as much about the discourse of a particular time and place as about the pathology of an individual. He calls for more attention to the historical and intellectual contexts in which collections are embedded, nothing that

> the objects of a collection do not represent the "self" in any private or simple way, for they may also represent systems of knowledge in whose names collectors act, hoping to claim agency and authority through the institutional acceptance of those systems. (p. 50)

This encourages us to read what began as Ferrer's own nostalgic fantasizing about a lost Spain in the 20th century as now a collective fetishizing of Don Quijote. The city places this symbol on top of her early trauma, the split from Spain she shares with the rest of the nation.

As a symbol of the feminine maternal, Quijote is *sacrificed* at the secular altar of the museum, just as the Virgin is sacrificed at the church. Kristeva refers frequently to the Virgin Mary as a symbol. In "Stabat Mater," she critiques "the incredible construct that the West elaborated by means of the Virgin" (1987, p. 256). She shows how the symbol of the Virgin effectively subsumes the semiotic into the symbolic. In return for sacrificing her son, the Virgin is made into an icon (given symbolic status) but at the cost of both the jouissance and the pain associated with sex, childbirth, and death. Patriarchy then asks women to identify with her (painless, joyless) body, which becomes a simultaneous identification with the symbolic order. Women who identify with the Virgin abnegate, sacrificing their own jouissance to the greater social good. They are reduced to the maternal function, excluded from sexuality, "a punitive chastity that seems to be the price women must pay for admission to the sacred—and to representation!" (Kristeva, 2011, p. 64). Don Quijote becomes another Virgin Mary. His semiotic aspects—his radical meanderings, his challenges to the systems—are sacrificed for the city-collective's greater good. He is stripped of his jouissance, deradicalized, virginized even, and set upon the secular altar of the museum-church for the city to identify with. The text that saved Ferrer's life and marked his birth from prison is thus silenced and spatialized like the maternal body, which is what Kristeva terms a "pre-condition for society" because it focuses or organizes violence: the one is sacrificed for the many (Oliver, 1993a, p. 40).

Back to space: We can now add a gendered layer to the museum site. The Iconographic Museum is located within a colonial home, and colonial homes in Mexico (as elsewhere in Latin America) were designed to control who entered and where they circulated, regulating space along race, gender, and class lines. Traditionally, to enter a colonial home thus involved moving through a series of layered spaces that limited visual or other contact with the wife, the highest and most ideal female in the home. For example, the large double doors (the *zaguán*) restricted entrée, as did the practice of conducting business in the front rooms rather than in the more intimate, inner spaces of the home. As both colonial home and museum, the Iconographic Museum is thus doubly a space that encloses, controls, and cuts off images' contact with the outside. An approving account of how the image of Don Quijote was moved inside comes from the museum's own website:

> Very fitting/correct that the Gentleman of the Sad Countenance, so celebrated in this city, should have in the city his residence, after having wandered on horseback through streets, plazas and theatres for many years.

This "museumification" of a street image controls and reigns in the untamed, outside elements. Like a woman, Don Quijote is moved out of the streets and plazas and established within a proper, colonial home. This fits traditional patriarchal constructions of the good woman as the one who stays at home (*en la casa con la pata rota*, as the Mexican joke goes, "at home and with a broken foot") versus the bad woman out loose on the streets.

The city thus sacrifices Quijote, making him into another Virgin figure with whom she identifies. By doing so, she also makes him into the sacrificing good mother that Spain was not and then uses this image to assuage current trauma provoked by tourists and other others. By reproducing his image rampantly, the city creates a Spanish spectacle that maps onto the spectacle of more contemporary tourist images. Previous trauma meets current anxiety in a complex manner that worsens both. By freezing Spain at the moment of separation and attaching Quijote to the wound, the city may be trying to make a character of her loss (Kristeva, 1989), but she is unable to complete the mourning process. As in the case of the Virgin, the connection between the word/image and the desiring body has been severed. The city remains stuck on this wound.

THE TEXT AS A VOYEURISTIC PRIMAL SCENE

As with most analysands, the city circles around in her narrations, and each retelling of the museum ticket text brings out both repeated elements and new nuances. In a subsequent session, her discussions of this particular text, the museum ticket, indicate that it represents a re-creation of the primal scene, which we can interpret as doubly voyeuristic. The tourist can be posed as the first voyeur, looking onto the city's primal scene and further objectifying her. While the other who returns the tourist gaze provokes anxiety, looking at a *representation* of the other allows the tourist to "realize that the picture does not change as our gaze changes," which relieves his anxiety (Lutz & Collins,

1994, p. 366). The tourist-viewer is thus a seer who is not seen, a voyeuristic agent of surveillance, which Foucault (1977) sees as the essence of power. In the ticket text, all of the gazes are closed. There is no communication between the characters represented and anything external. The city permits the tourist to take up this voyeuristic position of power; she becomes simply the desired landscape of Spanish colonialism, the object that he seeks.

It is also worth noting, if only as an aside, that the tourist other who either lost or discarded the souvenir ticket at hand is working out his own nostalgic desires. Goss (2005) points out in his essay on souvenir and sacrifice that a souvenir (here, the Quijote ticket) represents a fetish equally tied to memory, equally estranged from its original body. This resonates with Kristeva's general notions about images and what they do—the souvenir is nothing less than a reminder that we were somewhere, thus representing a futile attempt to find our place even as it reminds us we are no longer connected to our origins. The souvenir represents our modern distance from the semiotic (or the detachment of the sign from the drives; Beardsworth, 2004). So rather ironically and in a different way, even the tourist participates in Don Quijote's fetishization. Furthermore, like characters in a Kristevan novel, transferences abound between all of the relationships at hand—no one is spared their desires, nostalgias, and unresolved traumas.

The ticket also places Cervantes as the voyeur of the primal scene, however, which is more directly important to this analysis. Cervantes becomes the voyeur to his characters' union, yearning to be a part of what he is excluded from. His image is framed, but unlike the monarchs in Velázquez's *Las Meninas*, he is not framed in a mirror image—there are no reflections with or of the outside world. Furthermore, he is cut off from his own body—we have only the head—while Don Quijote and Sancho are flailing, gesticulating, alive. These two characters look at each other exclusively, in a reciprocal gaze, forming a loving pair. This aspect of the text suggests desire obtained and consummated as the tall dreamer is completed by his squatty, realist other.[17] As Prieto elaborates, "The voyeur's yearning actually restages the infant's longing for the mother, observed, or imagined, in the act of lovemaking with the father, the act from which the infant is excluded" (2000, p. 117). Cervantes thus has himself an "eye taco" to use the Mexican phrase (*echarse un taco de ojo*), which signals someone in a committed relationship who still looks at the other attractive people he cannot have, or consume. Desire is reshifted from the phallus to the eye, which sets up the pathology of voyeurism. Voyeurism thus represents a sort of holding place of desire, a functional (or dysfunctional) semisatiation. Like the icon, the text holds and freezes desire.

The ticket attempts to show the self having the (maternal) other it so desires. Nonetheless, we are reminded of the incomplete nature of this desiring

---

[17] Studies on this relationship are common. A. Weber writes about Sancho's role as comic and "ironic deflator" and also makes some suggestive comments about the Hegelian master-slave aspects of their relationship (1995, pp. 101–103). See R. A. El Saffar and D. de Armas Wilson (1993) for further analysis.

process because the lost maternal does not disappear; rather, the maternal continues to haunt at the margins. If Quijote and Sancho achieve independence from their creator and form a union between themselves to substitute the desire for the maternal, Cervantes (Spain) is still watching.

CRISES OF LOVE AND MELANCHOLY

The contours of the problem are coming into view. While Kristeva separates narcissistic and melancholic crises in *Tales of Love* and *Black Sun*, respectively, the city is not a textbook case of either. Rather, she displays elements of both of these crises that wrap together issues of love and loss and that tie into both her abundant textual production and her ongoing mediation of tourist desire and spectacle. And as Kristeva writes, melancholy is the corollary of the amatory state, and depression is "the hidden face of Narcissus" (1989, p. 5). From idealizations to despair, the subject keeps searching for the lost maternal.

It is quite plausible to imagine a Guanajuato-child abandoned by a Spain-mother and left ill-equipped to meet her early needs as part of the new nation. She is left without the protective lining (Kristeva, 1987, p. 24) of primary narcissism (this first experience of love that is maternal) that would permit her to create healthy relationships to others. Primary narcissism is a structure that facilitates the move into the symbolic. In the chora, the infant experiences an objectless identification with the mother at the sensory, bodily level. He experiences himself as one with the mother's love. Through this love, the infant also identifies with a loving Father (Freud's "father in individual pre-history"), or in other words, *the mother's desire*. The fact that the mother has another desired object that is not the infant is painful; however, it gives him faith that there is something else out there, that one thing can stand in for another, which will ease the fear of separation. Narcissistic identifications thus form the bridge over an empty, preverbal/presymbolic transitional space toward the symbolic.

Narcissus is Kristeva's enduring representative for the contemporary subject who fails to complete this process. Narcissus confronts the void between his not-yet-self and his image, and instead of identifying with the father, he remains mesmerized by his image, by the sign. He does not look away and elaborate the loss. He does not transcend by making the requisite preconscious "leap" into language (Kristeva, 1987, p. 41). For Kristeva, therefore, he is our unacknowledged suffering, our unspoken semiotic, our lack of love. This figure speaks to the spectacle-immersed West's incapacity to symbolize joy, pain, self and other, and disconnection from the body. The city, this lonely subject unable to love, fills the void with text, just as other subjects fill the void with TV images, drugs, illnesses … all of which only further close down psychic space. Narcissus is turned into a flower after his death, a flower shaped like two folded hands, to symbolize the need for reflection. For the analyst, Narcissus's psychic space must be reopened: not to move into, but to permit a reworking of these archaic identifications.

The city is staring into the void at these images of her supposedly Spanish self. She does not have the mother's love to ease her shift into the symbolic, and there seems to be no paternal figure, no loving Third for her to look up or out at. Who is the father? The new nation of Mexico? (The son that becomes the father, as Christ to Mary?) The father is hardly a reassuring, strong figure at this point, loving or not ... In the city's case, with the failure of both the maternal and paternal functions, she remains paralyzed in front of her unrealized idealizations like Narcissus. She papers over the void with a "cascade of false images" (Kristeva, 1987, p. 373) that meet tourist desires and that belie an addiction to the maternal Thing (the incompletely mourned mother, which will be addressed below). Don Quijote, therefore, is not the violent text of abjection, but a text of narcissistic depression. Through this text, the city achieves a semisuicidal reuniting with Spain, but she never makes the maternal into the abject. This failure to eroticize the maternal object will make it hard for her to love other others.

How does this situation dialogue (or not) with the work of Mexican psychoanalyst Santiago Ramírez? In his 1957 reading, he finds that Mexico suffers from too much mother and too little father. He refers to "uterine families" where the mother is abandoned and asexual, and the father is either pursuing pleasure elsewhere or simply absent. This sort of mother, he finds, sublimates everything into a Catholic model of abnegated motherhood. In the case of the city, however, we have both too little mother and too little father! The city keeps replaying the loss; she is in love with the image of Spain, and this image is used to cover up the void she feels. This is a pathological response but one that works to some extent, as images, like religious icons, also contain or control anxiety. While the paternal aspect of Spain may provide a Third for other Mexican city-subjects, and I do not wish to deny these more traditional construction of the maternal and paternal functions in terms of indigenous/Spanish, Guanajuato clearly has specific maternal issues. Like Kristeva's ET, exiled from psychic space, the city too is in want of love (1987).

Kristeva writes—to the consternation of some who misread this as essentialism, or the *only* option, which is certainly not her point—that women gain an opportunity to work through maternal issues and depressed sexuality when they become mothers (2011, p. 88). The provincial city attempts to do this as well, but she is unable to rewrite the traditional script and ends up reproducing the traditional, abnegated model. She sacrifices her body and desire just as the Virgin Mary and Don Quijote sacrifice theirs. As she welcomes weary tourists into her folds, listens to their anxieties, and offers them a bucolic respite from the überurban tensions of Mexico City, she becomes the good mother to the nation that Spain was not for her. But she does not resolve her own sexuality. Like the Virgin and the sanctified Don Quijote, she retains an asexual mode that impedes her ability to question, revolt, create. The language of these texts (visual or verbal) loses all affect as it is disconnected from the drives.

Therefore, to the extent that she has the architectural body of the mother (if Spain is the maternal), the city has indeed been unable to fully separate from the mother, mourn the loss, and retain female sexuality (the classic Kristevan understanding of woman's struggle). She becomes instead a subject who self-represses, someone who feels guilty and assumes the narcissistic wound as a flaw of the self. She internalizes the dead/abandoning mother, which yields an intense textual production but forecloses matricide, "that vital necessity for subjectivity" (Kristeva, 1989, p. 27). The city becomes addicted to maternal Thing, which limits her sexuality/desire and pleasure (p. 71). She will need to birth, expel, even kill off this black attachment. Only then will the city be able to speak her semiotic into the system and to love another other.

THE WOUND AS IDENTITY

We have moved beyond the city's more visible struggle to digest everyday otherness. The deeper dynamics of desire for the maternal and the presence of a narcissistic depression have been illuminated. The other is now Spain, deeply implicated in the city psyche. The city clearly experiences desire for Spain (albeit a nostalgic, remembered or invented Spain), fantasizes about this, and through the fetishizing of Don Quijote attempts to resolve this. At the same time, she encourages and cultivates certain aspects of the self through public texts that invite residents and visitors to support this effort. She works on her body as well, attempting to achieve a colonial Spanish "look" to reinforce this, which only furthers her positioning as the desired other of the contemporary tourist.

Unexpectedly and ironically, the city is still hungering for the maternal even as she sells herself as the site where separation (Independence) occurred, an issue that was notably ignored in the 2010 bicentennial celebrations. Does this cause shame or guilt? Tellingly, one analyst notes that shame "is a response to objectification, that is, a response to having one's status as a subject ignored, disregarded, denied, or negated" (Broucek, 1991, p. 8). In the separation process from Spain, which involves the beheading of the movement's intellectual authors, the city's subjectivity (conflated with the rest of the colony at this time) is denied. In essence, the city's wound becomes the crux of her identity, and this shows up most clearly in her texts about Don Quijote, a symbol of her unfinished separation process. The obsessive production of Don Quijote texts affords the city a strategy through which to contain the loss of the Spanish maternal and to control her own desire. The use of this image also points to an emerging pattern of depoliticizing and quieting of images that represent either ambivalence or rebellion (the Independence heroes, the Pípila, the Virgin Mary). This appears to form the city's modus operandi; she creates a fantasy version of these elements that conveniently leaves out their more radical potential.

The Don Quijote image is thus highly celebrated and highly controlled. Yet, the control is never fully accomplished. The museum ticket slipped out of the building or a tourist's hand and became trash—a blight on the pristine colonial body. The perfect tourist memento now becomes something that the city must tidy up. This self-surveillance bridges the bodily and the textual; in her attempt to maintain the colonial look, she also contends with her own internal editors that are obsessed with the idea of creating a perfect text. While the Quijote text is not the abject draft that horrifies all writers, it is a depressed one. Beneath this façade of tranquil perfection courses intense emotional pain as the city struggles to recuperate what has been lost. I wonder how else she goes about managing the intense editing process involved en route and what other unsightly things she might struggle to purify out of her texts. Our next sessions will probe further.

Four

Calladita, te ves más bonita
Analyzing Silences and Erasures

A certain sense of satisfaction seeps through me as I get ready for the city's next appointment. We are now getting into the thick of things and uncovering the roots of her troubles. The past is bubbling up into the present, something I can tell the city is reluctant to disclose too much about. When the office door closes, muting the sounds of street vendors, children rushing to school, and the occasional bank alarm, the silence seems to expand. I feel her wanting to *delete, delete* even as she speaks; she is hesitant, terrified even, to allow her past to fully emerge. It is not easy for her (or anyone else) to open up these tunnels into the past that has been sealed for so long. I have many questions now; however, I have to be careful to listen more than probe at this juncture. Within the sanctuary that psychoanalysis creates, will she speak more of the unspeakable? Will she talk more about this past that she has so carefully erased? Or will she remain silent? Either way, both the answers and the absence of answers will be telling.

The act of writing (a manuscript or a self) is full of editings and erasures, silences and absences. While the standard advice to writers is "write what you know," there are some things, of course, that we know all too intimately yet do not wish to recall, much less make public by writing about them. The city is no exception. "*Calladita, te ves más bonita*" is a popular saying usually used with children or, all too frequently, from husband to wife. It is translated as "quiet, you look more beautiful." Your most pleasing appearance coincides with your silence—the city almost seems to take this as a personal mantra. That which is not-beautiful or ambivalent must be edited out, sloughed off the city surface and deleted from the city's conscious like the trash-ticket. Indeed, the uglier events and darker side of the city are rarely spoken about, and people reiterate the phrase *aquí no pasa nada* (here nothing happens) to a carnivalesque degree, despite the fact that everyone is aware of cases of government corruption, the ever-nearing presence of narco-violence, and so on.

In the city's process of editing and reediting, what else gets taken out and made to "not happen"? As the city stays quiet and resists symbolizing what ails her, I examine some of the themes she chooses not to write about. This process of reflection—of reading between the lines of text she creates—reveals more of the deradicalization, purification, and repression that emerged in the previous session. These erasures also unveil a new theme (not written about) that will spur further questions about what lies beneath the city's physical and psychic surface. The need to narrate through these darker areas becomes increasingly urgent. Is silence a dead end or a fertile beginning?

ESTAS RUINAS QUE (NO) VES / THESE RUINS YOU DO (NOT) SEE

One text that the city reads on a regular basis is *Estas ruinas que ves*, by Guanajuato-born Jorge Ibargüengoitia. If Don Quijote provides the first emblematic character for the city's subjectivity, this novel, published in 1975 and winner of the Premio Internacional Novela México, constitutes a more recent identity text, although, again, among the well-educated parts of the population. While the full text of the novel is not posted on the city's surface, the novel itself is immersed in the details of the city's physiognomy. It names many local sites, albeit in pseudonymic form, that are easily identified. The entire novel is transparently disguised as taking place in a fictional setting called Cuévano, and local readers can pick out which café, which church, which house, and probably to some extent which event certain scenes refer to. Academics in particular make frequent reference not only to the book, author, and later film but also to the characters and places in the text. The name "Cuévano" also appears as the name of a local bus line and is written on the sides of these busses, and people refer to themselves as *cuevanenses*, residents of this (semi) fictional site. Ibargüengoitia (1979) notes in a later article that one woman even went around saying that she was "Gloria Revirado's mother" (Gloria being a main character) in an attempt to take ownership of some of the novel's eventual fame. Once again, the complex reversal—instead of a book that represents a city, the city now creates representations of the book, mimicking the previous chapter's discussion of Don Quijote's characters pictured in front of a representation of their author.

The title of the novel translates as "These ruins you see." Briefly, the novel narrates the story of the intellectual Francisco Aldebarán, born in Guanajuato but raised in Mexico City, who returns to the city to teach at the university. To some extent, the narrator's trajectory mirrors the experiences of the author, who also left the city at a young age and returns via this text. Aldebarán becomes enamored of one of his students, Gloria Revirado, who is engaged to an outsider trying to sell early computers to the governor. The narrator recognizes his old city; yet, he no longer forms part of it. He identifies Gloria as the face of the past that he yearns to possess, viewing her as the authentic and pure personification of *provincia*, of Cuévano. At the same time, as he pines for Gloria, he is told (erroneously) by a drunk friend that Gloria suffers from a heart condition, which has put her into the unfortunate situation where having sex would certainly kill her. As he laments this seemingly tragic state of affairs, Aldebarán enters into a rather raucous affair with the married Sarita, wife of a colleague.

How is the city portrayed in the novel? How does the city interpret this novel? A closer look shows that the revolutionary, semiotic aspects of the text are silenced in local readings. Ibargüengoitia portrays the city as a ghost town, as being in ruins. The word "ruins" in the title does not connote Aztec ruins; rather, it refers to the fate of most mining towns after the boom period has past and inhabitants have moved on. While the city of Guanajuato did not dry up amid the cacti like many of her more rural counterparts in nearby areas, the novel makes explicit references to the many things that the narrator finds in a state of deterioration. Benjamín Valdivia (2006) enumerates the novel's references to ruin: the barren mines, deafness and blindness in several individuals, imported food that never satiates hunger, a flasher-pervert, poor table manners, gossip, adultery—in short, architectural, physical, moral, behavioral, and other sorts of decline.[18] Ibargüengoitia also makes reference to the exodus of the city's upper class population. Tired of constant loss through flooding and the downturns of the mining cycle, the true elite (those who could afford to) moved out in the 1920s and 1930s. He writes, "They spoke of Cuévano as if they were speaking of someone on their deathbed … it's all to cry about, there" (1975, p. 72). This particular decline allowed a second- or even third-tier elite to usurp the place of the city's founding families. As one historian commented, those who own historical family mansions are usually linked back to the third or fourth cousin and sometimes even to the house caretakers of the actual aristocratic family of origin, making their supposed blue-bloodedness quite suspect.

Ibargüengoitia documents these ruins, and not always sympathetically. Despite his nostalgia, one also finds a perceptible tone of scorn as a worldlier, Mexico-City-raised Ibargüengoitia re-views his past from a more cosmopolitan viewpoint. For example, he makes fun of the frequent use of euphemisms to verbally paint over class inequality. At myriad points he also calls the city names, referring to her gossipy nature and labeling the city a *nido de víboras* (nest of snakes) and *manicombio grandote* (huge insane asylum). He ridicules a character who insists that the city's economic downfall cannot have anything to do with the Depression, thus refusing to see anything other than the local as important and playing on the city's sometimes insular outlook. Most frequently, he attacks what he views as a false morality, and this

---

[18] Historian Isauro Rionda Arreguin (1985) corroborates this. After the Revolution of 1910, he asks what was left in the city. His answer?

> A good pile of ruins and people sick with silicosis, water-filled mines, old deteriorated haciendas, little population, houses falling down, racketeer business, mining ghost towns, huge hollows in the subsoil and a few last names, that only live off memories. All of this and more was Guanajuato before 1950. City that more than agonizing, already smelled of death. (pp. 68–69)

could be read as the dominant theme in the book. This false morality emerges most clearly in the realm of sexuality, which brings us back to the female characters.

For a short novel, the frequency and range of instances of "perversion" (to use the term as the book does) is revealing. For example, early in the novel Aldebarán is drinking with friends at a bar, and an unknown man comes over and urinates on them. The same man gives Aldebarán a small box that turns out to contain pornographic pictures. One of Aldebarán's colleagues is a Peeping Tom. There is also the mysterious figure of *el ensabanado* (the one cloaked in a bed sheet), a flasher who roams the streets and terrifies innocent young women by displaying his nudity. Aldebarán himself begins an affair with a married woman. And in a scene central to the novel, he paints a slightly off-color image onto a restaurant wall that he and his university colleagues are helping to refurbish. He paints an image of a naked woman—who others then see as resembling Gloria—over an electric box (again the need to hide the unseemly), and he names this figure Mechanical Eve. The two switches on the box are positioned where the figure's nipples are. Also, throughout this scene, Sarita appears in a short smock that reveals the fact that she wears no underwear, something duly noted by the men present. Near the end of the story, Aldebarán finds himself dining at a hotel where a gay couple in the background appears to be conducting an affair. The author thus seems to go out of his way to include a range of sexual references that (1) have little to do with the plot and therefore seem out of place; and (2) should be further "out of place" for such an idyllic city of tradition, thus interrupting the superficial layer of nostalgic remembrances that readers easily identify in the novel. None of this is mentioned in local discussions and portrayals, however.

But what intrigues me most in terms of the city's analytical process is the portrayal of the two female characters in the novel. While they are posited as opposites, they turn out to be much less polarized than one expects. Gloria Revirado is seen by the narrator and locals as the pure female figure, a symbol of all that is good in *provincia*, and all the more tragic in Aldebarán's fantasies because her supposed illness would make sex (defilement) the cause of her death (again, the good woman/the good city as one who is separated from sexuality). Sarita, the adulterous wife, is not necessarily poorly viewed by society, as the affair is not public, but she is the "bad" woman to Gloria's pure one. She enters freely into an adulterous relationship with Aldebarán, which is documented throughout the book as a rather high-rolling, fun affair. This would all appear to set up the classic good/bad binary for women in Mexico specifically and in patriarchal societies in general. However, the reality is much more complex. Gloria Revirado (whose name literally means "reseen glory," i.e., a return to a glorious past) represents the nostalgic perfect past that cannot be possessed. But this perfection is only an illusion; she flirts with Aldebarán quite directly at various points in the novel, and at the end of the book it is revealed that she does indeed engage in sexual relations with her suitor and that the whole health issue has been invented as a joke. Does she perhaps represent an invitation to resee the history of the city with a clearer, more honest vision? To question local constructions of self as well as outsider/ national constructions of *provincia*? Is she not the personification of the Kristeva's revolt, an invitation to return, relook, reimagine, as posited in *Intimate Revolt* and beyond? Clearly, Gloria found a way to insert her semiotic desires into the symbolic without exiting from the system entirely. By looking to a Third, an outside lover, she also escapes the bowl-shaped city with its stagnated maternal-desexualized morals. And what about Sarita? Here is a woman living out her jouissance despite the fact that she is both wife and mother. The mother who enjoys her sexuality? What would Kristeva make of her character? What does Ibargüengoitia wish to claim?

The novel disrupts. The classic polarization of the two female figures turns out to be false, the boundary is blurred. Female sexuality is put into a happy crisis. Ibargüengoitia does not respect the usual constructions of good/bad female roles, and neither character comes to a bad end. While the novel provoked scandal at the time of publication, the contemporary city ignores the multiple insults leveled at her fictional counterpart, Cuévano, and claims the book as simple testimony to her provincial loveliness. "These ruins you see" are exactly the ruins the city pretends *not* to see. The city forefronts the beautiful buildings that attest to a past of genteel wealth, while backgrounding and denying the shabbiness or overall decay that characterizes other aspects of her physical self. Morally, as our subsequent sessions will show, similar moves are also employed to make her sexual self less visible. What stands out here, however, is that the novel's critique is lost on the city.

For Kristeva, novels offer the chance of resurrection, a cure for abjection and melancholy, an opportunity to work through and/or sublimate. The novel should be taken as "not an inquiry into source, to be glorified, but a composition-recomposition of the subject" (2011, p. 291). Ibargüengoitia does just this: he recomposes himself and reconciles his own ambivalent feelings about the maternal city of his youth. Kristeva further notes that "the novel is the only resurrection, the rebirth of those with no reference points, the promise of a flowering for those with no system, no home, for travelers" (p. 289). And once again, the traveling author can create a home through writing. The city-reader, however, does *not* undergo the same process. While the novel could have opened up a new space and offered the city a return, she refused to read it this way. Therefore, the author-other gains the opportunity to return and work through his issues, but the city herself is left playing the supporting maternal role with no addressee of her own to return the favor. The novel's transgressive message is ignored ("nothing happens"), marking yet another purification that maintains the usual images.

A similar process occurs with artist Diego Rivera, who like Ibargüengoitia was also born in Guanajuato and raised in Mexico City. It is unlikely that Rivera, with his radical politics and liberal sexual behavior, would have been idealized and shown off in the city. Rivera, arguably Mexico's foremost painter of the 20th century, left Guanajuato at the age of six, and while the city claims him now as her own, in actuality Rivera's family left precisely because his father found the atmosphere too stifling.[19] Both of Rivera's parents were schoolteachers, and while his father held political office and had interests in the mines, he was anticlerical and also edited a liberal newspaper, *La Demócrata*, which was oriented toward the plight of the working poor. This marked the family as decidedly not mainstream in this conservative city. Rivera himself later moved from Mexico City to Spain and Paris and, like his father, took on the cause of workers' rights, even becoming a member of the Communist Party. And as is widely known, the romantic adventures and experiments of both Rivera and Frida Kahlo would hardly fit with the city's traditional morality. The Rivera family did not return to Guanajuato regularly, nor did Rivera himself, and, indeed, the city is never represented in Rivera's paintings.[20] Yet, the city now claims him.

Both Rivera and Ibargüengoitia would have been unable to say (write, paint) the ideas they espoused had they remained in Guanajuato. Having left, both of these native sons are held out as icons of identity, but in such a way that completely silences both men's identities where they do not fit in with the city's sense of self. As Cronin finds,

> The Prodigal Son may be fêted by his father, but other family members feel only resentment. The promise of closure, of synthesis in return, becomes an open or festering wound. The traveller who has been to foreign parts is not only *unsettled* but s/he becomes on return an *unsettling* figure. (2000, p. 65)

The city employs silence as a strategy to resettle these figures, engaging in a type of translation of their worldliness back into local discourse. As Rivera became iconized as "the" painter of 20th century Mexico, Guanajuato opened his birth home as a museum in 1975. Within the museum, there is little direct allusion to Rivera's politics or less-than-discreet personal life; it is simply a museum that houses a range of his art. With respect to Ibargüengoitia, the author was killed in a plane accident in 1983, which to some extent prohibited any sort of reconciliation or future conflict. His ashes were eventually returned to the city, and a strange return it was, as one scholar comments (Argueta, 2006). In the ceremony, only about 30 people attended, and the priest officiating mentioned to all present that he had never read any of Ibargüengoitia's work. Argueta notes as well that, at the time of this event, neither the local university nor the local cultural institute had ever published

[19] Rivera formed part of what was known as the Mexican modernist school, along with the two other great muralists of the day, José Clemente Orozco and David Alfaro Siqueiros. This group's style was characterized by the use of color, scenes of intense activity, an emphasis on popular everyday life elements, and indigenous references.

[20] Rivera's *Día de las Flores* may represent Guanajuato, since this is a local holiday, but there exist reports of a similar celebration in Xochimilco (in Mexico City), so this is not definite. For an early yet fascinating consideration of Rivera's own maternal issues as they showed up in his art, see Mexican psychoanalyst Santiago Ramírez's 1961 essay, "Expresiones psicológicas en la plástica de dos pintores mexicanos."

any writing by Ibargüengoitia. Since then, however, the author's work has been featured in the 2008 FIC as well as at several important book fairs in town, and an unpublished play by Ibargüengoitia was also finally edited by the University of Guanajuato Press. Having been "cleaned up" through several decades of closed-eye readings, Ibargüengoitia is now an acceptable local hero and representative.

Cronin asserts that in these cases of redomesticating the traveler, "The purpose of the naturalising, fluent strategy is to efface the traces of travel, to make the text appear, in effect, as if it had never left home" (2000, p. 65). The city attempts to make Rivera and Ibargüengoitia appear as if they had never left, as if they had never traveled and met others, as if they were as pure and nostalgic as the city herself. In this sense, like the Pípila of the previous chapter who will burn no more Alhóndigas, and the decarnivalesqued Quijote, Ibargüengoitia and Rivera are also edited for in-town apparitions, and space continues to play a key role in how this is achieved. And in this move to devour her prodigal sons, the maternal city provides us with yet another scenario where the city offers the best of all possible worlds, a world where "nothing happens," and anything ugly (Ibargüengoitia's insults, Rivera's outlandish behavior and politics) is quickly erased and forgotten. Thus, the patterns identified in the previous sessions with the city-analysand are only deepened as we see more repressions, silencing, and purifying moves.

MINERS, RACE, AND UNACKNOWLEDGED SUFFERING

Another rather gaping area of silence in the city's texts and discourse revolves around the city's mining history. At each entrance of the city, one finds a statue of miners at work. At the formal entrance coming off the highway from León, the statue consists of two miners hammering and drilling. At the northern end stands a lone miner with his tools on his shoulder, in the middle of a tiny intersection flanked by a plaza and a gas station. Taken together, the pair of statues marks the city's boundaries and symbolically appears to contain her. Monuments close off space by defining interpretations and foreclosing alternative understandings (Farrar, 2000, pp. 11–12). What darker histories does the city attempt to obscure here?

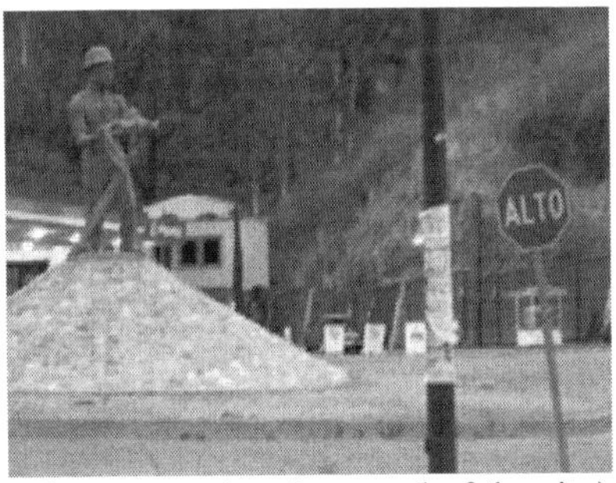

Miner statue (northern end of the city)

That the city is held between two representations of miners is not inappropriate, since Guanajuato owes its existence to its mining roots. Silver was first discovered in 1548 by Spaniard Juan de Rayas, and the Spanish Crown quickly sought to exploit this area's subterranean riches. As is commonly known in town, by the 18th century the La Valenciana mine (whose surface-level construction was shaped into the pointy form of the Spanish crown) was producing 30 percent of the world's silver. The resulting wealth gave birth to the city and made possible the lavish churches and beautiful architecture that would eventually qualify her for the coveted UNESCO patrimony status in 1988.[21] In her work on the mining history of Guanajuato, Ferry comments that locals describe the city as "born of silver," referring to roads made from silver, homes constructed from silver, and even themselves as surely having digested some of the mineral over time (2006, p. 298, p. 308). However, further investigation reveals that the history glorified in the city body also includes less-spoken-about instances and patterns of violence, hardship, racial shame, and economic desperation.

During the colonial empire, the mines demanded a steady labor supply, which created an ongoing challenge for Spain. Indigenous labor was consistently tricky to harness given the particularly bellicose nature of the semilocal Chichimeca group (a nomadic population that resisted Spanish control in what became known as the War of the Chichimeca). During the 1500s, as new mines were being registered in quick succession (over 40 by 1559, according to Blanco, Parra, & Ruíz-Medrano, 2000, p. 45), indigenous workers were often brought in from farther away to work as slaves in the mines. Less acknowledged in local accounts, however, is the fact that African slaves provided a small yet significant part of this labor force. While Mexico was never a large-scale New World importer of African slaves (the majority were sent to the United States and Brazil), epidemics and suicide created a dearth of indigenous labor, and, when indigenous slavery was later abolished, the Spanish Crown was forced to seek an alternative labor solution. African slavery was thus introduced to Mexico, not only as labor for the southern sugar haciendas, but also to address the problem of working the mines (Gálvez Jiménez, 1995, p. 19).[22] By the end of the 16th century, approximately 1,022

---

[21] The UNESCO proposal to include Guanajuato as part of the patrimony program states the following:

> Founded when the silver mines were opened, Guanajuato had a symbiotic relationship with them up to the 19th century. Its growth, the layout of its streets, its plazas, and the construction of hospitals, churches, convents and palaces are all inextricably linked with the industrial history of the region which, with the decline of the Potosí mines in the 18th century, became the world's leading silver extraction centre. (UNESCO, 1987, p. 39)

[22] While the first destination for slaves was the mines, many slaves were also sent to the sugar cane mills of Morelos and Veracruz and, to a lesser extent, to coconut and cacao plantations on the Pacific coast (Gálvez Jiménez, 1995, p. 19).

African or African-descended slaves were working in the Guanajuato mines (Blanco et al., 2000, p. 65).

In his lyrical book, *The Conquest of America*, Tzvetan Todorov (1982) describes the mining scenario. He quotes extensively from Motolinia, a Franciscan priest who wrote an important early chronicle of the conquest detailing 10 plagues (divine punishment) incurred by the Indians for their heathen ways.[23] Of the 10 plagues, three relate directly to mining. The first two mention the high death toll among Indians who worked in the mines due to the horrific conditions in which they worked. But the third provides a fascinating identification of the slaves as text; it is worth citing Todorov's paragraph-long description (which includes quotations from both Motolinia's chronicle and a letter from Father Vasco de Quiroga to the Spanish crown) to bring this point forward:[24]

> "The eighth plague was the slaves whom the Spaniards made in order to put them to work in the mines." At first those who were already slaves of the Aztecs were taken; then those who had given evidence of insubordination; finally all those who could be caught. During the first years after the conquest, the slave traffic flourished, and slaves often changed masters. "They produced so many marks on their faces, in addition to the royal brand, that they had their faces covered with letters, for they bore the marks of all who had bought and sold them." Vasco de Quiroga, in a letter to the Council of the Indies, has also left a description of these faces transformed into illegible books like the victims' bodies in Kafka's *Penal Colony*: "They are marked with brands on the face and in their flesh are imprinted the initials of the names of those who are successively their owners; they pass from hand to hand, and some have three or four names, so that the *faces of these men who were created in God's image have been, by our sins, transformed into paper* [emphasis added]." (p. 137)

Miners made into paper, slaves into text—this is the city's original surface upon which her history was written. This violent history is even more shameful because it challenges the local assertion that the city population has always been *criollo* (of pure Spanish descent), which is understood as the opposite of indigenous descent (despite sexual practices to the contrary). Therefore, not only is there an indigenous presence in the city's history, but also there is a significant slave narrative silenced over time. And there is an

---

[23] These included smallpox, death from the conquest wars, famine, mistreatment by intermediaries between the Indians and the Spanish, taxes, the violence of the mines, accidents during the building of Mexico City, the slaves, service in the mines, and the factions between Spaniards (Todorov, pp. 135–138).

[24] Father Vasco de Quiroga, or Tata Vasco, as many indigenous people called him, was an apologetic Spanish priest who wrote on behalf of the Indians, arguing that they were human and had souls worth saving, a subject of intense debate during and after the conquest.

African/Afro-Mexican component as well, with its own violent history. This is decidedly not something the city writes about. More unnameable and unspoken suffering in the city body …

City inhabitants refer constantly to the wealth of the mines and the glorious past that created the beautiful architectural façade enjoyed in the present. To some extent, past miners are seen as agents of this beauty, since they played a fundamental role in the city's early history. Yet the current miners—the live miners of today—are erased from view and rarely seen in the public space. More frequently, they pass in the mining company bus and are glimpsed in the tunnels in the early mornings and late evenings, shadowy figures whose helmets obscure their faces and make them all look alike—image over reality. On the few days a year that the miners emerge into the sunlight onto the main Plaza de la Paz, it is religion and ritual that step in to regulate their penetration into a space and time (*centro* area/daytime) that is normally shut off to them. The main day this occurs is the Friday before Holy Week—on the Day of the Virgen de Dolores (Our Lady of Sorrows)—and during the festivals for the Virgen de Guanajuato in May. The rest of the year, however, one rarely hears any news stories about real miners; nor do people speak of silver prices, as mining has ceased to be the city's main source of income. While some references to mining show up in tourist trinkets, actual miners are eerily missing in both discourse and text.

In his critique of the Museo Nacional de Antropología in Mexico City, Mexican anthropologist Guillermo Bonfil Batalla (1987) accused 20th-century Mexico for having built a tremendous monument to "a dead world," that of the indigenous groups. He describes a process of "ideological alchemy" by which the non-Indian Mexicans take ownership of this indigenous past, while the contemporary, live Indian is ignored, denied, or museumified (p. 91). One could easily accuse the city of doing the same with the miner and the mines. The dead miner of the past is immortalized in the two statues that hold the city; and the semidead mines that cannot produce enough silver are preserved as tourist sites. The current miner is ignored. When he emerges from the mines to the city surface, he represents the abject, the repressed that returns to haunt the city and remind her from whence she came; he is someone who has been down to see what is hidden and knows too much. The figure of the miner thus provides a semihidden, ambivalent text that lurks literally just beneath the city's surface-level beauty.

Mining is an industry that always suffers cycles of boom and bust, and these stories have also been taken out of the city's everyday texts. While the industry historically has suffered ongoing highs and lows, major crises on the eve of the Independence War's outbreak were particularly devastating. The years 1785–1786 witnessed both an economic crisis and a severe frost that devastated crops in the fertile low-lying areas of the region. This led to food shortages, which in turn provoked one observer to qualify 1786 as the "year of hunger" (Blanco et al., 2000, p. 99).[25] Plazas became "scenes of sadness and begging": the plague attacked many; and the city's morale was at a record low (p. 99). Soon after, another downward turn affected the economy. The costs of mining inputs rose considerably from 1800 to 1810, which provoked further shortages at the beginning of the war. After the silver heyday of the late 18th century, the War of Independence (1810–1821) thus came as a harsh and final blow, affecting mining drastically. Blanco, Parra, and Ruíz-Medrano (2000) stress that the violence that characterized this period was augmented by a regional agricultural crisis (p. 100). They also comment that, when the Alhóndiga was destroyed by the Pípila, not only foodstuffs and silver were lost, but significant quantities of mining inputs perished as well. Loss occurring right at the Alhóndiga? The site at which the break from Spain was staged? This is a hidden wound right on the city surface. Celebrated as the spot where the revolt began, when the Pípila burned down the door, the fact that the Alhóndiga has this second signification is rarely acknowledged.

Making matters worse, both the Royalists and the insurgents used the mines to finance the war, thus destabilizing every element of the process and creating a situation that would be difficult to recover from after the war (Blanco et al., 2000, p. 101). Anxiety and fear about outsiders also grew at this time; the rabble-rousing crowds, formed in large part by noncity residents, quickly spun out of control, and many creoles—the would-be instigators against the Spanish-born *gachupín* ruling class—quickly withdrew their support because they feared an uncontainable lower-class uprising (Grzegorczyk, 2005, p. 20). The city's ambivalence about Independence once again appears. She was left without her earlier sense of security, wealth, safety, and contentment (p. 104). A blow to the ego and a dismantling of her sense of subjectivity … Thus, while the taking of the Alhóndiga is retold as the heroic defeat of Spain, there is real loss, both economic and emotional, for the city.

What I observe in these seemingly unrelated stories of Jorge Ibargüengoitia's novel, Diego Rivera's work and life, and the miners is a pattern of more silencing. The other's difference (political, sexual, racial) is not recognized, but annihilated in popular memory and discourse. Origins, which the city so desires, are denied. Gloria Revirado, the miners, and Rivera, are all left unspoken, untold, not discharged and made meaningful.

ABANDONMENT AND THE COMPULSION TO REPEAT

Beyond this repression, which could be taken as simply more exaggerated conservatism to maintain the correct image, there lurks something deeper and earlier. Spain abandoned the city at the moment of Independence, withdrawing the financial support behind the mines. The newly independent State could not afford to take over the exploitation of the now-locally managed mines. With the subsequent War of the Reform (1858–1861), things worsened, and by the

[25] There is some discrepancy here: Lucas Alamán cites 1783 as the "year of hunger" (Joseph & Henderson, 2003, p. 176).

end of the 19th century the state saw a tremendous out-migration as mining work declined drastically. Foreign companies came in after this, but with the onset of the Revolution in 1910 they evacuated as well. Also at this time, as Ibargüengoitia has articulated, the upper and middle classes followed in their wake, which created a new elite with little claim to their position. Ultimately, silver itself abandoned the city. The Veta Madre (Mother Vein) from which the bulk of the silver was mined, was depleted, making silver into yet another abandoning mother. More recently, since 2010, many foreign tourists and students have abandoned the city in fear that the national-level narco-violence might make its way into her geography (although it has not). Abandoned first by Spain and then successively by foreign investors, miners, the elite, tourists, and silver itself, the city knows all too well that the other leaves even if she herself has not wronged anyone.

The city's experiences of abandonment go back two centuries and continue to this day, and this may explain why she maintains such an insular outlook. It is frequently said in town that residents do not imagine outside of this topography. As one saying goes, "*Para los guanajuatenses, el mundo se acaba detrás de los cerros*" (For Guanajuatens, the world ends beyond the mountains). One local scholar describes Gloria Revirado as being representative of the city herself: she symbolizes the authentic *cuevanense*, physically close yet at once distanced (Palacios, 2006, p. 101). Similarly, the categories of other are quietly vilified, yet remain strong: *fuereño*, *ajeno*, *de fueras*—these words are used frequently in daily language, and certainly more so than in other larger cities. Miners, foreigners, Indians, the elite—all enter into the same ephemeral, untrustable category. As a defense, the city allows them in but only so much—the psychic version of the colonial home that regulates entrée. Others can provide wealth, but they make poor objects of love because they leave all too easily.

The city cannot find love in her others; or to put it another way, she has *many dead mothers* … This is not atypical in these circumstances. As Kristeva has observed in her clinical practice, the depressed person ends up with "continuously disappointing adventures and loves" (1989, p. 13), and her "favorite partner or her husband is a fulfilling although unfaithful mother" (p. 84). Through the infidelities of the other, the city obtains perverse and melancholic pleasure as she relives her wound. Kristeva continues: "The sensory, sexual, fantasy-provoking ill-being of abandonments and disappointments" makes melancholy into an internalized black hole (p. 87). Loss is thus experienced as a psychic void, a crypt holding the dead mother. Citing Duras, Kristeva writes, "You think you weep because you can't love. You weep because you can't impose death" (2011, p. 247). The city's moves to deradicalize can be taken as masking more violent urges as she attempts to "impose death" by deleting. In this sense, she takes on the role of the bad mother whose instinctual emotions and aggressive feelings are neither tamed nor diffused through sublimation.

Worse yet, because the libidinal maternal bond with Spain is death-leaning (primary narcissistic depression is obviously prelibidinal because the mother was never made into an erotic object that could be recovered in language), masochism results. The pain and violence of the city's history are turned back on the self, causing the city to over-repress herself in unhealthy ways as she interprets these events as her own flaw. Like melancholy itself, the masochistic sexuality this all produces has also been metaphorized as a black hole or a void, which brings us to the mines themselves. Are the city's mines representations of these depressed voids and black holes? Are the mines this crypt that holds the dead mother and locks away the city's sexual self?

If things are bleak in *Black Sun*, her book on melancholy, Kristeva offers us a more hopeful association in *Hated and Forgiveness*. In this more recent work, she posits the black hole of the void now as the space of the Virgin. How is this? The Catholic Trinity (Father, Son, Holy Ghost) is a triangle of three points organized around a void. Without Mary, this triangle could not exist: she birthed the Son; through her love combined with the Word and the Holy Spirit, he came into being. Therefore, her absence is the "'hole' around which the filial/paternal symbolic revolves" (Kristeva, 2011, p. 181). Although she too has been deleted from the "ideal" (patriarchal) text, her presence has not been rendered unessential. The Virgin, continues Kristeva, denotes the unfathomable beginning we cannot picture, and virginity becomes the "space before space," the chora before the Word, "this nonplace, this unthinkable outside" (p. 65). Empty space made into psychic space … Even better, Kristeva writes, "I would like to imagine that the Virgin would urge us to dream to this point: before time, before the subject, before the beginning, which is the beginning of desire" (p. 65). Can the city dream back to this union she is so missing, to the "before" of her narcissistic depression and melancholic sexuality?

A LA LLORONA DREAM: VEILED SOLUTIONS?

The following text, back in the public realm and ostensibly part of the tourist spectacle/discourse, comes to the city in a dream. She struggles to describe it, and she is reluctant to talk about what it might mean, but at least she shares it. She provides the following image:

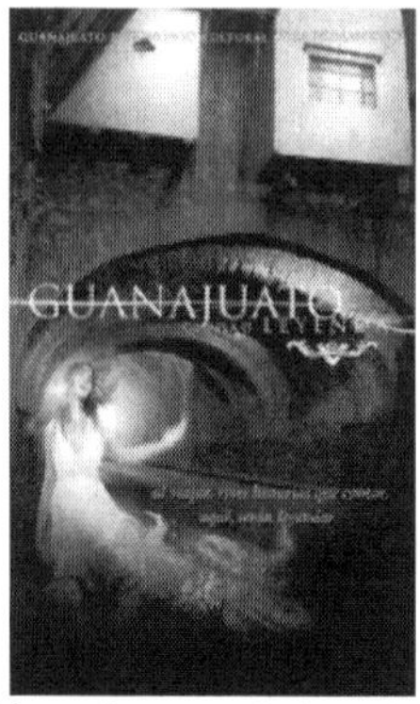

"City of Legend" brochure

In this brochure image, a white figure with an outreached hand beckons to the tourist-viewer. At the superficial level, we find—not surprisingly—what hints at yet another purified, deracialized image. Although the somewhat phantasmagorical woman inviting us into the city in general, and the tunnel specifically, cannot be a tourist (a tourist cannot be a guide), she is exaggeratedly white, thin, and blond. She is dressed in white, and the bottom half of the dress dissolves into dark, abstract figures. She seems to mark a halfway point between the semiotic world of the tunnel and the legends she mentions in the caption, and the symbolic of the outside world in which she is still positioned.

What she immediately recalls, of course, is the figure of La Llorona, Mexico's "patron ghost." La Llorona is a woman dressed in white who wanders through both urban and rural areas, usually near water, and who cries inconsolably for her children. She is often taken as a more recent version of the Mesoamerican goddess, Cihuacóatl. Cihuacóatl, also dressed in white, appeared at the time of Moctezuma and was one of the bad omens witnessed on the eve of the conquest, which collectively foreshadowed doom. Cihuacóatl wandered the streets crying out, "My children, my children, what will become of you?" which is taken as a warning about the bloodshed and tragedy about to occur. La Llorona does not appear until the colonial era, and she is generally portrayed as an indigenous woman who gave birth to several children of a Spanish man, who then abandons her for a woman of his own race and class. Crazed with grief, La Llorona drowns her children and herself in a river. Henceforth, she haunts these areas, crying out for her children in regret. She also seduces men who cross her path, drowning and killing them as well. Adding yet another layer, she is frequently linked to the indigenous Malinche, lover of Cortés, who is understood in Mexico as a traitorous mother, who sold out her children in her desire for Spain. Indeed, in contemporary speech the word *malinchista* refers to a person who prefers the foreign (lover, capitalist goods, or anything else) to the Mexican.

The figure on the brochure thus calls up multiple maternal associations, albeit within the indigenous versus Spanish construction. Situated at the entrance of the tunnels (which often flood and which were old river causeways, thus symbolic of the female Mother Nature who can destroy), she seems to be poised at the edge of the feminine. From a pessimistic angle, we can ask, is she simply a somewhat weaker (paler), contemporary (spectacle) version of the indigenous maternal represented by the figures discussed above? Is she the monstrous and abject La Llorona who murdered her own children? Is she the Eve-like indigenous Malinche whose desire provoked the downfall of Mesoamerican not-yet-Mexico? The spectacle's own *malinchista* call to prefer the tourist to the local? Dream symbols are always overdetermined, and all of these interpretations are possible. I am tempted, however, to read her as a more benevolent mother urging the city to return to her origins instead of preferring the foreign tourist spectacle. After all, she is leading the viewer into, not away from, the tunnel. Into, not away from, narration. The slogan says, "Traveling, you live stories to tell, here, they will be legends."

The fact that the narration is posited as a legend opens several layers of meaning. First, the city is known as a site of many legends; the varying alleyways all have specific legends associated with them, which are amply played up for tourists as both folkloric tales and ghost stories. Second, legends are generally understood as stories from the past that are not always verifiable, which could parallel the psychoanalytic perspective in that the subject's truth is more important than any objective truth. Third, the word legend is etymologically associated with speech, logos (Freud's "soft voice" of the intellect), and knowledge. For Kristeva, to narrate is to know, and to speak is to intervene into the symbolic, and these multiple roots make the slogan technically redundant, but doubly strong. The need to narrate is, of course, one of Kristeva's preferred themes. As she comments after having helped one analysand return to symbolization, "By creating the 'logos of the soul,'" the patient was able to "provide himself with a new body" and recover his own intimacy (1995, p. 26).

Finally, a legend is also a guide to symbols on a map: If we are studying the city subject's "psychic map" (Kristeva, 2011, p. 171), perhaps this figure is offering herself as a guide back through the feminine tunnels to meaning. She may be silent, but she is pointing us toward bodily symbols, trying to encourage us to read them. She is also promoting travel, asking the city to engage in the vertigo and displacement of a transference relationship. Is she, then, perhaps the good mother, the indigenous mother, the mother who wants to release the city into language and who offers to listen to the stories she might speak?

The traditional La Llorona figure is unable to access any means of reparation; she is like Mallarmé's Narcissus, the "watery prowler" (Kristeva, 1987, p. 134), an exile from psychic space. But this white-dressed figure provides more hope. At the shadowy bottom of her dress, we see a series of dark, somewhat abstract figures. One of these appears to be an upside-down woman: It is as if this woman is giving birth to the "monstrous" maternal, expelling her finally … We can read the oneiric figure as one who offers the city a chance to expel the melancholic, monstrous maternal, to come back to language and narration, and to enact what would constitute a psychic rebirth. If the void discussed in this session with the city is the feminine and the maternal, this "gaping cavern in everyone" (Kristeva, 2011, p. 65), perhaps we are now seeing where it will be transformed into psychic depth.

The city silences quite a lot about her past. She covers up the violence, the racial mixing, the poverty, and deviances from her own ideals. This work takes place within or behind the images and texts she uses to promote those positive attributes she aspires to embody. The Ibargüengoitia novel becomes a symbol of the city's intellectualism and romantic or nostalgic identity; Rivera a symbol of her Mexican-ness; the mines her wealth and Spanish legacy. These efforts to foment certain interpretations at the expense of others nonetheless take their toll on her psyche. Her self-imposed repressions betray her repeated lacks of love as well. She is being pushed to the limit, and things look grim after this session. Is she not deleting herself in the process? Analyst Alexander Stein writes that silence "quiets the din of the present, and liberates us to hear the past; what is revealed, embodied and embedded in silence, is regression itself" (1999, p. 413). The city is drowning in her melancholy and must return to the symbolic. The final Llorona text signals that the return to the feminine is urgent indeed, and it can be read as a hopeful sign amid an otherwise dark scenario. I conclude this session wondering if the city might find a way out via sexuality and a return to the feminine underground as La Llorona appears to be suggesting. We seem to be on the verge of something.

Five

Releases and Returns

Sex and the (Provincial) City

```
The last sessions have left me concerned about the depth of the emotional problems that are emerging. I consult with a local colleague, a psychologist, before seeing the city again. Her impressions match mine, and she adds a strongly voiced opinion that repression of sexuality is what drives the city psyche. The previous sessions have made it clear that the city must reconnect with her sexual self; and I decide to explore this more, wondering if here, in the realm of everyday sexuality, the city will find an escape from such rampant repression. She certainly has contact with ideas very other to traditional norms; might sexuality and the means for managing it provide a fertile area in which to uncover signs of revolt? When the city returns to my office, I hurry through the usual chatter about the chilly weather and immediately begin the session. I begin by asking her how she manages the pressures to be ideal and what strategies she might use to relieve some of these tensions. I am surprised and hopeful when she pulls out multiple texts. We seem to have moved out of the silence.
```

We are fast approaching the necessary crisis. We will talk about one more series of texts before I offer the city my own displacements, transferences, and interpretations to consider. Previous sessions have repeatedly drawn attention to the city's tendency to domesticate, silence, purify, and repress. The last session, however, showed the city reaching the limits of her ability to contain all of this tension and signaled that the necessary route back to psychic health should take her through the feminine body. Today, I finally broach the topic of sexuality. Psychoanalysis, of course, is based on the notion that sexuality matters and is intimately connected to thinking and participation in the symbolic order. Whether repressed or expressed, understandings about the self as a sexual being, shaped in early childhood experiences, affect the adult life that results. I therefore ask how this modern city negotiates her traditional upbringing in the face of change. As I discuss the city's sexually themed texts for signs of how this negotiation plays out (and for what I hope will be signs of transgression and release), I notice that she has turned to writing in foreign languages. I wonder how language, place, and sexuality will come together here.

During this phase of work I undertook analytic supervision with a female analyst who worked with both men and women ranging from professionals to poor victims of domestic violence to upper-class youth at a conservative private school staffed in large part by nuns. When I asked her what she thought the city's most common psychological problems seemed to be, based on her own cross-section of experiences, she thought only a moment before replying that, in her opinion, the city was most affected by a deep fear of sexuality, male and female.[26]

She attributed this to the prominent role of the Church in people's daily lives, Catholic guilt, and parental and societal pressure on young people, all of which combine to construct sexuality as something to be repressed. If Guanajuato has any desire of her own, she said, it is to maintain the image of herself as virginal, pure, perfect, that is, free of sexuality. This fits everything that has been emerging in the sessions thus far. It also fits my view that the city plays a traditional maternal role for her others, a role inscribed in Catholic discourse that denies the female subject desire (or that would make desire into a transgression). Inarguably, the city's rejection of the naked FIC poster and her making of Don Quijote into a virginal icon reinforce this.

Equally true is the Catholic Church's stronghold in the state of Guanajuato. While 90 percent of the country is still Catholic (Aguayo-Quezada, 2002, p. 66), in other places the influence of the Church has suffered a generation-long decline related to the Church's inflexible views on birth control, divorce, and homosexuality, on the one hand, and the incursion of many new Christian religions, on the other. Guanajuato (both state and city) has not been immune to these pressures; however, the entire state is recognized as one of the most Catholic and conservative of the nation, something attested to in the fiercely opposed responses to abortion, homosexuality, and so on, both in the newspapers and in everyday conversation (Lamas and Bissell, 2000, pp.17–19; Meyer Cosio, 1993, p. 10; Newcomer, 2002). While the expression "*obedezco pero no cumplo*" (I obey but do not comply) is used occasionally here as in other places to signify the quieter noncompliance with such things as weekly Mass, abstention from premarital sex, and even the prohibition against birth control, it is fair to say that, in this small-town setting

[26] Note that not every psychologist I spoke with during this research identified sexuality as the most prominent problem of the city; for example, one underlined the split from Spain, and another kept referring back to the effects of economic hardship. All, however, were quick to link repression and sexuality with both the dynamics of local social life as well as with the topographical specifics that permit easy vision of what occurs in the city.

preoccupied with class and social image, people tend to be noticeably less vocal about their deviations from expected practice.[27]

SEX, TABOOS, AND THE USE OF SPACE

If we accept the assertion of the psychologist that sex is the city's main taboo, the expression of desire becomes a transgression that the city otherizes as incompatible with the ideal image she seeks to cultivate. The city achieves this in part by spatializing sexuality and removing it from her bodily margins. How does she do this? While some informal prostitution exists among poor women, the official story (yet another oft-repeated one that constitutes the city's sense of self) is that there is no prostitution in Guanajuato; and, unlike other Mexican cities, it is true that there is no red light district. Instead, formal prostitution is relegated beyond the city's margins to other nearby cities with strip-clubs and brothels. A long string of what are called "autopark" hotels are also scattered between the multinational businesses and semirural remnants of agricultural work that line the highway on the way to León, a large industrial city half an hour from Guanajuato. These hotels, designed for quick trysts, are visible from the road; however, their wide entrances are built to quickly usher in entering cars and then hide them from view, furthering the hotels' illicit character and protecting the privacy of the transgressor. Tellingly, the vernacular for this stretch of highway is the "Bermuda Triangle," not because of any triangular shape, but because, as one informant put it, "Cars go in and then *whoosh*, they disappear." In this space, a rather devouring one, what happens is quickly made invisible, erased from reality.

An intriguing parallel separation of good from bad exists with material things as well. Local residents have long rejected allowing U.S. businesses into town. While part of this is economic, because big businesses would ruin the predominantly family-run operations in town, there is more to this. The American megastores are viewed as eyesores of northern influence that do not fit into a colonial, small-town façade: The huge chains are ugly, unelegant, and impersonal. The city fulfills her desires to access these global goods (consumption desire directed at the other of foreign products), but she does so outside of her pristine borders, much in the same way she directs a desire for sexual pleasure to the hotels outside her city limits. Desirous of imported goods, residents who can, regularly head to León (population over a million) to shop at large U.S. businesses, ranging from Home/Office Depot, Costco, and Walmart, to McDonald's and other more upscale restaurant chains. Its U.S.-style shopping mall, named the Plaza Mayor, is full of American fast-food and boasts an indoor ice-skating rink, which furthers its northern look and feel. For city residents, shopping in León and purchasing membership to Costco or Sam's Club stores affirm their economic standing and status as upper class. Yet ironically, the megastores also permit the

[27] Indeed, my personal observations indicate that people expend much effort to give the image of having complied even when they have not.

ongoing construction of the city-self as quaint, small, and traditional and of the big-city-other (León) as unsafe, industrial, ridden by foreign business, even slightly sleazy.

If León is constructed as other, Mexico City is even more other. I asked the psychologist who had argued that sexuality was Guanajuato's key "issue" how the city could maintain such a pure/traditional image when much of the media comes from and reflects the lifestyles of Mexico City, a megalopolis highly attuned to global trends. Mexico City is only four hours away, after all; it is hardly "another world." In particular I wondered how local adolescents could watch mainstream Mexican movies and *telenovelas* full of teenagers openly engaging in casual sex and then not claim the same right to be open about their own lifestyles in *provincia*? She was quick to answer that, in her opinion (which I do not fully share, but find interesting), local people viewed things in a black-or-white fashion: Mexico City was bad; Guanajuato was good. She carried this idea further by arguing that local inhabitants (not just adolescents) lived "a schismatic existence" with no room for negotiation in between these extremes. By rejecting the big city, local teens did not have to make a choice or address the contradictions between their idealized behavior and their actual practices. This is only one opinion, of course, one that would demand much more exploration before making any definitive pronouncements, but it resonates with the patterns that have emerged. Compared to Mexico City and other large urban areas, local residents are quick to repeat that "*aquí vivimos en la gloria*" (we're living in heaven here).

Officially, then, sexuality is shuttled off to the bars, clubs, and hotels of non-city spaces. In Spanish, a husband's second household with a mistress is referred to as the *casa chica*, the small house that will never challenge the status of the *casa grande* (big house) occupied rightfully by the legal, Church-recognized wife. By displacing sexuality, the city thus conceives of herself always as the "big house," while these spaces outside the city become the *casa chica* where transgression is relegated, hidden, and essentially disappeared. But sexuality and desire do not disappear so easily; what remains within the city space must be accommodated somehow. The city is certainly exposed to different conceptualizations of sexuality through the others who visit or move to the city; through the university, which is not so subject to local repressions; and through the media, which are saturated with sexual imagery and which report larger national-level debates over sexual issues. As a result, whether to maintain or challenge traditional norms, the city must confront her sexual others: those who speak their desire, those who have different practices, those who might desire her. So the city returns to text, but she tells me that she has been writing in other languages … This is potentially a good sign. Foreign language offers the writer/speaker a place in which to experiment; the signs are more open. Where the mother tongue fails, will the city find freedom in which to rewrite her desire in these other languages?

The city's foreign language base is modest; Guanajuato is not a multilingual city per se. There is no indigenous language base either. As a university and tourist city, however, certainly many inhabitants speak or read some another language as a part of their professional lives. There is also intense exposure to U.S. media, and tourists visit year-round, which brings in a considerable amount of English and other languages. One thus occasionally observes texts in Japanese, English, French, and German posted alongside of the usual texts in town. Within the middle class and more elite social groups, it is also becoming increasingly common for people to drop in English words (much in the way Americans used to do with French) to show their own cosmopolitan-ness: words such as *drinks*, *shopping*, *fancy*, *nice*, *coffee break*, the academic *abstract*, and the expression "*oh my god*" show up frequently (and sometimes incongruously) in local conversations, even though all of these things can be (and are) expressed in Spanish as well. While, in other cities, the presence of English-language texts might simply be taking as cosmopolitan posing or acquiescence to American tourists' monolingualism, in the case of this city, something else seems to be going on.

OTHERIZING SPACE THROUGH LANGUAGE: BAR NAMES AND BAR FLYERS

The first set of texts the city shows me consists of bar names. Bar names frequently appear in English posted on the locale's door, but one also finds bits of English (and occasionally other languages) on the bar flyers posted on public bulletin boards and handed out on the streets of the downtown area in the evenings. To consider the bar names first, one bar that she mentions is called (in English) the Why Not? Why not indeed? This name, visible from the street, gives a certain care-to-the-winds attitude to the bar space. Another is a bar called Whoopees, which means nothing in Spanish but which has a certain sexual connotation, of course. I believe that by not translating the bar names, the city is making these sites into othered spaces. Desire is set up because "the foreignness of the language of others generates its own enigmas, speculation, desire to know" (Cronin, 2000, p. 58). Moreover, place names are not translatable; as proper nouns, they "have a signifier and a referent but no signified," which means that their meanings cannot be transferred (domesticated) into Spanish easily (p. 29). There is no chance of purification and deradicalization. We can speculate that perhaps this allows the city to take a risk, as what happens in this other-languaged space cannot be translated into the native-language norm outside …

On an ongoing basis, the city also writes within the bar flyer genre. These small and ephemeral texts are handed out on the main pedestrian streets of the *centro* and often lack dates, times, and addresses. They assume that the reader knows where places are located and whether or not the "tonight" of the text has already passed. The readers, therefore, constitute a specific group of bar-goers, including both locals and foreigners, who are repeat attendees at these locales. The images, colors, and styles used in these texts range widely, but trends come and go, and it is possible to identify patterns within this genre. For example, it is not unusual for the flyers to include images of young foreign women, yet the photos are quite frequently asexual, showing touristlike photos of foreign women sitting in front of local monuments not connected in any way with the bar at hand. This creates a rather incongruous separation of the "who" from the "where," which begins the work to make this all somewhat unreal. At other times, the faces are superimposed onto text about the bar, and sometimes the faces are not referred to anywhere in the text, which again disconnects somewhat. The flyer pictured below, however, proclaims, "*Todo el mundo está en el Guanajuato Grill*," which translates doubly as "Everyone is at the Guanajuato Grill" and "'The whole world' is at the Guanajuato Grill." While the text is in Spanish (signaling that it is directed to a local audience), the visuals show what seem to be a Mexican, an American, and an Asian woman to support its claim.

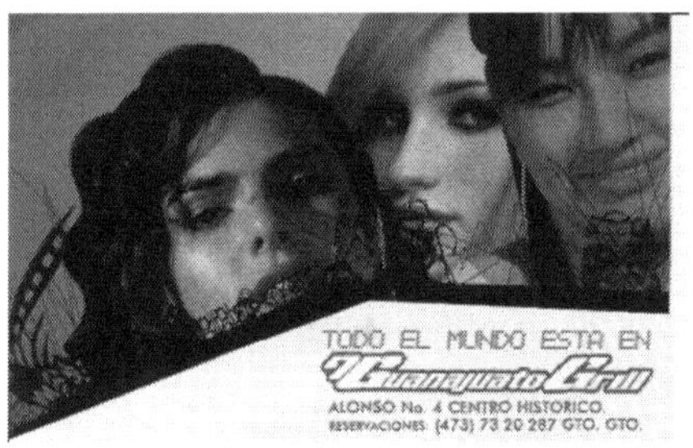

Everyone is at the Guanajuato Grill

This text effectively brings the world to the city and, specifically, into this space, which again has an English name (it is referred to as simply El Grill). It invites the barhopper to step inside this local site while simultaneously re-creating it as magically cosmopolitan. The space becomes everything that city is not: worldly, anonymous, not so intimate.

In another text about a popular bar with an English-language name, the Barfly, the city creates the flyer from a photograph of a Parisian street sign with arrows pointing in different directions to the Louvre, the Théâtre du Palais Royal, and the Comédie Française, with the bottom sign pointing to the Barfly. The city thus locates the bar linguistically and, albeit through fantasy, geographically as *not here*. Rather, it is transformed into an oasis of "away" where sexuality, foreigners, and other taboo things are permitted.

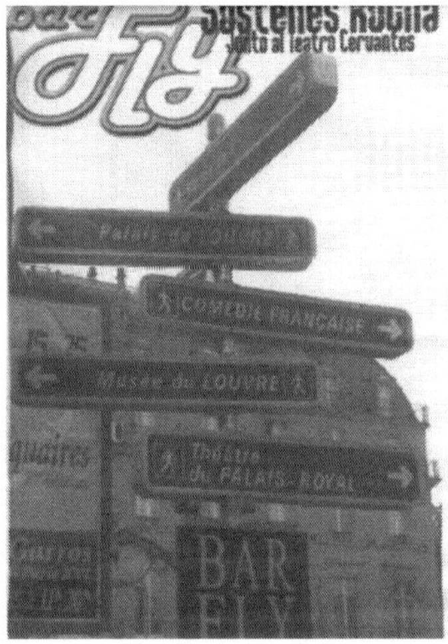

Barfly in Paris?

The whole world is at the Grill, and the Barfly is in Paris … We see quite a fantasy taking place in the city's use of other languages on publicly posted/distributed texts. She is using her imagination, whether to cover up and deny desire or to find an outlet for it …

Italian psychoanalysts Amati-Mehler, Argentieri, and Canestri have observed that the recounting of one's life in a second language makes it less real. At times, this provides too much distance in therapy, which impedes any sort of cure. The other language can serve as "a form of defense to guarantee a certain degree of emotional detachment and of control regarding instinctual infantile vicissitudes" (1993, p. 51). Stephanie Delacour, the protagonist of Kristeva's detective novels, exemplifies this: Whenever she readjusted to speaking Santavarvaran, she said, "her life was like that of a dazed Frankenstein monster: she did everything but was touched by nothing" (Kristeva, 1998, p. 177). At other times, however, Amati-Mehler et al. find that the switch to another language can provide a helpful distance (and create a safe space) from which the analysand can begin to come to terms with what ails her:

> We were able to understand how an analysand, by speaking about the conflicts and anxieties of his childhood in a second language learned in adulthood, could construct a kind of "safety barrier" against the tumult of primitive emotions that would immediately have been evoked by the words of his mother tongue. (1993, p. 2)

Does foreign language create a safe space from which the city might speak? I am not convinced just yet where this other-language writing may be taking the city, but I am pleased that she is trying new things in her writing.

This may be the sign of a first step back into the symbolic. A look at several more texts is necessary.

MORE SPATIALIZING OF DESIRE THROUGH LANGUAGE: THE DAY-AFTER-PILL TEXTS

The city's next set of texts concerns the day-after pill, a hormone-based pill that prevents pregnancy after intercourse has already taken place. In 2006, the day-after pill (*la pastilla del día después*) was formally approved by the Ministry of Health for inclusion in all states' basic medicinal supplies (*la canasta básica*) that health units should provide. While the day-after pill has been controversial in Mexico in general, in Guanajuato the public outcry was especially fervent, as conservatives viewed this as both an endorsement of premarital sex and an abortive measure (although scientifically, it is not). Nevertheless, the pill is available locally for over-the-counter purchase and, according to one pharmacist I spoke with, both the flyers advertising it and her supply of pills disappear as quickly as they arrive. As the texts will show, desire is once again assigned to the foreign.

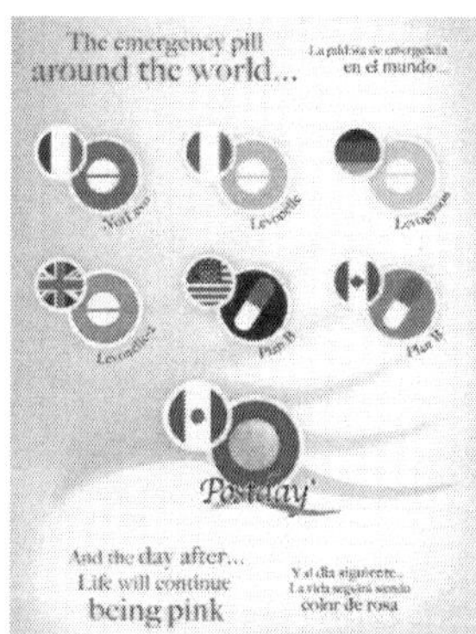

Bilingual day-after-pill flyer (front)

The front of this text is straightforward. It shows how this day-after pill is packaged around the world (although notably in countries from the global North), with text in both English and Spanish, displaying world flags next to the name of the pill in different countries. The immediate reading is that to take the pill is to be global, to be modern. If the whole world is at the Grill, the whole world now takes the day-after pill, which works to destigmatize sex. The slogan offers a "pink life," which in English means very little but in Spanish signifies good, happy, romanticized, or otherwise perfect. This leap from taking the pill in the city to participating in a global practice seems to effectively skip over (transcend) the cultural incompatibilities between traditional Mexican understandings of female sexuality and this particular form of birth control.

A consideration of the flip side of this advertisement is even more revealing:

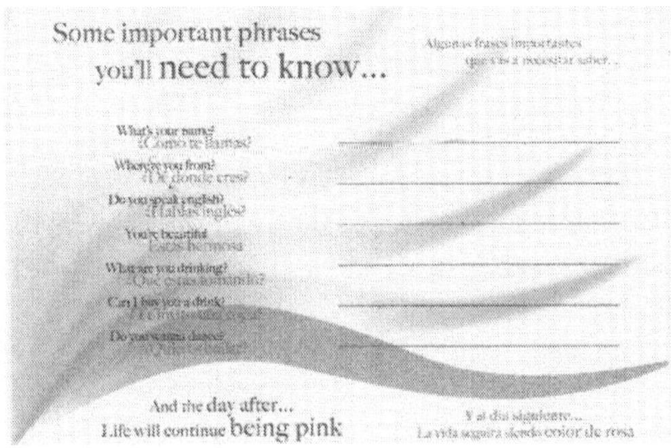

Bilingual day-after-pill flyer (back)

The text included is displayed in bilingual form, English and Spanish, and, as on the front, the English font is larger than the Spanish, despite the fact that we are in Mexico. The flyer offers "important phrases you'll need to know." Need? The phrases that follow are pick-up lines in English with the translation in Spanish; and, given both the word "beautiful" and the gender-agreement of the Spanish, it is clear that the English is spoken by a man, and the addressee is a woman. This flyer appears to offer the woman a guide to understanding the questions that would lead to a sexual encounter, the aftereffects of which would then be counteracted by the day-after pill. Is this possible? Is this an invitation to get accidently pregnant? Even more outlandish is the fact that this flyer is designed as a postcard (to send to *whom*?); the postcard genre implies that whatever occurs will be sent away, told to someone not here … It also includes spaces to write down the answers to these questions: What's your name? *My name is X.* What are you drinking? *I'm drinking a Y.* Do you wanna dance? *Yes I would like to dance* … And life will still be rose-colored and perfect because your transgression as "not-here" cannot cause a problem. Again, *no pasa nada*, nothing happens!

Conveniently, the question "Do you have any birth control?" is left off of this list. This strongly reinforces the idea that sex is too illicit for female adolescents to plan, even while teaching them how to get into the situations that presumably lead to sex. The message seems to say "be modern, but not too modern"—a small retreat or simply a way to sell more pills? The message implied about foreigners is clear as well. Women are told that a sexual encounter with a foreigner, whom they will not understand, is acceptable, since foreign men do not stay long enough (or speak enough Spanish) to kiss and tell. The fact that women are permitted a sexuality at all is something, but only within the context of much control.[28] Foreigners thus comply with both modes

[28] This maps onto two generations of local stories about foreigners serving as temporary sources of romantic and sexual attention, stories that are wrapped up in changing

of permissible sexuality—they are spatialized (not from here but from there) and ephemeral (here only a short time).[29]

"Leaving the mother tongue is a way of finding another space that is not occupied by the mother, by her language, thus finding an identity that is not that of the mother" (Cronin, 2000, p. 61). By switching to English, the city thus exits the constructions of sexuality she has been given (or that she has inferred from) her Catholic, Spanish mother. Here is another opportunity for Kristeva's matricide, the necessary separation from the mother that proceeds the move into the symbolic of language. Fittingly, her character Stephanie labels her transition from French into Santavarvaran as nothing less than a process of death, resurrection, and rebirth, noting that the new language affects "her senses, organs, and sex," a "slow, lazy, and sensual" process (1998, p. 177). The other-language of these texts may thus offer the city the possibility of such a separation and rebirth.

In a final text from this series, the city returns to monolingualism even while she maintains the day-after-pill theme. In this text, she provides a different scenario. While the sexual partner in the bilingual text is clearly a foreigner, in the monolingual text, the sexual partner is a local, which radically alters things.

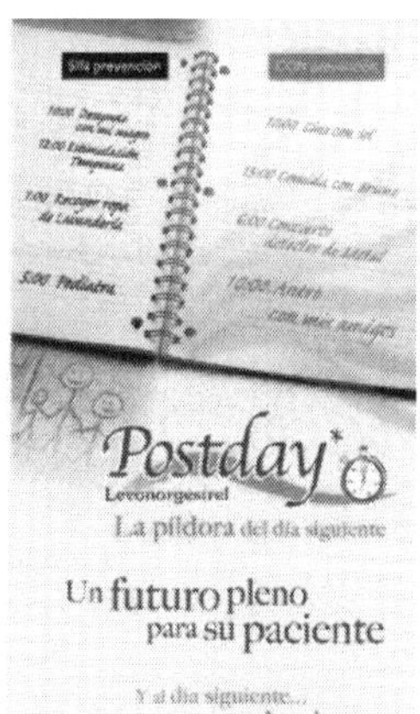

Monolingual day-after-pill flyer

The left-hand column of the datebook (in black-and-white) reminds would-be users that an unplanned pregnancy leads to a day filled with the

gender norms as well. The way these stories are told, in the previous generation local women resented the arrival of more-liberal foreign women who would take away their potential boyfriends. Now, both sexes manipulate the arrival of tourists as opportunities for ephemeral relationships.

[29] In everyday slang, young people also use the expression "un free" to signify a quick sexual relationship that doesn't count or hold any commitment. Again, the English otherizes the experience; there is no easy Spanish equivalent.

following activities: breakfast with the mother-in-law, early stimulation (a sort of pre-preschool for babies), domestic errands such as picking up laundry, and, finally, an appointment with the pediatrician. In short, the day begins and ends with obligations. The implication is that, should you have an unplanned baby, your future will necessarily include both marriage and conformity to a traditional role that clearly includes housework, childcare, and the universal issue of trying to please a mother-in-law. While there is obviously a husband involved, in that there is the presence of the mother-in-law, it is noteworthy that the husband appears not to have a role in any of these parental duties. There is also no mention of school or career. But most visible (by its invisibility) is the fact that the city has left no room for single motherhood as a viable option. There is no evidence whatsoever that indicates the city will challenge the equation of pregnancy=marriage=conformity to rote gender roles.

In stark contrast, the right-hand, pink side of the brochure displays the hypothetical schedule of the young woman who does take this pill. Her day begins with a cinema date with one man, progresses to lunch with another, moving on to an evening concert to see a group called Metal Detector, and, finally, a night at the bar with friends. There is no obvious reference to the relationship that led to the pregnancy; apparently this man has long been forgotten and erased into the past. Again there is no reference to school or career (the relevance of which will be taken up below), and the slogans (in pink to reinforce the pink side of the text) assert: "The day-after pill. A full future for your patient. And the next day … life will still be rose-colored." Within the flyer and on the back cover (not pictured), the fact that the pill is not abortive is stressed several times.

The city's monolingual text communicates several things. First, this is text written for adolescents, since a single older woman would presumably be working and less likely to be planning cinema outings at 10:00 a.m. or heading to what sounds like a heavy-metal concert. We can read into this the unspoken assumption that women beyond adolescence would not find themselves in the situation of the needing or desiring the day-after pill. Is this meant to imply that women beyond adolescence would not ever have spontaneous, unprotected sex, or that they would be so grateful for a child that they would not recur to the pill? Would they get married instantly and take up residence in the left-hand side of the brochure? For that matter, local married women find themselves accidentally pregnant on a regular basis, whether they are complying with the Church injunction against birth control or not; they are not addressed in this text either. Evidently, the reader of this text is limited to being in this adolescent age group.

By setting up the pink column as a list of purely fun items, the text defines (and strives to prolong) adolescence as a period of sexual freedom. With no school and career references, the text creates an image of adolescent womanhood as simply being a free moment before the demands of traditional adult womanhood (wife and mother), no matter which side of the pamphlet the adolescent falls on, which reinforces the idea that this is a brief and particular phase of life somewhat outside of the norm. The lack of emphasis on thinking and preparing for the future is furthered by the fact that the brochure does not openly (on the cover) encourage adolescents to plan for future birth control needs. Sex, which in this scenario has led to a pregnancy, is represented as *unplanned and accidental*, which serves to denormalize it: ironically, the cinema and the bar are scheduled into the datebook, but sex is relegated to being a surprise and an aberration, even as unplanned pregnancies are expected enough for a company to manufacture day-after contraception.

The city's texts appear to suggest some deviance from the norm, but they simultaneously foreclose other options and keep things inscribed neatly into the acceptable order. The same traditional schism of good-woman/bad-woman (virginal/sexual) is now reconfigured as a tightly confined choice between good-traditional and good-modern. As a teenager you may aspire to the "rose-colored life" of fun social outings and multiple relationships, but if you end up pregnant your only option is to erase the fact quickly or to fit back into the traditional mode, which preconfigures a "return" idea I will take up below. It also subtly teaches young women that they may "sow their oats" in adolescence; but not afterward. This corroborates Kristeva's understandings about the construction of maternity as incompatible with sexuality and pleasure. Within the patriarchal system condensed into the Virgin icon, women "will not be able to accede to the complexity of being divided," she writes in "Stabat Mater." They will always have to choose between asexual maternity or the "fallen" of the sexual (1987, p. 248).

Once again, the city's patterns are put into relief. What I see emerging in her texts on sexuality is a set of otherizing practices that spatialize desire. Desire for material goods and sex is displaced into more acceptable spheres and onto more acceptable objects (outsiders, prostitutes, other places/cities, anonymous hotels) that do not threaten the city's own pure body or, in other words, the status quo of her subjectivity. What cannot be displaced is correspondingly reimagined, fantasized, and translated into other languages that provide a more open linguistic space into which the taboo can be channeled. Adding to this rather shocking degree of control via spatialization (*outside of town, within the bar labeled as elsewhere, with someone foreign*) is a parallel *temporalization* of desire that further regulates female sexuality.

As the pills texts make clear, the sexual subject is the adolescent one, but this is complemented by several other time-related maneuvers. In the morning, the main *centro* area is tranquil, pedestrian, and dotted by schoolchildren rushing to class, businesspeople going to work, and many late breakfasters in the Jardín. At night, however, the graceful downtown is transformed into bar spots, and professionals are replaced with teenagers. Bar attendance runs until the wee hours of the morning, but by 7:00 a.m. the city has brushed signs of alcohol, trash, sex, and anything else unsightly off the surface. Sex thus belongs to nighttime. The FIC offers heightened contact with outsiders, the more appropriate partners, which directs sexuality to the month of October. Finally and in most detail, one local source noted that even the marginal autopark hotels follow a schedule: At 11:00 a.m., he said, society ladies take their gardeners or workmen to the hotel; at 5:00 p.m., the husbands of these ladies take their secretaries; at 8:00 p.m., university students drive in with their girlfriends; and at 11:00 p.m., the partyers finish the hotels' booming daily business with whomever they encounter at the end of the evening. Once again, time and space come together. A phase of life, a month of the year, a time of night … how could the boundaries be more clear? It is now possible to see that the recalled FIC poster constituted an attempt to add a new time-space for transgression. The poster was being hung up semipermanently during the day, before the festival, in the main downtown of the city. Here was an attempt at transgression that met with failure because it did not conform to the rules. Had it been hung only in bars, rather than intended as the public representation of the festival, there would probably not have been such a public outcry.

The implied binaries that the city has constructed (here versus elsewhere, night versus day, etc.) take away and relieve the ambiguity that sexuality incarnates. Her spatial and temporal moves, complemented by forays into foreign language, further separate sexuality from the proper city self. This all comes together to reinforce the bad woman/good woman binary that continues to underwrite gender constructions in Mexico, as these highly regulated escape routes exist. Anthropologist Martha Lamas puts this into perspective:

> *El insulto de "putas" se dirige a mujeres que se salen de la estrecha norma de la doble moral, comercialicen o no su actividad sexual. También es "puta," aunque no cobre, la rebelde, la que se acueste libremente con quien quiere o la que no acepta una relación.* (2007, p. 315)
>
> The insult of "whores" is directed at women who stray beyond the narrow norm of the double morality, whether or not they commercialize their sexuality. Also called "whore" is she who, although she does not charge, is a rebel and sleeps freely with whom she chooses independently of whether or not she accepts a relationship.

The day-after-pill flyers might let a (young) woman sleep with whom she pleases, but they do not allow her to be the one who chooses not to accept a relationship should she end up pregnant. This must be tempered a bit: In actual practice single motherhood is no longer scandalous, and families in the city, as elsewhere around the country, are much more supportive of this option than in the past. What is important here is that the city continues to write this norm in an idealized fashion despite these changes. There is a noticeable gap between public presentations of self and private practices, which speaks to the ongoing power of traditional discourses.

A RETURN TO THE NORM

These texts reveal an anxious city body full of fantasies. The city projects her unacceptable desires onto foreigners, and foreigners thus represent a certain taboo persona (in Kleinian terms, the bad object). The city attributes her own sexual desires to these others, displacing the shame onto the figure of the unknown foreigner, which sometimes even prompts this figure to behave as imagined, that is, to engage in more liberal behavior than he or she might at home. The foreigner becomes or absorbs the undesirable part of the city self that she cannot accept.

For the many local residents who have traveled elsewhere, it is possible to suggest that foreigners symbolize what they renounced to come home, which then casts foreigners into a certain *unheimliche* role. Foreigners—and here I equate the term "foreigner" with outsider, whether national or international or othered for other reasons—could represent the city resident's sacrificed sexuality that accompanies a move back into the symbolic world of a city that keeps constant surveillance turned on herself. Although previous experiences with outsiders in other cities or countries means that their behaviors do not shock or deeply offend (after all, many locals have seen and perhaps have engaged in these things in other sites), foreigners in town may be taken as representative of what was sacrificed in the return. This calls up a range of emotional responses, from anxiety to envy to resentment. *Are they me or not-me?* Adding to this is the intimate geography of the *centro*, which means that outsiders must be made sense of every day in shared and close quarters.

In *Black Sun*, Kristeva writes, "We love the other, we hate the other, we embed the other within ourselves out of love, we hate ourselves with this other within. What we don't like of the self is what we dislike in the other" (1989, p. 11). In other words, the city projects "disowned aspects of self" (Grant & Crawley, 2002, p. 18), her own unacceptable desires, onto others. Following Klein, Kristeva would see this as projective identification, "the projections of the good and bad components of a not-yet self onto an object not yet separated from it, with the aim less of attacking the other than of gaining a hold over it" (1989, p. 61), which refers to a "substratum of an unsuspected sexual desire" (p. 11). If women (and provincial cities) have a depressed sexuality, Kristeva understands that they prefer to devour the other, to hold it in the mouth, in pieces chewed up, rather than to lose it completely (p. 12). Is the outsider not this? Is he not just a Spain substitute being held in the mouth—the compulsion to repeat—a way to hate, love, and not lose the other again? Not quite digestible? Not quite rejectable? But one who will abandon her later …

Kristeva follows a Kleinian understanding of projections /introjections, but I refer to analyst Thomas Ogden's (2005) three conditions necessary for a successful experience of projective identification, which offers a straightforward model for this process. First is the displacement of the unwanted part of self that threatens. This is ejected into a proximate space, projected into someone/something with whom there will be interaction, so that this unwanted object or part is not lost forever. The city projects her taboo desire into spaces fantasized as other, into interactions in another language (making situations less real), and into foreigners themselves (who are passing through and play a specific role that locals cannot).

The use of other languages, as noted above, has its dangers and benefits. From their clinical observations of female, multilingual patients, Amati-Mehler et al. state the following:

> It seems to us that by substituting the language of their childhood with a new language—the conveyor of new thought and affect routes—and by adopting a cultural and emotional context not mortgaged by the archaic conflicts, they not only rendered a service to resistances and defenses, but they also created new passages that provided them, albeit at the cost of deep and painful splitting, with valid and structured introjections on which to reorganize their adult feminine identity. (1993, p. 71)

For those who cannot travel physically to another site, or for those who have traveled and returned, they can now travel to the fantasized foreign context of the otherized bar and the other language of the pill texts, thus opening the "new passages" referred to above and experiencing the splitting as well. The bad or taboo part of the city, her desire, is separated from her usual Spanish-speaking, rest-of-the-city self. These spaces "not mortgaged by the archaic conflicts" thus open a possibility and keep desire near enough so as not to lose it completely.

Ogden's second condition is that the recipient person/object is pressured to experience his or her own self in such a way that corresponds with the projected fantasy. In this case, the local space permits the projection—the bars self-identify as transgressive spaces and collude by producing flyers that reiterate the otherness of desire, using foreign language as one way to do so. This allows the city to control space and to maintain her ideal, pure self, which is then opposed to other spaces understood as decidedly less pure. For the city's female adolescent as well, her acquiescence to the postcard fantasy interaction with a foreigner, undertaken in English, also shows how these created spaces "work." She is not propositioning her would-be partner in Spanish, but in English; she is temporarily other to her own self as she does this.

And some foreigners, although this is said more symbolically and should not be overstated, play a return role here: They accept the construction of themselves as passing, ephemeral, fun, liberal … even if they do not necessarily see themselves as such at home. As Kristeva herself observes, the foreigner frequently enters into a libertine state, released from his or her *own* repressive societies: "Foreigners continue to be those for whom sexual taboos are most easily disregarded, along with linguistic and familial shackles." But she also points out that the foreigner's words in the new language

> are centered in a void, dissociated from both body and passions, left hostage to the maternal tongue. In that sense, the foreigner does not know what he is saying, the foreigner can utter all sorts of indecencies … since his unconscious shelters itself on the side of the border. (1991, p. 32)

Even the foreigner's seemingly easy escape from repression may not last.

This brings us to the third condition for a healthy projective identification process. Projective identification can only mark a "pathway for psychological change" if the feelings are reinternalized in some modified form made possible during the other person or object's containing of them (Ogden, 2005, p. 21). For the projecting city, this could happen if the bar sites performed a different understanding of sexuality that would enable the city to reunderstand desire as a now acceptable aspect of the self. Or it could happen if the monolingual text allowed for a nontraditional choice instead of reinscribing the consequences of an unplanned pregnancy back into the status quo. Or finally, it could happen if the city could link the freedom available in the other-space of the bar and in the otherness of her interaction with the hypothetical foreign sexual partner into a protest against the conservative norms of the city.

But this does not occur—what happens in adolescence, in the bar, or out of town, remains contained in those specific time-spaces. While the different language moves cited here attempted to open up change, the monolingual pill text reproduces the impossibly split woman because it so clearly forecloses sexual desire/pleasure for the woman who becomes a mother. This means that the moment of opening for the adolescent is transitory and is not linked forward to a challenge to existing norms and prohibitions. The question that remains is why, if some options for transgression are available, even if they are regulated to certain spaces and times, does this not produce a stronger challenge to the status quo? Why do these temporary adolescent rebels return and reproduce the norm (in appearance if not always in action) as adults? To some extent of course, adolescence in many places could be seen as a swerve slightly beyond and then back to an eventual adult norm, but this seems extreme. The city seems to endure a violent self-repression as these digressions from the norm produce guilt, regret, and denial.

A common saying directed at daughters when prohibiting something is "*Para que no te pase lo que a mí me pasó*" (So that what happened to me doesn't happen to you), a saying that connotes some amount of guilt and certainly regret. Another psychologist echoed this, noting that, in her experiences in town, the mother who transgresses norms feels so much remorse that she reins in her daughter even more in order to spare her the same experience, something she often does without ever admitting her reasons. As Freud states,

> The pleasure of the impulse constantly undergoes displacement in order to escape the locking which it encounters and seeks to acquire surrogates for the forbidden in the form of substitutive objects and

> actions. For the same reason the prohibition also wanders and spreads to the new aims of the proscribed impulse. Every new advance of the repressed libido is answered by the prohibition with a new severity. The mutual inhibition of these two contending forces creates a need for discharge and for lessening the existing tension, in which we may recognize the motivation for the compulsive acts. (1918, p. 51)

Without wanting to go so far as to label the city compulsive, the impulse toward what is prohibited does appear to be met again by a refortified prohibition, even if it is self-generated. Concerning returns and prohibitions, Kristeva (2011) offers a more extreme example: She discusses the character of the female Palestinian suicide bomber schooled in the West and torn between competing discourses of the traditional and the secular, which produces (in the examples she cites) frustration, melancholy, and an inability to reconcile school with life. She cites a study that revealed the high level of education of these young women and that illuminated the tremendous abyss between their two worlds of school and faith. The bombers were offered spiritual redemption in exchange for their return to the norm, and they took it; often, the desire for Law is stronger than the individual desire to transgress even when one has been exposed to alternatives. Women who "travel" elsewhere (even through the othered sites of adolescence and foreign language) thus seem to be pulled back and "resettled" like Rivera and Ibargüengoitia.

While the city's young people transgress, they do so by the rules, which may include going somewhere else and enjoying a temporary respite from them. However, in the psychologist's opinion, a tremendous number return to the city more convinced than ever that their parents were right, that the traditional way is the superior way. Despite increased access to educational and professional experiences in other cities or abroad, she hypothesized that today's youth would continue to raise their children from an orientation of guilt, thus perpetuating the situation. While young people in other parts of Mexico propose other options to themselves for adult lifestyles, in her opinion this was less common in the city. And then—fascinating to me—she came back to a spatial and bodily interpretation. "Perhaps it is because there is no horizon here," she said.

Admittedly, this exploration of the city and her specific texts yields only a small part of a much larger story, that of sexuality in *provincia*. If I were working beyond the one analysand, there would be much more to work with, and one could draw out significant ethnographic data about how all sorts of sexual practices and deviances are organized in everyday life, which would complicate the overall picture. There is also an important class bias here that must be acknowledged. First, my city-analysand is widely constructed as middle class and professional, which distinguishes her greatly from many, if not most, Mexican cities where the middle class is shrinking. Secondly, the upper class traditionally sets the ideals that neither they nor the popular classes truly comply with; however, it is at this more middle- and upper-class level that I see the city engaging in extreme efforts to maintain appearances. For this reason, a focus on adolescence that targets those with the money to go out to the clubs at night (those who read the flyers and go to the mainstream downtown bars, those who attend university, etc.), leaves out adolescents from lower classes. While the former constitute the dominant class that sets the norms and creates the more powerful discourse in this somewhat affluent city, they represent, of course, only one aspect of the city's overall subjectivity.

It would also be remiss not to emphasize that, as in other sites, a critical element at play in the city has been the failure of the sexual revolution. As another local psychologist lamented, important feminist advances were made in the work world and in the policy arena; however, the "revolution was never fully realized in the household," which then produced shame on the part of those who had attempted to move outside the traditional, conscripted models of femininity. This echoes the spatial nature of this whole discussion: It is commonly said that the sexual revolution occurred "*de la puerta hacia afuera*" (from the door outward), which means that, despite changes in the outside world, much less changed in the intimacy of the domestic world behind closed doors and within gender relationships. In Guanajuato, we see this clearly: Outside the city, the expression of desire and sexuality is accepted. In these pockets of other local spaces remade as "not here," desire finds a place as well. But in the "real" space of the city, outside the bars and within city limits, the revolution is not invited in. With no bridging of transgressive space to everyday life space, no change is possible. What we see here remains a defense.

The city's careful management of transgression creates almost as much tension as it would appear to liberate. I am deeply worried.

Six

Transferences

Of Cities and Analysts

In working through the FIC poster incident, I had found the city's at least partial refusal to be written by tourist desire something to admire, even as she purged a text I found refreshing. She seemed to be asserting a certain caution that protected her subjectivity. Our subsequent sessions, however, have left me increasingly concerned about the depth of her anxieties. I am worried that she might not be able to transgress, that she will not question the spectacle or the standard perceptions of closed, repressed *provincia*. While there seem to have been novel, new spaces, and other potential paths to transgression here and there, she has consistently missed taking them to a full revolt and rebirth.

A text that appeared on a large billboard at one of the entrances to the city summed up where I thought the city seemed to be stuck. Imposed upon a collage of city images, the slogan on this text read "*Guanajuato te va a encantar*," meaning "Guanajuato will enchant you." This is a play on words, since the same verb for "enchant" is also used in children's games of tag, where it means "to freeze" you. This is how I felt: that the city was enchanting, bewitching, but freezing people into certain ways of seeing, writing, and being in this space. For tourists, she was simply a set of signifiers that conformed to traditional constructions of passive femininity. And for herself, worse still, she seemed to be frozen along with her virginal Don Quijote on the loveless wound of her melancholy. Was she incapable of speaking back? Would there be no addressee to listen to her? No chance of revolt?

My heightened anxiety and, soon after, more negative and judgmental assessments of the city's mental `state, make me realize that my countertransferences have been ignited.`

What follows is an interlude in which I delve into the transference relationships that will—if all goes well—open up the city's crises to new possibilities for resignification. I begin by setting out my own fears and negative projections that I find the city suddenly eliciting in me. After considering the role of transferences in the analytic process and Kristeva's particular understandings of these, I then examine how we both project onto place—onto the city and Mexico, in my case, and in Kristeva's onto East-West constructions in her theory, her fictional Santa Varvara, and her portrayals of Byzantium. From this, it becomes clear where the rest of the analytical process with the city needs to go. I finish ready to offer her an interpretation; or, to move from a maternal position of listening to a more paternal one of making something from what she has said (and what she has not said) over the course of our sessions.

LIBERATE YOUR EMOTIONS?

While the "enchanted city" billboard provoked concern, it was another poster that brought out a stronger and more negative reaction. The text in question was a poster that was seen in many different sites around town. Produced by the state government and state tourism bureau, the particular poster photographed and included below was hung in a local plaza, pinned up on a kiosk of mostly official notices.

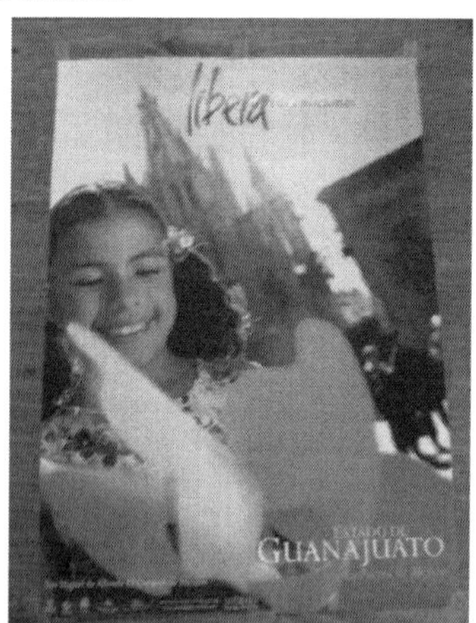

"Liberate your emotions"

The blurry background depicts the main Catholic Church in San Miguel, a neighboring city that most tourists visit in conjunction with the city of Guanajuato. In the foreground, in much more focus, is the gleeful face of a little girl, clearly Mexican, holding balloons or maybe paper flowers—they are also blurred. The text above is written in a multicolor, wavy font and reads "Liberate your emotions," which is the slogan for the larger ad campaign to which this poster belongs. The second and only other line of text is not a full sentence. It simply reads, "State of Guanajuato, door to Mexico."

How, I wondered, with growing anxiety, could I take this poster seriously? Was the city mocking the analytic process? She was self-repressing on all fronts, trying to maintain her clean and orderly self, stripping Don Quijote of his carnivalesque aspect, denormalizing desire, and hiding from the buried sexuality of the abject mines. Liberating emotions, as the city surely has realized, is not a clean and orderly process; such a task involves messiness, confrontations with the ugly and the threatening, and unknown amounts of chaos. More directly, her use of the Church as the key image to go along with this call to liberate is both strange and troubling. How could one conceive of a relationship between the Church and liberation when the Church is one of the most repressive forces at play in the city's emotional makeup? Is she about to run away from analysis and effect yet another return to the status quo of Catholic *provincia*? Finally, positing Guanajuato as a "door to Mexico" is a questionable choice for a landlocked state that does not sit on either border. Who or what lies on the other side of the door? What border or threshold is this meant to symbolize?

For the tourists, this image might work. They could see the city/state as a door into the lost nostalgic and into the (penetrable, female) provincial body that symbolizes all of these things. Passing through it, tourists and other outsiders encounter an idyllic past and an escape from the drudgery of what many consider to be a comparatively soulless urban existence. With the poster understood this way, outsiders can indeed liberate their repressed emotions related to the lost mother symbolized by *provincia*, and *provincia* is constructed yet again as a welcoming female/maternal body. With respect to the Church—a rather baffling image, as the Catholic Church (especially in this conservative city) is not generally portrayed as a place to go to liberate your emotions or anything else—perhaps it suggests that tourists could or should also liberate themselves through a return to the spiritual and family-oriented emotions that urban life tends to squelch. While Kristeva adamantly does *not* call for a return to organized, institutional religion, she does posit the decline of the Church as a meaning-bestowing figure as a major source of modern melancholy. This could simply be a more Mexican resolution, as institutionalized religion still holds strong for many.

Crouch, Aronsson, and Wahlstron comment, "In encountering space the tourist also encounters her- or himself" (2001, p. 255). Travel is constructed here as a physical symbolization of a return to what has been lost, a way to complete what is lacking in the everyday life of urban existence that constitutes the symbolic order par excellence. While tourists reconnect with repressed drives and engage in behaviors that they would not enact at home, such as "uncontrolled" sexuality, excessive drinking, even vandalism and other such things, locals who reside in the traveled-to space cannot follow suit because for them nothing is anonymous, and there would be consequences for such acts. Therefore my negative reading is that the city may provide an opportunity for her other to return to the provincial-maternal, to work through his issues, and to experience psychic rebirth, but she does not seem to have this opportunity herself. One sees an ironic parallel with perhaps what is one of Kristeva's most polemical issues. Her theory has been criticized for not providing women with a way out even as it makes room for men to disrupt the symbolic through poetic language while retaining their positions as speaking subjects (see Oliver, 1993a, for the critique, although this predates Kristeva's trilogy on the female genius, which does provide female examples). The provincial city, at least in the case of Guanajuato, thus suddenly appears to do much the same. Was this it? Was this going to be the only role for my female city? A provider of the lost maternal for others while she stagnates in her own troubles? Who would return the favor and be her comforting addressee?

I found myself reaching an untenable position in the analytic process. I began to see the city in terms of the quintessential stereotype of both *provincia* (closed-minded, repressed) and Mexican womanhood (silenced, abnegated). She now seemed to epitomize Octavio Paz's assessment of Mexican femininity in *Labyrinth of Solitude*, still the best-known work on Mexico's national character both in and outside of the country. Paz wrote Mexican women as closed, masochist, passively resentful, and dangerously enigmatic, which made male insecurity all the more reactionary and violent. Women's split anatomy, he argued, made them both vulnerable and virtuous, ideas that were supported and reinforced via the Church, patriarchy, and writing about the nation both within and beyond Mexico. Suddenly the city seemed to fit this uncritical caricature of Mexican femininity all too well. She was the receptacle for urbanity's needs, a hollow channel (tunnels and mines) for others' desires, yet lacking both her own desire and a site into which it could be displaced.

While I found city's writing fascinating, often funny and quirky, I was not finding the clear examples of resistance I had expected. I was not seeing any proposals for alternative ways of being, and—given the predominant role of bar flyers in all this text, a category representative of youth culture in particular—this lack of creative critique stood out even more. Instead, I found the city employing defenses such as displacement and projective identification, denying certain aspects of the past, and engaging in a tight regulation of sexuality that co-opts any attempts at true transgression. Not every analysand is capable of change, but in this case I cannot stop at such an interpretation. I cannot write the city as yet another suffering, abnegated-mother female figure incapable of resistance.

And indeed, if this were a book strictly about gender, this would be unfair, since women of course do resist from different class and rural/urban positions throughout Mexico! It would also be necessary to underline that women gain something (even at the expense of a larger loss) from their reification as sacred mothers; women gain respect, a sense of purpose, a sacredness (Kristeva, 1987), which means that not every Mexican woman who has acquiesced to at least some of this discourse is seething with rage and resistance. The role of sainted, suffering mother is held in such high esteem that conforming to it provides a strong sense of identity and value even as this role has been positively "edited" in recent decades by women's increased participation in the workforce and in politics. These age-old stereotypes entrenched in Catholic discourse have thus been dismantled without being discarded. It would wrong, then, to conclude that the city is just a stereotypical female entity trapped in a male-controlled symbolic system, underwritten by religious convictions, without pushing further.

While my reluctance to stereotype the city has been a constant presence in this process, at the other extreme I was now embarrassed at the depth of my desire to find what I wanted. Mexican gender constructions are often more different than similar to those in the United States, and I regularly insist to my students that feminism is not defined worldwide in U.S. terms, exhorting them to critically consider things before dismissing either Mexican women or feminism in general (the result of which has meant that my own identification as a feminist fits Kristeva's unlabeled position more than a North American one, which I believe she rightly characterizes and critiques). Yet here I was, disappointed that my female city was not living up to my own quest for a Kristevan rebel questioning the status quo. She was no Stéphane Mallarmé or Melanie Klein, no Hannah Arendt, and certainly no Colette or Georgia O'Keefe! I began to think of the city as having very little to say, which then only redoubled my anxiety about the power issues involved in my own complicated positioning as outsider and as analyst.

As a result, I found myself suddenly taking on the city's silence and reserve as my own. I felt with her the feelings of being constrained and suffocated. I began to feel devoured and invisible and offered no resistance other than being quiet about my concerns, instead of inviting anyone to dialogue. I edited my responses about my research; most of the time, I simply stopped mentioning my work except when asked about it specifically. Not speaking, not opening. I was allowing myself to play into the complex problems suffered by the city. One could even say metaphorically in Kristevan terms that I was at risk of abandoning language for a more melancholy state. This state of course affects all writers at some point when we doubt the validity of our ideas, but at this moment I felt my own intense need to re-become a speaking subject, an embodied one at that, who would *not* disappear and who would not quiet parts of the self. Would I ever be able to say in public, especially as a foreigner, "This is what I'm researching"? That I disagree with the way some things are? Once I noticed that I was starting to experience the city as the city experienced the city, adopting the very reticence I criticized, I pulled back.

OF TRANSFERENCES AND COUNTERTRANSFERENCES

These negative feelings and crises are normal in the analytic process as one's own issues and vulnerabilities become activated; and indeed, they are absolutely essential to the resolution of analysis. As the analysand transfers and projects her patterns onto the analyst, the analyst eventually finds her own psychic issues animated in response, and this two-way dynamic opens up the psychic space in which to work. To distinguish both sides of this, the term "transference" refers to the analysand's tendency to displace previous relationships onto the relationship with the analyst.

> More precisely, in the analytic situation, the analysand, through transference, metaphorizes the analyst into the place of his or her desire. The analyst comes to occupy the position of that desire, and his or her refusal to comment directly on the associative chain of the analysand serves as the surface on which the analysand in turn comes to recognize the nature of his or her own desire. (Forter & Miller, 2008, p. 14)

Kristeva concurs; in *Tales of Love*, she writes that, "for analysis to happen, one needs to the loved and hated other" (1987, p. 14). The analyst thus provides a stand-in other with whom to work out the issues created by the analysand's real others. Transferring, the analysand will believe that the analyst will act as his previous significant others have acted, positioning himself to once again repeat his traumas (Grant & Crawley, 2002). But by responding differently, the analyst breaks the patterns, thus forging an opening for change and making possible different "endings" and resolutions.

Countertransferences, in contrast, are what the *analyst* projects into this relationship, and they are equally important. An analyst may experience a range of emotions, including "drowsiness, boredom, anger and impatience, sadomasochistic enactment, fear of losing the patient, fear of working with the patient, erotic feelings, rigidity, envy and insecurity, overidentification" (J. S. Hall, 2004, p. 51). While Freud referred to these moments as the therapist's blind spots, one's unconscious reactions to the treatment process, contemporary analysts tend to argue that *all* aspects of the analyst's life come into the office and must be managed within the therapeutic relationship (Forter & Miller, 2008). Moreover, they advocate digging into the sources of these reactions, seeing consciousness of one's countertransference as essential to a successful analysis. The analyst must check but not repress her own emotional involvement, desires, and anxieties (Holmes, 2005). As Kristeva comments, in the thrust of these transferences, "I am in osmosis with the patient's unconscious discourse, possessing it as much as it possesses me" (2011, p. 296).

Relke (1993) observes that women psychoanalysts have historically brought these issues to the fore, noting in particular the early work of British analysts Paula Heimann and Margaret Little and taking into account Melanie Klein's work as well. Kristeva is no exception; she actively insists upon the crucial and positive role that transferences and countertransferences play in the analytical process. She has explicitly defined transference relationships in terms of love and forgiveness. In an interview, she said,

> For me to understand my patient, a certain form of love is necessary. This love is not idealization but an accompaniment of the loved subject in his or her traumatisms and states of dereliction. But this is an accompaniment to bring him or her out of this situation. It is "the wager on rebirth." (Rice, 2002, p. 286)

Kristeva threads the theme of forgiveness through her work over time, examining forgiveness in her literary studies of Dostoyevsky, in her biographical study of Hannah Arendt, and in her work on psychoanalysis as well. She takes pains to make clear that analytic forgiveness is not the same thing as the forgiveness of confession—a pardon, or reprieve from someone with power to grant it. She argues "that giving meaning beyond the nonmeaning of the anguished patient's trauma empowers the patient to be born again just as a forgiven subject finds new life and starts over following a pardon" (Rice, 2002, p. 279). The interpretation of the analyst is offered back as a *gift* (taking the French *pardon*, "par-don" meaning literally "through-gift"). Analytical listening thus opens up suffering, pulls it back toward the surface, and lets the patient transcend (2002, p. 282). This perspective is especially fitting in the context of the contemporary crisis in which the most common ailment Kristeva has observed in the consulting room has been, precisely, this inability to represent, to narrate.

Transferences thus form an essential part of the therapeutic process, and the analyst must take the time to unravel her own emotional engagements instead of simply pushing them away in a doomed attempt to stay neutral. What transferences were coursing beneath my sudden pessimistic evaluations of the city and her possibilities of progress? Here, it is worth remembering that she is not a human subject but a city subject. While everyone projects onto others, it is also true that, as human beings, we project onto space, as both theorists of architecture and psychoanalysts have long observed. As Langan (2000), Leach (2003), and others have stated, we introject the physical world, which structures our possibilities for being, and we then project this back onto the space around us. Leach argues that "the environment must therefore serve as a kind of 'screen' onto which we would 'project' our own meaning, and into which we could 'read' ourselves" (2003, p. 79). He also states that national (and, by extension, I would add local) identity is cathected onto objects, which permits statues, monuments, urban landscapes, and so on to embody subjectivities that we then reread back to ourselves. These projections onto spaces and places, common as they are, cannot be taken as neutral in the analytic process.

SPATIAL PROJECTIONS AND TRANSFERENCES

What desires were behind whatever I wished to find in the city? It appears that the city had metamorphized me in part as the tourist looking for the "real" Mexico in *provincia*; but unlike my tourist counterparts who bought into the colonial façade, I wasn't finding it. My "real" Mexico was something quite different. A rereading of anthropologist Guillermo Bonfil Batalla's *México profundo* (1987) allowed me to flesh out what it was I desired for this place. Bonfil Batalla, like many other Mexican intellectuals of the 20th century, portrays the nation as split, but he provides a contemporary nuance to his analysis by going beyond the strictly Spanish/indigenous divide that politically had ceased to exist before the 20th century. Instead, he extends this to a more encompassing "Deep Mexico" (*México profundo*), which is contrasted to what he labels "Imaginary Mexico" (*México imaginario*). Deep Mexico is the "real" (i.e., authentic) Mexico, the indigenous Mexico, the nation with roots that predate the conquest. These roots are still highly present in both rural and urban areas in the form of cultural practices of all types (which he sets out in detail). Imaginary Mexico, on the other hand, he defines as a middle/upper-class illusion, a superficially modern Mexico that imitates the United States or Europe and that does not actually exist. Imaginary Mexico has always followed the Westernizing project (as imagined by Spain and then by capitalist modernization), while Deep Mexico consists of those who were left out, the subaltern groups who were never invited in to these processes and who, to this day, do not identify with the imaginary nation promoted by the powerful classes. Bonfil Batalla's discussion is cultural in nature, and he refers to the range of symbolic practices embodied by each Mexico to outline what one could see as each Mexico's subjectivity.

In reality, is not Bonfil's Imaginary Mexico simply the Mexico of the Debordian spectacle? A site of images, appearances, surfaces … I could easily locate the city's sometimes humorous attempts at cosmopolitanism within his depictions: this dropping of English terms into daily language, as mentioned in the last chapter, and the insistence on serving non-Mexican food at cultural events—one is rarely served a *botanita*, a Mexican hors d'oeuvre, but instead a stale processed canapé, which is perceived as exceedingly upper class and elegant. Such everyday practices among the middle and upper classes situate the city within Imaginary Mexico; to no small degree, these groups consistently pretend to be more "modern" than provincial reality allows for, and those who fit into these constructions (who are not the majority, of course) tend to name-drop about brands of clothing and places they have traveled to. In contrast to these characteristics, my Deep Mexico I identify as firmly located in the south where my family (in-law) resides. Consistent with Bonfil Batalla's descriptions, my Deep Mexico has recent indigenous roots, retains some of the Nahuatl language, cooks beans and *mole* in clay pots large enough to sit in, adds hot chile to everything, is humble to the point of self-deprecation, and laughs quickly no matter what the situation. I maintain this image despite the fact that I know of the darker aspects of life that exist there: the ever-growing population of abandoned children thanks to heavy out-migration, the proliferation of what seem to be increasingly perverse relationships in small towns, and situations of domestic and other violence that are overlaid with both the blackest aspects of folk magic and quiet links to organized delinquency.

Despite this and perhaps because of this, I hold onto my imagined and nostalgic image to compensate for what I find in the city and as a relief from the current national news, which hovers between the extremes of modernizing spectacle and narco-terror. Thinking through Bonfil Batalla's romantic splits, it became clear that I was projecting something similar onto my assessment of the city. This metaphorized me too into the maternal of colonial-era Spain, a figure asking the city to become something that only exists in a nostalgic memory of the past, in other words, something impossible. Like Stephanie Delacour, the protagonist of Kristeva's novels, who goes as far as to label herself "just a Byzantine," and personalizes her own romanticized ideas about this past within the present as "my Byzantium" (2006, p. 86), I seem to be constructing my own Byzantium in Deep Mexico. Deep Mexico, Imaginary Mexico … another split in which neither side is truly real: both exist within each other.

Kristeva too has her issues with geography. Throughout her oeuvre, she speaks of the crisis of the contemporary *Western* subject. Where does the West end and the East begin? Who is the Eastern subject, and what are *his* contemporary crises? Where does Kristeva—from Bulgaria—locate herself? Obviously, Kristeva's specification of the Western component forestalls at least some accusations of universalizing that have been leveled both at her and at psychoanalysis in general. She is quite clear that she is writing about Europe and the United States, which then allows her to make wide claims about the psychological impacts of patriarchy and Christianity. However, her work does raise intriguing questions about the crises of the rest of the world, especially in Eastern and Southern locations. These questions emerge visibly in her recent novels; however, they also arise in one of her earlier books. In 1977, Kristeva published *About Chinese Women*, a work she wrote after a visit to China with other members of Tel Quel. Dejected with the failures of the leftist movements of 1968 Paris, they had traveled to China with the desire to find something more hopeful in Mao's Cultural Revolution. The book has been widely criticized by Gayatri Spivak and others as romanticizing both the East and the situation of Eastern women in particular. China was presented as the feminine chora (Hattori, 1998, p. 123). As another critic summed up, "The China described in Kristeva's Tel Quel articles and in her book *About Chinese Women* is an imaginary one, and her writings contain little or no analysis of actual events" (Sjoholm, 2005, p. 13).

While Kristeva would later abandon this project as the Cultural Revolution turned bloody and tragic, at the time she wrote the book, she was attempting to critique the West from the standpoint of the East, not engage in a cultural study per se of China. Notwithstanding, her portrayal of China is laced with a certain amount of geographical fantasy. Chinese women are written as an archaic, Eastern, more authentic version of womanhood (and of female subjectivity) than what Kristeva was seeing in Europe at this time, and she seemed quick to parallel her own Eastern European roots with those of China. To some extent then, this book may indeed position Kristeva as a nostalgic immigrant searching for some sense of roots and connections in a geography to which she has no direct claim (as I seem to be doing with Deep Mexico). To equate her Bulgarian identity with something Chinese seems to push this generalized notion of "East" too far.

This critique surfaces again with the publication of her three detective novels that take place in the fictional Santa Varvara, and especially in the final novel, *Murder in Byzantium*, which takes on Byzantium as a complex condensation of past-present identifications. Held up in contrast to Paris and Europe, Santa Varvara and Byzantium have been read as essentialist Eastern sites, whether romanticized or demonized. For some, these works simply further their view that Kristeva romanticizes the East and uses her own Bulgarian background to distance herself from the Western crisis. She is also criticized as portraying the East as Europe's abject and then positioning herself as French, as having "overcome" her roots. One of her harshest critics, Dusan Bjelic, writes that Kristeva "has rushed to disown her Bulgarian identity" (2004, p. 2) and has created a portrait of the Balkans that associated them with "all things dirty, polluted and uncivilized" (p. 1). He goes on: "She formulates a principle of geo-aesthetics that divides European nations into those, like France, which have an aesthetic of the public sphere and those, like Bulgaria, which do not" (p. 2).

Bjelic draws his examples from Kristeva's well-known essay, "Bulgaria, my Suffering," identifying positive associations with France (language, order, good taste) and negative ones with Bulgaria (corruption, a national language she finds lacking). It is possible to identify similar constructions as these in her novels if one compares descriptions of Santa Varvara to Paris. In *Possessions*, Santa Varvara is "macabre" (1998, p. 9) and greets Stephanie with "convulsions and other signs of the devil" (p. 18). In *Murder in Byzantium*, Stephanie labels the city a "paradise of mafia groups and sects" suffering from "runaway inflation, the dizzying corruption, the chaotic administration, the absence of political direction, and therefore the absence of any future" (2006, p. 2). In Paris on the other hand, Stephanie is at home: "No more opacities, dramas, or mysteries. Everything obvious, transparent, in the open," and "there's not an inch of the landscape that doesn't reflect the fact that, here, being is immediate and logical" (1998, p. 162). It is—perhaps—not entirely wrong to argue that Kristeva also splits her geographies defensively.

Oddly, along with the geographic East, Mexico has been orientalized and made into the Europe's abject as well. From the early period of the conquest through the 20th century, intellectuals have, at times, bizarrely referred to Mexico as "oriental," and the indigenous population both historically and to date is frequently posited as the non-Western aspect of Mexico. This is meant in terms of developmental models, of course, but this still ignores the fact that the indigenous sector is implicated in the national in one way or another; and geographically, the term is absurd. To mention just one example, Octavio Paz writes:

> The impression we create is much like that of Orientals. They too—the Chinese, the Hindus, the Arabs—are hermetic and indecipherable. They too carry about with them, in rags, a still-living past. There is a Mexican mystery just as there is a yellow mystery or a black. (1961, p. 65)

He goes on to say that Mexico is ambiguous, promoting both attraction and repulsion; in other words, he seems to be calling Mexico (situated West of Western Europe) Europe's abject (pp. 65–66).

On the other hand, Kristeva may also romanticize Bulgaria and Byzantium as the chora, the source of the semiotic to which crisis-ridden subjects must return. Margaroni (2009) has suggested that this could be seen as a redemptive move, since Byzantium has always been poorly portrayed in Europe as anti-intellectual and decadent. Kristeva may, therefore, as Bjelic argues in another article, use her exile "as a biographical template for this liberatory process" from the maternal that all subjects must go through (2008, p. 373), but Kristeva also calls upon the semiotic element to enliven her language and thought. Speaking French as a Bulgarian, she writes,

> A surge that is not made up of words but has a music all its own imposes an awkward syntax on me, and these unfathomable metaphors that have nothing to do with French politeness and obviousness infiltrate my calmness with a Byzantine unease. (Kristeva, 2000b, p. 167).

The foreigner always infuses the second language with "the archaic rhythms and instinctual bases of his native idiom" (Kristeva, 2002, p. 241). In other words, "his difference seeps through" (p. 241). To sum up these different statements made by Kristeva and the different perspectives of her readers, it is clear that Kristeva at times distances herself from her roots and constructs the East/Bulgaria as *less than* Western Europe. And it is equally apparent that, at other times, she claims the feminine East and its semiotic excess and possibility of revolt. How much of this is typical of the exiled/expat writer? Are Kristeva and I both making fantasies of geography into our lost maternal?

One thing is certain. Kristeva is conscious of this double positioning, and she is consistently careful to identify herself as always the foreigner; to no small degree, she elides representation and categorization in this way—is this her way of getting around the West's tendency to control and subdue the feminine through representation? Her critics "cannot decide whether Kristeva is a vulgar Bulgarian or a Parisian elistist; she is both and neither," concludes Bjelic (2008, p. 371). Her own subjectivity, as she writes it, lies resolutely in the in-between, a theme brought out in the novels. For her character Sebastian Chrest-Jones, searching for his Byzantine roots, the airplane is his between-space, his high-tech semiotic garden. "The transit zone was his secret garden hideaway whose uncertainties he savored during his out-of-time hallucinations, which migrants frequently experience at irregular intervals" (Kristeva, 2006, p. 12). Kristeva's bilingual and migrant characters also find a refuge between languages, in what resists full translation, in the "infralinguistic hiding place that I believe to be the true habitat of foreigners like Stephanie, Sebastian, Wuxian, and Julia Kristeva," she writes, including herself (2011, p. 282). As Stephanie asks, avoiding a permanent location, "Do you want my address? I'm living among the geraniums" (2006, p. 62). She resides in poetic language, in music, in the unsayable. As a whole, Santa Varvara and the range of characters who appear in the novels are constructed as much more *between* than as purely Eastern; Kristeva carefully avoids such black-and-white positioning, sharing with them some of the freedom from symbolic representation she has claimed for herself.

SANTA VARVARA AND BYZANTIUM

Kristeva does not psychoanalyze her fictional city of Santa Varvara, but it is worth thinking about *that* city's subjectivity and possible psychic anxieties. Santa Varvara is portrayed in slightly varying ways across the three novels. In *The Old Man and the Wolves*, Santa Varvara is an ex-communist city, similar to Eastern European sites, struggling to create new forms of social and political life while facing institutional inefficiency and corruption. In *Possessions*, the city has become something much closer Kristeva's every city of *New Maladies*: "a sprawling metropolis with glass and steel buildings that reach to the sky, reflect it, reflect each other, and reflect you ... What might one do in such a city? Nothing but buy and sell, goods and images, which amounts to the same thing, since they both are dull, shallow symbols" (1995, p. 27). Santa Varvara is now the bustling spectacle of consumption, of false images, of surfaces. And by *Murder in Byzantium*, Santa Varvara is the essence of the global village, having lost most of its singularity, and seems immersed in a larger subjectivity crisis.

Complementing these varying identifications, the name "Santa Varvara" permits several interpretations, as various scholars have commented (Davis, 2002; Greaney, 2008; O'Grady, 2002). First, Santa Varvara invokes the barbarian tongue attributed to Asia Minor migrants by the Greeks—the barbaric aspects of violence and corruption that make no sense, like the "bara bara" of the migrants' language. It also alludes lightly to the Californian Santa Barbara and former soap opera of the same name; again the spectacle and consumerist element lurk. And finally, O'Grady (2002) has provided a series of provocative interpretations suggested by the figure of Saint Barbara herself. To summarize from her work, Saint Barbara is a Catholic saint martyred somewhere between the second and seventh centuries. Barbara was a motherless girl whose father enclosed her in a tower to keep her pure. While he is away on a trip, she discovers the Catholic faith, destroys his religious idols, and adds a third window to the tower in order to represent the Trinity. Upon his return, he beheads her for her disobedience, but then bursts into flames (or is struck by lightning), leaving only a pile of ashes behind. Barbara is made a saint as a martyr for her faith.

O'Grady first provides a possible reading that would see Barbara as a Kristeva—the (Freudian) father's daughter, estranged from the maternal/feminine, stuck in the tower. But then she counters this with a liberatory story of challenging patriarchy; after all, Barbara is sainted for the patricide that occurs! O'Grady reads this as Barbara's harnessing of paternal power as she searches for the lost maternal. In most representations, she is posed in front of the tower but holds a chalice (thc only female saint to do so; p. 57), which symbolizes her connection or her ability to reconcile both sides. She is neither stuck in the tower, nor does she fully recover and return to the maternal. O'Grady concludes that Kristeva exemplifies the same third way and in-between space that Santa Varvara also symbolizes. In O'Grady's interpretation, Santa Varvara represents the dislocation of the modern subject because it is a place with no place. Bridging East and West, the fictional city finds itself in a sort of exile just as Stephanie Delacour finds herself, and Santa Varvara too must resituate its subjectivity on a regular basis, something that sends the city into "convulsions," as noted above.

Santa Varvara is now decidedly not the East in any limiting fashion. Rather, Santa Varvara is contradictorily everywhere and nowhere at once. As Kristeva writes, "Santa Varvara is in Paris, New York, Moscow, Sofia, London, Plovdiv, and in Santa Varvara too, of course" (2006, p. 64). But she also affirms that the "the world is incompatible with Santa Varvara; I know nothing from it translates here" (p. 61). As a potential analysand, Santa Varvara certainly fulfills the criteria of the contemporary subject in crisis. That city is disconnected from a place-based body; while there are mentions of a beach and flowers amid the descriptions of urban problems, the reader cannot form a mental picture of the urban landscape. Hilly or flat? Old or new architecture? Green spaces? Abandoned lots? Elegant shopping malls? There is no clear city body, nor are there any other references to the invented city's singularity; of her specific history, we know nothing. What are her maternal and paternal elements? What gender is the city? Santa Varvara does not appear to be representing much … Is she/he actively confronting the spectacle? A full analysis of Santa Varvara is not possible of course, without more information, but the questions are worth posing.

What does become clear is that places are constructed as contradictory, heterogeneous, complex subjects. While some of Kristeva's work can be harnessed to launch accusations of either denigration or romantization, the city and her inhabitants/characters are all figures of the in-between and the multiple, which, I believe, constitutes an attempt to repair the split, not deepen it, if only by keeping things complex. Things Byzantine, as Kristeva will emphasize, resist easy representation, making them both appealing and potentially liberating. So rather than name and categorize, Kristeva rewrites the East and West as mutually within each other. If Santa Varvara is not on the map, neither are Bonfil Batalla's constructions—Deep Mexico and Imaginary Mexico exist in the same space and time despite their differences, and yet no one can plot these locations out topographically. Most importantly, what we are seeing here is that Kristeva is conscious of her projections onto space. Stephanie, for example, says of one character, "Brian, I possess him, though in reality he's completely alien to me" (Kristeva, 1998, p. 18), and then says of Santa Varvara much the same thing: It is "as though I were inhabited by another person, who I'd rather ignore but who in fact possesses me" (p. 15). Similarly, the Byzantine historian Anna Comnena becomes for Stephanie the embodiment of the past and of place, "Anna Comnena, my Byzantium" (Kristeva, 2006, p. 86). Woman becomes a place. From all this, it is clear that place possesses people who possess place, setting off another endless cycle of transferences.

Kristeva positions Santa Varvara in the murky borderlands between East and West; but while her Byzantium initially seems more Eastern, it too is hard to locate on a map in her portrayal. In the novel, Byzantium is considered as a historical, metaphorical, and current place, and to some extent it sets up a range of associations that Kristeva plays with freely. Byzantium, of course, refers to the Eastern Roman Empire that ended with the fall of Constantinople to the Muslim Ottoman Empire in 1453. Yet like most things ostensibly in the past, influences linger on. The Orthodox Christian religion is still practiced, and not only Kristeva, but Byzantium researchers, have identified other cultural influences in present-day border areas between Europe and the ex-empire (Bodin, 2011). On the one hand, Kristeva identifies Byzantium as a decadent and corrupt civilization on the brink of collapse and as a place/period of religious fanaticism. On the other hand, Byzantium becomes the semiotic, the sacred, the transgressive that Stephanie (all Western subjects, Europe) need to connect with. Because Byzantium is a future anterior, that which was and that which might yet be, we again are moved to draw a parallel with Deep Mexico. Isn't Kristeva, like Bonfil Batalla, asking us to look back, to return, to reopen the past in order to imagine better alternatives for the future? Not to re-create the past, but to bring forward its semiotic?

A final but crucial similarity that I find between Byzantium and current Mexico must also be brought out because it will clarify, at least in part, something about how to read Kristeva's *Murder in Byzantium* and what advice we should take from it. Kristeva uses the Europe-Byzantium juxtaposition as a metaphor for the current encounter between Europe and conservative Islam. While she has been critiqued for portraying Islam as oddly (or uncharacteristically for her theory) homogeneous, dogmatic, and fundamentalist, she does draw an interesting parallel between the religious crusaders of Byzantium and the fanatical element of Islam that includes the suicide bombers (see Almond, 2007, for the critique). She seems to suggest quite directly that Europe, like the previous Byzantine civilization, may be on the verge of crisis if it does not find a way to communicate with its Islamic/Eastern other. The difficulty of generating these increasingly urgent dialogues is monumental. Indeed, the need for larger levels of dialogue has not been overlooked by the psychoanalytic community, a part of which works directly with political, ethnic, and religious conflicts by having the involved parties rethink national trauma, grief, reparations, and the like; the work of Vamik Volkan comes to mind in particular.

Is Mexico not facing something quite similar to this potential collapse? Having immersed itself (albeit in an extremely unequal and divided way) in the consumerist spectacle of Hollywood, conspicuous consumption, and the like after the economic crises of the 1980s and NAFTA's ratification in 1994, Mexico is now facing its own potential demise in the mind of many intellectuals and regular folk as organized violence has taken its toll on the nation's subjectivity. In my view, the narco-presence offers another example of fanatical allegiance (of the obsessive love that Kristeva describes in *Tales of Love*) with a quasireligious overtone. Its members have created an all-encompassing lifestyle that includes a particular vocabulary, style of dress, musical preferences, alcoholic preferences, tastes in real estate and décor, and so on, which situates them in a very specific version of the Debordian spectacle. Loyalties are also extremely important; allegiances are managed as family-like, with certain deceased leaders (such Arturo Leyva Beltrán, for example) remembered as father figures and one faction named La Familia (the family). Befitting this, betrayals are cause for murder, much along the Italian Mafia model. Furthermore, the mass violence of horrifying types and quantity has been unilaterally combined with the maintenance of Catholicism. While they do not kill for religious reasons, the "practitioners" of narco-terrorism wear crosses, attend and sponsor masses, and set up their own altars with specific protecting saints to watch over their illicit practices. And like a suicide bomber, anyone entering the narco-business is ready to die for his cause, even if his cause is capitalist or power-related in nature, rather than spiritual.

Not surprisingly, this violence now represents a spectacle in its own right, as "crime has become theatrically media-friendly" (Kristeva, 2000a, p. 5). Everywhere the narco-news is on the television, in the newspapers, and spoken of constantly, and telenovela-style dramas on national TV channels further glorify the men and women of organized crime. And like in Europe, Mexico's desire to revolt against either spectacle, the one of images or the one of untenable violence, is constrained by the crisis in authority that Kristeva brings out in both *Intimate Revolt* and *The Sense and Non-Sense of Revolt*. In these books, she asks whether or not revolt is still possible in a spectacle society where no one takes responsibility, where it's not clear who is in charge. This is another failure of the State to play a healthy paternal function … Who exactly should one revolt against? It is most certainly not clear in current Mexico who "the bad guys" are and how to identify this corruption that penetrates all levels of society. As the media culture turns violence into banal entertainment, psychic space is again closed down, leaving the contemporary subject numbed and unable to question. As the journalists have been saying since early 2010, Mexico has entered into "collective psychosis," which is the Kristevan condition of an inability to symbolize anxiety, loss, and trauma.

TINY REVOLTS

What solutions does Kristeva offer to contemporary "vulnerable Byzantines and recorders of the modern Crusades"? She insists that the answer lies in "asking Byzantine questions—is there anything else to do?" (2006, p. 65). She advocates for sharing our vulnerabilities, which links the social back down to the intimately personal space of the individual analysand in the consulting room. This can be taken as one of her greater strengths or greater weaknesses, but her approach is openly targeted at the intimate level. She encourages acknowledging one's vulnerability as a subject while recognizing others' vulnerabilities as well, arguing that "psychoanalytic listening to vulnerability could take on political meaning" (2011, p. 44). While she is referring in this particular reference to the case of the disabled other in France (a far cry from the self-other relations with narco-terrorists and suicide bombers), her point is well taken. By listening and sharing trauma, by making art, designing buildings, writing novels, one ignites what she has called "tiny revolts" (2002, p. 5).

These "tiny revolts … preserve the life of the mind and of the species" (p. 5). In *Intimate Revolt*, she writes that the novel "is privileged terrain for such an exploration and its communication to the greatest number" (p. 5), and she states, "I consider my book [here she is referring to the recent publication of *Possessions*], among so many others, as a low form of revolt. But are other, higher forms really more convincing?" (p. 4). Writing (creating) constitutes a means for displacing authority from the system back onto the self, to regain control over one's own narrative while paradoxically maintaining oneself open to the other who will read, respond and challenge. This solution enacts, admittedly, a huge leap down from global and national politics, trauma-inducing as they might be, to the level of a writer more humbly concerned with expressing his or her own semiotic to disrupt less volatile symbolic orders. But given the nature of my city-analysand and my interests in her particular crisis, this gap will be left open. In an interview, Kristeva stated that writers and artists provide an essential challenge to the status quo:

> One cannot change the mode of communication in a country, or in a society, without having experienced a fundamental disappointment. And the artist is the one who changes the codes. A photographer, or an artist, or a poet, will not use the clichés, but change the clichés. In order to achieve this, they must have felt disgust, rage, or at the very least a disappointment which they have endured, which they have transcended, and which they have gone beyond. So, I believe there is a core of disappointment, related to melancholia, but not necessarily ending up as a medical case. Not all artists are stuffed with antidepressants or locked up in psychiatric wards! (Huitfeldt Midttun, 2006, p. 168)

To change the clichés is to challenge the status quo of language itself, which in turn constitutes being a genius and transcending. This brings us back to the city: If the city is not challenging the sociohistorical conditions of her identity just yet, could she? Are the paths toward such a challenge perhaps embedded in her femininity? What sorts of bodily elements might serve as resources, and can they be mobilized in ways that do not redraw the boundaries of East and West that Kristeva occasionally sets up, which parallel the North-South ones at play in Latin America?

Through the transferences and countertransferences that inform our relationships with people and place, I have traced out at least some of the key elements in this dynamic as it unfolded between me and the city-analysand. Through her own transferences, the city metamorphized me into the tourist, searching for a geographical maternal that was more imaginary than real. At the same time she made me into Spain, the maternal who also holds the city up to an impossible image. These projections fed into my own intellectual desires to find signs of rebellion (to not write *provincia* is stereotypically traditional), and my personal desires related to Deep Mexico identifications. Perhaps not surprisingly, during this period I felt myself rather desperately wanting to move to some other city, which situated me as the abandoning mother-miner-foreigner who leaves when things get difficult. What the city needs at this juncture is a response from the analyst that does not include abandonment. What I need at this juncture is to recognize and then gently push away my countertransference desires to flee. I do not wish to be an exploiter and abandoner of the city, and I am increasingly aware that the elusive "someplace better" may always remain a desire that will never be satiated. I need to find a way to disengage from these projects and return to my task as analyst. As Kristeva says,

> For if I do not really love my patients, what could I understand in them, what could I tell them? Countertransference love is my ability to put myself in their place; looking, dreaming, suffering as if I were she, as if I were he. Fleeting moments of identification. Temporary and yet effective mergings. Fruitful sparks of understanding. Provided I move away. (1987, p. 11)

One way to "move away" is to write, of course. Swartz (2006) offers a fascinating reflection about the potential third voice that comes through in case notes, creating a distance between an analyst's formal notes—"coded in clinical neutralese, language that slips the practitioner into a white coat of distance and objectivity" (p. 428) and that is used for billing and legal purposes—and her private notes, which can provide "a powerful tool for self-reflection and scrutiny" (p. 431). Swartz then ties this into the question of representing another's voice, a question that plagues ethnographers in the same way. How to represent an often oppressed other's voice without imposing the official, power-laced account of the analyst? Referencing Bakhtin and notions of the carnivalesque and dialogue, she states that for subaltern clients to speak with the therapist "they must be given a voice suited to the task of subversion, disruption, ambiguity and contradiction" (p. 435). Working with unconscious material, she continues, is highly carnivalesque and this material must be allowed to play out on its own terms.

> Theoretical and professional writing must not capture the voice of the client and like a bird in a cage, command her to sing. The voice

> needs to be allowed the possibility of disrupting and subverting, questioning and rendering incoherent the "official" version of the notes. (p. 437)

Swartz's subsequent strategies for operationalizing her concerns return to language. She calls for poetic writings of case notes, defining this as writing that includes repetitions, incorrect grammar, broken sentences, and metaphor, all of which release the analyst from "the need for particular outcomes" (p. 438). My own notebooks were certainly full of poetic writings; and while I had ignored much of this in favor of Swartz's more clinical language, I now looked more closely at what was going on in the margins of my note taking. The recurring themes and questions were there, and they seemed to be asking to be unrolled into something fuller. I began to try to get at these complex folds between self and other through creative writing; more specifically, I tried to "switch sides," first by thinking about the sensual nature of city space, even as she denied it, and second by writing into the essential female icons and figures in the local and national repertoire, thus pushing myself into the murky space between self and other. The resulting book of poetry that emerged from this crisis period, which has since been published (Rodríguez, 2009), thus constituted my attempt to plunge into these issues and to work through some of my transferences onto this place.

Kristeva writes into her analysands as well. In *Colette*, her voice occasionally merges with her that of Colette, her protagonist-analysand. She is not trying to become Colette; this is neither desirable nor possible. But stylistically, one can read this as a temporary possession and transference, part of the attachment of love that enables the analyst (or researcher of any type) to become passionate about the (research) subject. If she is philosophical with Arendt and analytical with Klein, Kristeva with Colette waxes poetic and "digests" this figure from a synesthetic position. For example, after citing a passage from Colette, Kristeva responds in the text, "Necessarily, naturally, it is on that palate, in my voracious mouth, that the words live" (2004, p. 204). She connects at a sensorial, corporal level to her task of reading Colette and then "moves away," returning to psychoanalysis in the book's final chapter, "Is There a Feminine Genius?" She is showing us via example how writing mirrors the transference process of moving into and then distancing oneself from the analysand. And she foreshadows the discourse on "dispassionizing love" that will come in subsequent work, in particular in *Hatred and Forgiveness*. What the three geniuses do in their own lives, Kristeva does here: She sublimates the passionate transferences her analysand/research subjects provoke in her, transforming them into a more serene, dispassionate love that can be symbolized for her own readers.

Referring to the transferences involved in psychoanalytic practice, J. S. Hall aptly observes that "each therapist will hear a patient with different ears" (2004, p. 45). The analyst must recognize and then disconnect from (without denying) her own vulnerabilities and transferences, thus becoming for the analysand "an other who does not judge but hears my truth in the availability of love, and for that very reason allows me to be reborn" (Kristeva, 1989, p. 205). In this manner, the analyst slowly disconnects and then approaches the possibility of being able to offer a new interpretation back to the analysand. This is what comes next.

Seven

Revolt, They Said

Two Virgins, One Indian Princess, and the T-shirt Girl

Okay, back to work. The city is on the way in, and it is time for each of us to return to her respective role in this relationship. I pull my chair closer to the keyboard, push up my sleeves, and briefly take stock of where we are in the analytic process. I've been hearing the city discuss her life and writings over a long period of time. I've been listening to how she focuses her energies and paying attention to what she chooses not to think about as well. I've also submersed myself into and reemerged from the dynamics of transference and countertransference. I am ready to begin responding more creatively and hope to offer a possible interpretation for the city to mull over. The power of the semiotic, which I see as the key force that could bring the city to a disruptive writing, will dominate in my analysis.

While the previous sessions did not find the city actively engaging in the semiotic disruption I had hoped, at this point I return to the question, *could* the city challenge the symbolic if she wanted to? Does she have the resources and thus the potential to radically disrupt the status quo? Insight is liberating, but my own belief is that simply recognizing the contours of a problem is not quite enough. The city's issues with which she struggles have been illuminated, and the crises have been productively reopened through the transference dynamic. At times, when an analysand is struggling to symbolize, Kristeva will use her imagination in order to gently draw the subject back toward verbalization. For example, in one case she comments,

> I offered Didier my own fantasies, which his paintings elicited in me. While we were pursuing this path, however, an imaginary and symbolic contract was established between us. Even though he found my discourse "reductive," "oversimplified," Didier began to accept, adjust, change, or reject my interpretations of his collages, he could give his own name to the phantasmatic that lay behind his cool technique. (1995, pp. 19–20)

By offering the analysand words with which to work, the analyst gives him something to ground himself into as well, a base from which to launch a return to language. I now take on Kristeva's musings on intimacy, creativity, and revolt in order to plunge back into the city's psyche and suggest a possible route to revolt, leaning heavily on her textual and bodily resources.

In *Intimate Revolt*, Kristeva defines revolt as, not only "a protest against already established norms, values, and powers" (2002, p. 3), but also as "return/turning back/displacement/change" (p. 5). To rupture is to renew, she affirms, to move out of an automated, unquestioning stance, "to avoid ossifying into the mere act of managing business" (Kristeva & Petit, 2002, p. 86). She defines a route to revolt that includes two key elements: intimacy and questioning. The intimate is "what is most profound and most singular in the human experience" (Kristeva, 2002, p. 44). It is located at the borders of sexuality and the body, language, and creativity. Oddly, intimacy in the psychoanalytic and literary context does not mean verbally articulating one's inner thoughts to a trusted confidante or reader in a safe environment. Intimacy does not mean sharing everything, or necessarily saying much at all! In *Murder in Byzantium*, Stephanie Delacour admits that she does not reveal her own wounds, loves or personal traumas, "for I am convinced that intimacy blossoms in the unsaid" (Kristeva, 2006, p. 69). And even this, as a notion of Kristeva's, is somewhat unsaid and deflected, since it comes out of the mouth of a character.

The sentence that follows reads, "Intimacy speaks indirectly, transmuted into figures and parables, numbers, symbols, and allusions, and all that is Byzantine" (p. 69). Does this not imply that the semiotic, personal, and intimate messages today's analysands need are right there in the text? I read this as an invitation to turn back to the city's key symbols and iconic texts in the realm of the preverbal. Symbols function to hold a place; somewhat like the analyst, they provide containers and pauses in which to suspend meaning. For Kristeva, symbols retain their intimate character because they sit at the border between the symbolic and the semiotic, whereas language (the process of verbalizing a symbol) involves movement and disruption. Symbols provide necessary mooring points for modern analysands who are desperately searching for meaning amid the barrage of images. Therefore, a partial answer to uncovering "the intimate" for the city would be to turn to her own "figures and parables, numbers, symbols, and allusions" that make up these preverbal energies. Perhaps this is the realm in which to locate the semiotic elements necessary for disruption.

So my task now is to plumb the city space for symbols, myths, and icons—in short, I will rifle through this subsection of her textual repertoire to look for ways out of silence and repression, for ways into a fuller expressive life. "The image," writes Kristeva, "has an extraordinary power to harness your anxieties and desires, to take on their intensity and to suspend their meaning" (1995, p. 8). As I have found thus far, the city's images of the no-longer-transgressive Don Quijote, the Pípila who never again ushered in any revolt, the abject miners, and other such figures have indeed contained her anxieties and fears of transgression. I now ask, however, what would happen if I *unharnessed* not only the city's anxieties and desires but also the images themselves? If "Guanajuato enchants," as the last text promised, these once-frozen conflicts are now ready to be opened up in the analytic process. I hope to find a way to disenchant the city, which would allow her to move toward a more fully human existence.

THE UNHARNESSABLE, UNREPRESENTABLE VIRGIN OF GUANAJUATO

The first icon I will discuss is already at least partially unharnessed. She is the city's own Mary image, the Virgin of Guanajuato, and she is a loose cannon of sorts.

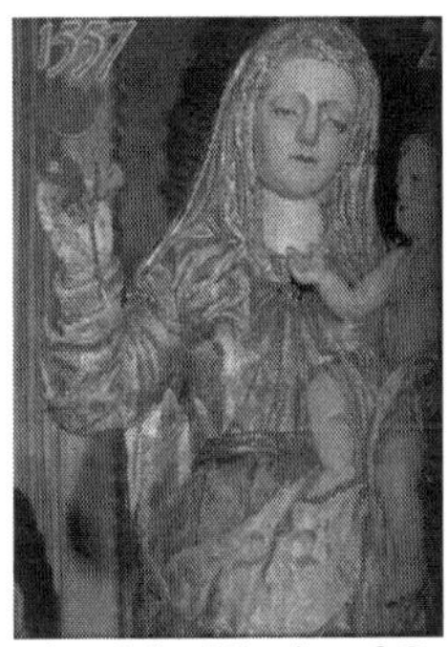

Poster photograph of the Virgin of Guanajuato statue

The main statue of what was eventually named the Virgen de Guanajuato (Virgin of Guanajuato) is 1.15 meters tall and normally stands in the main church, the Basílica, on the Plaza de la Paz. The image represents the Virgin holding both Christ as a child and a staff, and the entire piece was carved out of a single piece of cedar. Originally, she held a wooden rose from which dangled a rosary, a detail that was replaced with a gold staff (which one cannot help but read as a shift from female to male symbolism). In 1557, she was sent as a gift to Guanajuato by Spanish King Carlos V. It is said that she is the oldest Mary icon in the New World; before coming to Mexico, she had been hidden in a cave during the Moorish invasion of Spain, where she remained for eight centuries. Miraculously, she emerged from the cave completely intact—the wood neither rotted nor splintered after centuries underground. A Virgin who knows the underground female world of caves—how similar to the city's mines and tunnels—and yet here she is, back on the surface of the symbolic world.

As the local story is told, when the Spaniards carrying the image reached what is now Yerbabuena (an outlying community currently about 20 minutes from downtown), they were so lost that they settled down for the night. In the morning, a miracle occurred: Two doves appeared and led the group directly into the city, a divine act guiding the Virgin to her new home. The image was housed at different chapels for 131 years, and occasionally in shelters for indigenous people, until she was finally installed in the main Basílica in 1696. The city's Virgin thus begins as a stranger and a foreigner, as a woman emerging from a cave to move into a new symbolic; and yet, she is also linked nostalgically to Spain at the time she arrives.

The Virgin's trajectory is unusual given her ancient cave origins and, to a lesser extent, the fact that she was housed among Indians at first, but there is a second part to this story that is fascinating from a Kristevan perspective. Many years ago, when I first moved here, I had looked for a small icon of this local Marian image. Over and over, I was frustrated in my attempts and wondered why images were not sold at the market or in the finer craft stores of the city. I found all sorts of images of San Miguel (the neighboring city's patron saint), of the Virgin of Guadalupe (the national patron saint), and a host of other common saints and virgins, but never the city's. After a round of unsuccessful attempts to visit the main Basílica's own religious store, I finally found it open. I went in thinking that surely in this baroque site of stacked-up religious paraphernalia I would find Virgins of Guanajuato in varying mediums. I found nothing. While the elderly woman in charge looked around for an image under and among the other sacred souvenirs, I asked her why it was so challenging to find an image in the city.

"Ah," she replied, "it's because the Virgin of Guanajuato doesn't allow herself to be represented! If someone makes an image in clay, it breaks in the kiln; if they carve it out of wood, it splinters; in glass or ceramic, it shatters." She affirmed that the Church had starting commissioning works from far-away places because local artists would no longer attempt to create anything in her likeness. Too much effort and too many costly materials to produce something destined to fail … Since then, this story has been retold to me many times, and indeed there is an observable dearth of Virgin of Guanajuato drawings, paintings, sculptures, and so on, which stands in stark contrast to the national industry of Virgin of Guadalupe paraphernalia (which runs the gamut from key chains and portraits to salt shakers and tattoos). The only images of the Virgin of Guanajuato that one can find tend to be photographs; nothing bodied or material.

Surprisingly, however, the woman in the shop was eventually able to produce a small plaster image—"the last one I've got, made somewhere farther up North, you're lucky since I almost never receive these anymore," she said. It was about seven inches tall and resembled the original one well enough, it seemed to me. Two weeks later, I took the icon with me to a conference in the States along with other examples of Mexican icons. I kept it carefully on the hotel dresser and then wrapped it in clothing in the suitcase when I was ready to come home. When I unpacked back in town, the statue emerged from the suitcase with one of the black horns missing (the Virgin is often portrayed as literally stepping on the symbols of evil). I emptied out my suitcase, but the broken pieces had vanished. Another case of refusing representation? Anger at having been brought home after traveling? Since then, I have kept this broken icon in my home.

For Kristeva, that which is not represented retains power, while that which is represented loses its power through the very process of representation. "It is not possible to say of a *woman* what she *is* (without running the risk of abolishing her difference)" (1987, p. 234). Kelly Oliver explains,

> When represented, the unrepresentable woman becomes what she is not. The existence of the unrepresentable upon which representation rests is denied; and the representation of that unrepresentable, woman, is a fetish. … It seems necessary for feminists to represent women in order to work for the emancipation of women from the oppressive representations of them in patriarchal cultures. But for Kristeva this is to once again fetishize her, or refetishize her, and thereby render her powerless, completely coopted by the Symbolic. (1993a, p. 108)

As we have seen, the Virgin Mary is Kristeva's preferred example of how this occurs because she effectively loses her semiotic, disruptive, and female body as she is denied both sex and death. The Virgin of Guanajuato thus appears as a powerful symbol of the unrepresentable. Rather uniquely, she neither rejects the symbolic nor sacrifices all of her humanity to become a part of it.

She is also out on the street. Although it is not unusual in the ritualized practice of Mexican Catholicism to see saints being paraded through different urban neighborhoods, the Virgin of Guanajuato is especially mobile. She is regularly marched in processions from church to church, from the *centro* to outlying barrios. She is most mobile in the months of May, called "María's month"; in August, which marks the anniversary of her arrival; and in November, during another set of traditions called the Illuminations.[30] While Don Quijote was "rescued" (like a damsel in distress) from his roaming, and his revolutionary potential was squashed as he moved indoors to the museum, the Virgin of Guanajuato was not taken fully through this process, and she retains her liberty to move outside of the institution that would control her. She is the first protagonist of my emerging interpretation, a unique icon that resonates uncannily with Kristeva's more abstract speculations.[31]

---

[30] An important painting in a hotel on the main Jardín depicts the first parading of the Virgin and dates this tradition back to 1810, the year the Independence War began. In 1810, she was marched by the Insurgent forces and in 1811 by the Royalists. Neighborhoods would keep their windows lit (illuminated) as a show of faith, as well as coming out and encountering the Virgin on the street, a tradition still practiced.

[31] The Virgin in Guanajuato is thus tinged with something a bit dangerous, and this is not the first time a Virgin icon has become a bit ambivalent. The Independence uprising was organized under a flag bearing the image of the Virgin of Guadalupe. While on the one hand, the use of Guadalupe signaled the existence of an emergent Mexican (i.e., non-Spanish self), not everyone was happy about this. Guanajuato's Lucas Alamán wrote at the time, "What a monstrous pairing of religion with murder and robbery"

THE INDIAN PRINCESS WHO WANTS TO BECOME HUMAN

If the Virgin thus retains several shreds of her humanity, the following myth orients us further toward her desire to be fully human. There is a commonly recited legend about an indigenous princess that is intimately related to the city space; it is more of an oral text than a written one; however, several versions of the myth exist in small books of local legends (e.g., Torija & Olmos Fuentes, 1998).[32] These inexpensive and often brochurelike anthologies of legends are sold at magazine kiosks, and they constitute the sort of text that tourists buy and that locals tend to have lying around the house, drawn out when relatives from other places come to visit. The story consists of two parts, both of which offer significant analytical material.

Part 1 of the story establishes a mythic history behind a dominant element of the local landscape. The highest and most striking peak of the otherwise softly contoured mountains that surround the city is called La Bufa (literally, "the buffalo," as it is shaped like the wide rounded hump of a buffalo). At the top of this hill is a cave in which can be found representations of both pagan and colonial-Christian motifs. The myth claims that in the early colonial period, an indigenous princess was turned into a snake by a jealous husband who had noticed a young shepherd observing her. He stashed her away in the cave, but this act was avenged in part by her father, who killed the husband and then built within the cave a city designed to duplicate and thus compete with Guanajuato's emerging opulence. The "enchanted city" of the cave boasted streets of gold and silver and would only be attainable by the man who could rescue the princess.

The princess is turned into a snake as punishment for attracting sexual interest.[33] She is sent into a cave, which represents both the female abject and the unconscious. A return of sorts, and this place also recalls the mines, which are similarly dark, female, and full of riches. The father (her Law) avenges the death by shooting a (phallic) arrow through the jealous husband, but he is not able to undo the spell cast upon her. As compensation, he builds her the city's double—an unreachable, enchanted yet lovely place. It is easy to interpret this

---

(Joseph & Henderson, 2003, p. 173). The use of a religious icon to rally fighting against the Law represented by Spain broke the bond between the symbolic patriarchal order and the Church—no wonder the fear ... The rallying cry yelled every Independence Day to date, "Long live the Virgin of Guadalupe and Death to the *gachupines* [Spaniards]," "still resounds in my ears with a frightful echo," remembers Alamán (p. 173).

[32] Versions of this myth exist elsewhere in Mexico, but the version told here is recounted with the unique local references of the city, a tendency that is not uncommon when the same myth is told in different regions. For example, most towns have a localized version of the Llorona myth as well, with the attending details and place-names similarly adjusted to local history and geography.

[33] In both Mesoamerican and Spanish-Catholic symbolism, a lowly earthbound snake in a high-up mountain cave is out of place. Things are not where they should be.

double as the city's unconscious, not only because of the usual symbolism of caves, but also because the interior conforms to an other-worldly mapping of the city body … Here also, perhaps, is an original split that occurred around the moment of the city's founding or birth, which relegated the indigenous feminine to the abject spaces. As Amati-Mehler et al. remind us, myth "is also an enunciation of the law, a demarcation of the limit, an indication of the boundary" (1993, p. 17). The story enacts the boundary between the conscious and unconscious, the real city and the fantastic one, the abject and the not.

One can also read this as a sign that the city, as the embodied consciousness of the "West," has lost touch with her inner, indigenous, unconscious riches. Her psychic space is unreachable, caught under a spell and even more inaccessible in terms of terrain. How to gain access to the unconscious and its riches? Or as Kristeva would ask, how to reopen this psychic space we no longer know how to get to? The answer supplied in the myth appears to be by rescuing the abject female/semiotic and by integrating her power into the symbolic. (Doesn't this echo the La Llorona brochure figure beckoning the reader into the tunnel?) Only then will the cave be reopened.

Part 2 of this story opens with a poor shepherd walking his horses through the mountaintops of this area. Suddenly, a beautiful woman (the Indian princess) appears on his path. She begs him to carry her to the altar of the Basílica, home to the Virgin of Guanajuato, to break the spell that hangs over her so that she can become human. In exchange for this, she will give him access to the enchanted city, the silver- and gold-plated copy of Guanajuato, and all its riches. The only condition? That he not turn around and look at her, no matter what people may say as he descends into town carrying her on his back. Already thinking about how his fate and status would change for the better, the shepherd eagerly accepts and begins the trek downward. As he nears the townspeople, they yell out comments about the monster he is carrying on his back. Finally, unable to resist amid so much scandal, he turns around to look at the woman. In this second, she is transformed into a snake and slithers off his back and into the mountains. The shepherd turns into a stone peak of the mountain (now called *el peñon del pastor*, or"the shepherd's peak"). The enchanted city remains unfound, waiting forever for someone to break the spell (Torija & Olmos Fuentes, 1998).

Again we find significant analytical material. The indigenous (and presumably non-Catholic) feminine must be brought to the heart of the city *centro* where the city digests so many others currently. Specifically, she must be carried to the altar of the Virgin herself. Others are watching, and their own horror and shame are projected onto the once-beautiful princess since they cannot bear to gaze upon the abject feminine. If the feminine could be rescued, the shepherd would gain a full life of riches, which while material in the literal sense could certainly also signify sensuality, self-knowledge, and other such things. The fact that gold and silver are highlighted references not only the local mines but also the less tangible feminine riches that have also been depleted by modern society as the city occupies herself with more masculine concerns, such as economic development through tourism and so on.

The shepherd cannot bear the pressure of those observing their journey toward the church, and when he turns to gaze at the princess both undergo a transformation, albeit not the one either had hoped for. The princess returns to being a snake condemned to the cave. The shepherd turns to stone, literally becoming a rocky mountain peak, because he stared into the female abject. Like the warrior that looked at Medusa and turned to stone, the wife of Lot who looked back at the city and turned to a pillar of salt (all equally phallic in motif), he freezes. He is transformed into city space, albeit a (super)natural one versus a built part of the environment. The entire process crumbles, and the enchantment endures. The abject remains in the cave, and the city carries on without benefit of this inner wealth.

The disenchantment of the princess is supposed to occur at the altar of the church. The Spanish-colonial reading might view this as a sign that humanity is restored by God and that the princess is doing the right thing by moving toward Catholicism. However, from a Kristevan perspective, the Church seems ill-suited to restore female humanity, since it has specialized in taking away women's human aspects! Through ritual, the Church has enacted a patriarchal devouring of maternal power by freezing the feminine into icons, yet despite this the Church as a site of masculine authority can be put on trial as well. In the forward to Eve Ensler's *The Vagina Monologues* (2001), Gloria Steinem provides a fascinating connection between the Church and the female body, the very element it usually fears. While a physical church is commonly described as the House of God (read male, Law, etc.), its body, nonetheless, is female. Steinem writes,

> In the 1970s, while researching in the Library of Congress, I found an obscure history of religious architecture that assumed a fact as if it were common knowledge: the traditional design of most patriarchal buildings of worship imitates the female body. Thus, there is an outer and inner entrance, labia majora and labia minora; a central vaginal aisle toward the altar; two curved ovarian structures on either side; and then in the sacred center, the altar or womb, where the miracle takes place—where males give birth. (2001, p. xvii)

She goes on to argue cogently that patriarchy has thus allowed men to take over the birthing process—male priests sprinkle water ("birth fluid") on people's heads, rename them, and promise re-birth (p. xviii). Steinem also comments rather acidly that this explains the Catholic Church's age-old efforts to keep women from becoming priests; the men are in there co-opting female power that they are, not surprisingly, reluctant to give back. As we have seen in the case of the Virgins thus far (and the virginal Don Quijote), the body is thus sacrificed for the word through formalized ritual. But here in the city, our Virgin of Guanajuato is not representable, so there is an unexpected hole in the way things should be that Steinem could not have expected.

The Virgin heads away from the church to maintain her humanity, while the Indian princess needs the altar to become human. Kristeva underlines the fact that the diminished role of religion in modern life creates a lack, as people no longer have this age-old system to provide symbolism and meaning (no matter how patriarchal). The princess, then, may be seen as returning to obtain a dose of this meaning. She is coming out of the cave, off the mountain, back into a world of people, and back into the real city versus her imaginary cave version of the city. She, too, is looking for meaning in the symbolic, even as she has the potential to greatly disrupt it. Taken together with thc Virgin of Guanajuato, we find here yet another folding together of what should be opposites coming together within the city's bodily space.

What if the Indian princess had made it to the church? Was her part-humanity seeking to merge with the Virgin of Guanajuato's own lingering human aspects? These two stories together seem to illustrate where the city is right now. These unresolved issues of the female abject, love, and incomplete humanity are almost opened; the riches of the cave await.

OUR LADY OF SORROWS (AND SWORDS): THE VIRGEN DE DOLORES

On the Friday before Holy Week, Guanajuato celebrates the Día de la Virgen de Dolores (Day of Our Lady of Sorrows). Here we have the classic Stabat Mater image: Mary mourning her sacrificed son. Custom dictates that on this day altars be positioned in thresholds of both homes and businesses. The altars include representations of the Virgin that show her cloaked in a shawl of dark purple, which symbolizes mourning, and with a gaze directly downward, enclosed in her sorrow.

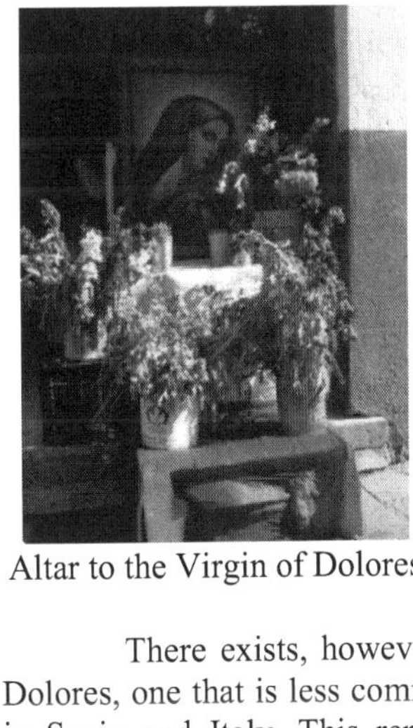

Altar to the Virgin of Dolores

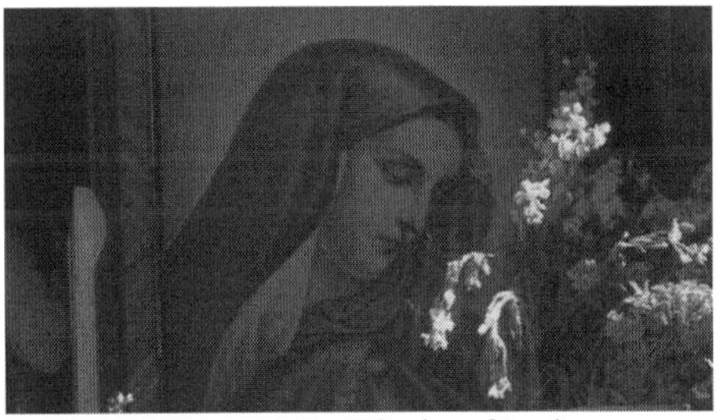

Close-up of the Virgin of Dolores

There exists, however, another representation of the same Virgin of Dolores, one that is less common yet present in sites around Mexico, and also in Spain and Italy. This representation depicts the Virgin of Dolores with seven swords going through her heart, swords that represent the seven sorrows she has suffered: Simon's prophesy; the flight to Egypt; the loss of Christ at the temple; her encounter with Christ on the road to the Cross; the moment he dies on the Cross; the moment he is lowered from the Cross into her arms; his burial). It is hard not to view the swords as potential weapons with which to castrate patriarchal power.

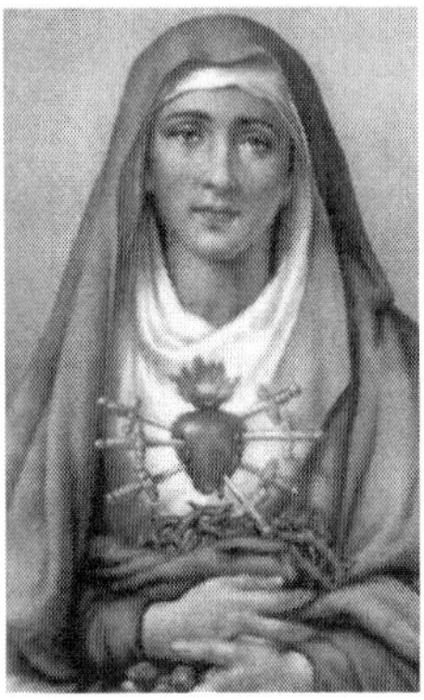
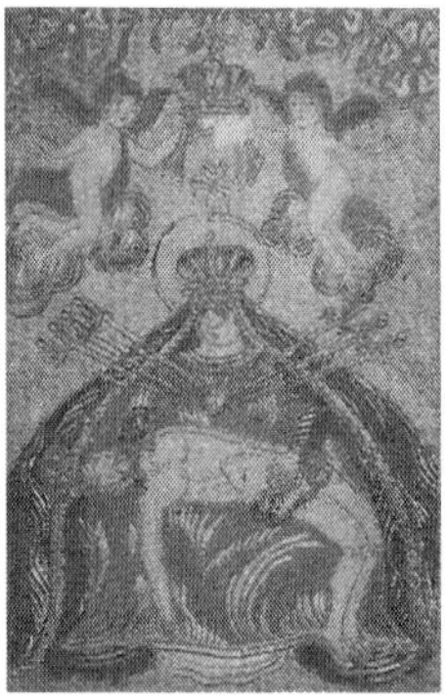
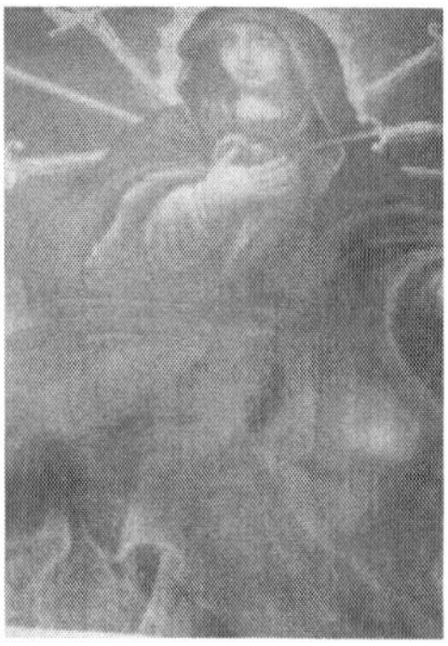

Images of the Virgin of Dolores (Our Lady of Sorrows) with swords[34]

An armed Virgin? We now have three figures clamoring for revolt. The indigenous princess wants to move into the church to restore her humanity. The Virgin of Guanajuato wants to move out onto the streets to further avoid representation. And the Virgin of Dolores hovers with her swords. What we can read in these symbols (the interpretation that I offer to my city-analysand), is a triple-voiced (polyphonic) and urgent call for a new discourse of maternity/femininity/*provincia*. They also serve as reminder that the contemporary Western subject still needs some sense of the sacred or, in other words, a sense of meaningfulness in a context where the spectacle has left a void. The three figures are each in touch with her respective semiotic potential; each attempts to inscribe herself into the symbolic to recover a fuller humanity with both pain and pleasure, and each is positioned to at least partially rewrite the traditional discourse of maternity/womanhood.

Further making this psychic shift available, the sites in which this could all be enacted have been specified: change will occur on the street and at the altar. And the city is offered not one, but two cyclical dates to keep this possibility open eternally: the Día de la Virgen de Dolores and the Día de la Cueva. On the Día de Dolores, the abject miners come up and out of their dark lair and take to both the street and the church. And on this same day, women

[34] The first and clearest image was found online at http://members.chello.nl/~l.de.bondt/OurLadyofSorrows.htm; the second, a photo of a stained-glass work at an exposition in León, was featured in the local newspaper; and the third is a photograph I took of a poster-sized image hung outside the main Basílica during Holy Week celebrations.

are permitted into the mines, breaking dramatically with accepted practice (Ferry, 2005). We see here a staging of a perfect carnivalesque moment. Nothing is in place. Spatial and social rules have been turned on their head. Ratcheting up the tension yet another level, at the surface of the mines—as well as all over town in both public sites (storefronts, parking lots, shopping plazas) and private homes—city dwellers encounter the semiotic "tears and milk" of the Virgin (Kristeva, 1987) as they are given water (the traditional *aguas frescas*, or freshwater juices) and *nieves* (sorbet) at these small altars.[35]

Milk and tears serve as a leitmotif in Kristeva's "Stabat Mater." In the section on the cooptation of female pleasure and pain—entitled appropriately, "What Body?"—she writes, "We are entitled only to the ear of the virginal body, the tears, and the breast" (1987, p. 248). Tears and milk become "the privileged signs of the *Mater Dolorosa*" (p. 249) and "the metaphors of non-speech" (p. 249). The city's inhabitants and visitors approach the altars to this Virgin of Dolores to partake of her tears and milk, thus coming into contact with the Virgin's remaining semiotic or bodily elements, a situation fraught with power and disruption. In effect, "the Mother and her attributes, evoking sorrowful humanity, become representatives of a 'return of the repressed' in monotheism" (pp. 249–250). While I observe a power-heavy carnivalesque opportunity here, it is important to note that this is only my own interpretation. One historian who wrote part of the official government-sponsored webpage for the city finds simply a moment of nostalgia:

> *La transformación que se realiza ese día en las calles y en las minas de Guanajuato, hacen del tiempo y el espacio destinados a la vida cotidiana en esta ciudad colonial, un espacio sagrado donde la población recupera su identidad original de ciudad minera.* (Zaldívar, n.d.)
>
> The transformation undertaken on this day, in the streets and in the mines of Guanajuato, make the time and space designated for daily life in this colonial city into a sacred space in which the population recuperates its original identity as a mining city.

Again, the origins … Zaldívar seems to imply that the city goes back to her mining days, which I would interpret here as synonymous with "the good old days" and wealth, a reminder of the origins of the city's beauty and well-being. Yet lurking in this quote are signs of something else. The space is made sacred, Zaldívar writes, suggesting the potential to look at one's origins within the safe space that religion provides, albeit outside of the physical doors of the church in this case. I see this as an unearthing of semiotic resources and a possibility for the future.

If the Día de Dolores opens up one time-space at the limits, the second and strongest moment for reconnecting with the past and the semiotic occurs on July 31. On this day, every year, city dwellers trek up to the myth-

[35] While the *nieves* are traditionally water-based, they have a creamy consistency.

filled cave that could be disenchanted to celebrate the Día de la Cueva (Day of the Cave). Shops close, work is suspended, and tradition reenacted. This trek to the cave, however, has another layer; it is also the saint day of San Ignacio de Loyola (Saint Ignatius of Loyola). In 1624, the Church formally approved a motion to make Saint Ignatius the patron saint of the city on the condition that the city celebrate his saint day, July 31st. Within the cave, there is a painted image of the saint next to a silver frog. The frog is generally taken to represent the city, not only because it is silver in color, but also because the indigenous meaning of the word "Guanajuato" (*Quanax huato* in the *Purépecha* language) is "hilly place of the frogs." It is suggested that San Ignacio is protecting the city and her riches against the "pagan" forces, a local parallel to the story of how he fought the devil in a cave in Spain.

Near him is another Catholic painting, one of the Virgin with a snake at her feet, which again recalls the common image of stomping out evil. However, the Catholic imagery, as noted earlier, is accompanied by indigenous paintings as well. These include several red-toned, symmetrical paintings that are most likely Otomí in origin and possibly related to petitions for rain.[36] We find these images within the cave at the spatial limit between what is inside the earth and out, at the spiritual fold between the Catholic and the indigenous, and at the margin between male and female icons as well. Kristeva makes somewhat extensive reference to Saint Ignatius of Loyola in *Intimate Revolt*, pausing on his "loquela." Loquela she defines as "the infraverbal but nevertheless discursive sign of the affects of the soul," and "a prerepresentation, an embodied speech," an ecstatic inner sound that precedes representation (2002, p. 47). Here in the cave is Ignatius himself—in the chora, with his prespeech and his tendency to tears that he shares with the Virgin. And in front of him are the pagan/indigenous symbols. In this site of multiple splittings—male/female, conscious/unconscious, Catholic/pagan, good/evil, past/present—is reconciliation now at hand? The city's inhabitants must go up to meet this site to gain back their unconscious riches and access the semiotic, while the enchanted princess must come down to gain back her humanity. Every year a new opportunity… Self and other passing en route, trying to help each other, within these bodily city spaces, to become whole.

The city becomes a convergence site between these limits. There is a phallic Virgin armed to castrate patriarchy (the Medusa-esque Dolores) and a streetwise Virgin (the Virgin of Guanajuato) who refuses representation and retains some of the female body/pleasure. At the surface fold, the mines meet the city, public meets the private of storefront/homefront altars, and city dwellers meet the abject feminine. They encounter what has been repressed in the semiotic symbols of tears and milk, which they then consume.

[36] The official city website, http://www.guanajuatocapital.com/guanajuato/index.php?option=com_content&view=article&id=170&Itemid=348&lang=es) credits anthropologist Ana María Crespo's "La pintura rupestre en la Cueva de San Ignacio" (1981), presented at the X Congreso Internacional de Ciencias Prehistóricas y Protohistóricas, Mexico City, for this insight.

Furthermore, there is an enchanted princess who wants to become human and who holds the key to the semiotic unconscious of the city. And consciously or not, city dwellers hike up to the cave once a year in an attempt to reconcile their indigenous/Spanish, pagan/Catholic, past/present, and other binaries into some more palatable whole. They are all positioned on the myth that would reconcile the fantasy underground city with her aboveground real city and rcpair thc split.

The scene is set to break the spell, to free the not-fully-human city that (as the billboard said) "enchants us" and that frustrates me, the analyst who desires a more radical city. The city is therefore representing this limit where the semiotic meets the symbolic, where sign and the body relate, something that Kristeva finds the West unable to do. If a different response—*a question*—were inserted here, the repetition could be broken, and the city could be freed from endless repeating, symbolized by these centuries of climbing up to the cave and played out in her myriad repressions and silences. Kristeva proclaims revolt as a way to open up psychic life and, like most analysts, she advocates for the conflict needed to engender change, underlining the need to return to these tension-filled, tenuous limits:

> This is where we are: we can either renounce revolt by withdrawing into old values or indeed new ones that do not look back on themselves and do not question themselves or, on the contrary, relentlessly repeat retrospective return so as to lead it to the limits of the representable/thinkable/tenable (to the point of possession), limits made evident by certain advances of the culture of the twentieth century. (2002, p. 7)

Return and revolt produce conflict and angst. There is no doubt about this. However, they also make possible jouissance. The city may find her genius potential right here in these bodily resources that have not been overly commodified and, in the case of the indigenous princess at least, are not melancholic. Could the maternal love from the Virgins meet the princess and carry femininity over to desire and the symbolic? Will the city reinterpret these elements *not* as nostalgic and romantic, but as a question? She seems to have what she needs to respond to her others from a much firmer sense of her own subjectivity.

GET THEE TO THE GARDEN

I offer the city a final scenario to consider. Kristeva writes about the "need to create a space for an 'inner zone'—a secret garden, an intimate quarter, or more simply and ambitiously, a psychic life" (1995, p. 27). The city's most creative center is not the square *zócalo* (plaza) of traditional Latin American cities. While there is a main trapezoid-shaped Plaza de la Paz in front of the Basílica around which Church and government power are represented, the city's true center is the Jardín de la Unión. Situated in the middle of the symbolic city *centro*, the Jardín could be interpreted as the city's potentially semiotic inner garden, the point of union between the semiotic and the symbolic.

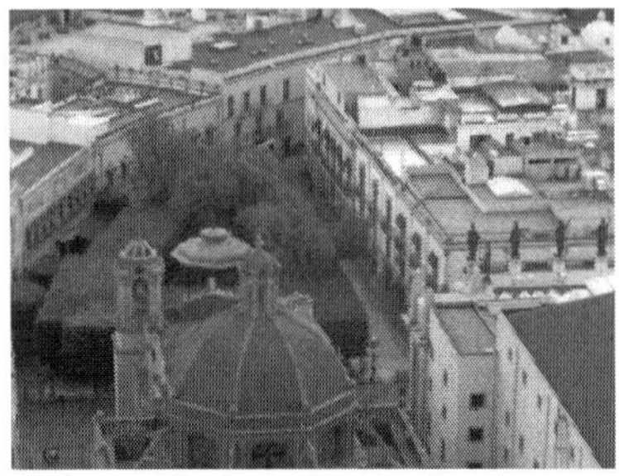

The city's Jardín de la Unión, her inner garden

Not only is the Jardín a site surrounded by old family businesses and the main theater, a place in which good manners and social norms are reproduced, but it also constitutes a site of jouissance. It is full of live music and competing food scents—the body is still present—and it is topped by the city's main theater, the Teatro Juárez, which is protected by rooftop statues of the female muses. Imagination thus finds its own church and altar in this site; and, as a site full of others, there is someone to signify for and to. Furthermore, and relevant for our city-author, the Jardín constitutes a key site where text is posted and reposted, layering up the city's past and present in an overlapping, endless flutter of words. It is notable; however, that the abject miners never march through the Jardín to penetrate the true city center, and the renegade Virgin of Guanajuato is not paraded through this space either.

What would happen if the Virgin were to eschew the church altar where the female body is sacrificed and frozen into an icon, reject the Plaza de la Paz, which represents patriarchal power, and instead arrived at the more feminine Jardín? The seductive inner garden of the city … could the nocturnal possibilities slip over into daylight? Could these multiple spatial and social ambivalences allow the Jardín to be a perfect Kristevan site where the semiotic and symbolic come into uneasy but life-giving contact? Positing the city body as female, the triangular, lush Jardín represents the vagina. Here, as a site of cultural reproduction, this metaphor is refortified. If the Virgin of pleasure, revolt, displacements, and nonrepresentations that the Virgin of Guanajuato embodies could make it the "interior garden" (Kristeva, 1995) of female sexuality, she would inscribe the female city subject's "cavernous interiority" (Kristeva, 2004) with pleasure. The melancholy void could be transformed into a site of jouissance with others.

I finish this gathering of icons, symbols, and spaces with a live girl, a composite who is, nonetheless, real. A young girl probably around 20 years old innocently (or not) wanders through the streets and Jardín. She is wearing a T-shirt that was seen on the streets quite commonly about two years ago, in the middle of the research process for this book. Her T-shirt reads, "*No soy virgen pero sí hago milagros*" (I'm not a virgin, but I do perform miracles).

In my mind, this unnamed and multiple girl (since the T-shirt showed up regularly around town) represents the miraculous feminine genius. She embodies the would-be sacred woman capable of being a mother with her sexuality-slash-humanity restored. She can walk through the city's Jardín and assert her own potential to act, as her body takes back the jouissance that the Church and repressive local society would try to take away. Kristeva writes that the word "miracle" has roots in the astonishing, the strange, the marvelous, and the act of laughing. What is miraculous "presents the intimate while allowing it to remain enigmatic" (2011, p. 58). This is the discharged but never fully captured semiotic; the invisible but important female jouissance. Through language displayed on her own body, the T-shirt girl writes revolt.

This is tremendous. Along with Kristeva, it moves us from the ears-and-tears of the Virgin and representations in Western art of her draped, sexless body, to a recovered feminine. Writing about Georgia O'Keefe's work, Kristeva (2011) seems to ask, don't you see the sensual nuances? We might well ask, don't you see the voluptuous city? In O'Keefe's landscapes, Kristeva finds that the hills "assume the aspect of a living fabric, a mons veneris filled with blood and fluids rather than a mineral conglomerate" (2011, p. 242). Are the city's hills also ready to be transformed from a "mineral conglomerate" of melancholic memory into the living, sexual, sensual body of "blood and fluids," everything she was so reluctant to acknowledge at the beginning of the analysis?

REVOLT, THEY SAY

Geographer Steve Pile states that "spatiality shifts around real, imaginary and symbolic co-ordinates" (1996, p. 169). Here I have identified several coordinates that the city possesses within her own spatial body—her myths and symbols, geographical landmarks, and told stories—which are real, imaginary and symbolic, although it is not always clear which is which. Symbols harness our anxieties, and myths establish limits that constitute a necessary "prerequisite for desire and knowledge" (Amati-Mehler et al., 1993, p. 18). This desire, personified by the resignified female figures of this interpretation could catalyze an effort for the city to reconcile her surface self (embedded in economics and national-level traumas and needs) with her unconscious, female, and semiotic aspects of self. In order to revolt, the city must access the archaic elements in her bodily history. She must relinquish the failed ideal of virginal motherhood devoid of sensuality and desire and write her way through the tiny spaces and openings in her local icons back to her own body.

Amati-Mehler et al. go on to say that any given myth (and I would add symbol, etc.)

> forms part of a symbolic universe inside of which it displays all its potential symbolic virtualities and produces its effects. These effects depend on the privileged connections it interweaves with the other elements of the same universe. (1993, p. 16)

Psychoanalysis claims that you can interweave more than one pattern of connections, and therein lies the emancipatory potential for constant rebirths.

We have reached the deciding point in our analysis. "The verbalized interpretation implies a choice that severs and thereby liberates unconscious thought from the traumatic scene where it was stuck" (Kristeva, 2011, p. 148). In Kristeva's example of the artist-analysand Didier, at the end of treatment, he gives her a painting as a return gift. But now, it is a painting that signifies and a painting that he is able to discuss and explain to her. He had gained "access to his psyche," and he had renewed "a psychic life with and for another person" (1995, p. 26). It is now time to see if the city is ready to make the inner shift that precedes any outer shift, if she will truly unfreeze her images.

Eight

Tales of Love and Life After Analysis

Of Art, Opera, and Halloween

The city's final visit, at least for a while. Outside, the jumble of houses is interrupted by the brilliant outbursts of purple *jacaranda* trees that mark each spring. This energy seems to magnify as the office door opens and the city comes inside. She has a lighter step, and she holds out some of her writing for me, which I accept with excitement. I am already anticipating pouring over it after our appointment. I am anxious to read these texts to see if, indeed, she has been creatively reconsidering her ideas about self and other and, more importantly, asking herself new questions. We reminisce about her original presenting problem and I ask how she is doing with the host of others with whom she continues to interact every day.

Any more nausea, I ask? *Anxiety? How is your writing evolving*?

I am pleased when she smiles in response …

For the Kristevan analyst, the contemporary Western subject suffers from what she has termed "new maladies of the soul," catalyzed in large part by the Debordian spectacle. As both Debord and Kristeva have argued, the spectacle's deluge of images mediates social relationships, squashes creativity, and takes over the subject's ability to think and feel. Singularity, the particular emotional and physical experiences of each subject, gets discounted as the generic mass-produced image in its myriad media forms takes over. As a result, the subject becomes detached from language, unable to express pain or pleasure. She is left practically anesthetized and cannot question or respond. For the female subject, the set of psychic crises produced by the spectacle only compounds an existing crisis within the patriarchal society of the West. Patriarchal religion has already abjected women's sexuality, pain, and pleasure, robbing them of a place in society, through manipulations of the figure of the Virgin Mary. Reduced to her maternal function, the female subject is left with a sexuality that is abject, sacrificed, denied. This disconnection between the sensing, sexual body and language (the Word) is thus simply redoubled with the onslaught of the spectacle. These two crises, combined with the individual contours of each analysand, make the treatment of the female subject especially complex.

When my city-analysand came in for analysis, it was immediately apparent that she could be situated within this double crisis. She is threatened by the untiring spectacle in which images reproduce other images and mediate how people relate to her. Over the course of our treatment period, I have watched her try desperately to become the image of tourist desire (perfect Spanish colonial tranquility, pure provincial tradition). These moves distance her from her body, deny her desire, and, at many times, impede a creative response and revolt. Furthermore, constructed as female within Mexican national discourse, the provincial city also endures the asexual, abnegated maternal prescriptions of Catholicism. The city has thus offered a fairly representative contemporary female subject, even as the particulars of her traumas, her body, her desires, and her variant of the spectacle are, of course, unique to her alone.

Having traversed the conflicts of transferences and countertransferences in the necessary crisis our encounter provoked, it is now time to see what the city has done with the interpretations I have tentatively offered back to her. Psychic change takes time, of course, and it would be illogical and unethical to conclude that, after my analysis, the city "suddenly" changed and wrote herself a happy ending in which self and other tensions existed no more. Furthermore, the Kristevan subject only permanently resolves her subjectivity with death, so a lifetime of crises provoked by one's others is an essential part of being alive. But I believe that the city has resignified an impressive part of her psychic content and that she is questioning and responding to the symbolic order from a position of corporal and emotional singularity. In fact, she seems to be enacting the prescriptions of Kristeva's latest work toward a new discourse of maternity/femininity.

As we move to the end of our analysis, I am not without some ambivalence. How does one evaluate whether or not a psychoanalytical interpretation has been successful and when it is time to end? Like any other kind of research, analysis could go on forever, since the subject evolves and the surrounding context constantly changes as well. Psychoanalyst Karol Marshall follows Freud's advice that, when enough of the repressed and the analysand's resistance to examining it have been brought to light, repetitions become unlikely, and analysis can be brought to an end. Through her reading of Harari and Moncayo, she adds, however, "I might say that analysis does not end when it ends" (Marshall, 2000, p. 943), since both parties carry the resonances of this process into whatever comes next. Marshall also suggests that even the term "analysis" seems rather outdated, proposing instead "psycho-exploration" (personal communication). This seems appropriate for the city. From a critical standpoint, the term "analysis" sounds analogous to mining. It implies an attitude where one would say to the city, *Sit still, I'm going down and plan on rooting around until I find this "thing," your unconscious, the roots of your problems, and once I find it, I'll bring it up and refine it, make it better.*

In reality, this book's process has been much more akin to Marshall's exploration metaphor; I have meandered purposefully through the city's history, psyche, texts, and streets in order to read something about her unconscious and think through how self and other are worked out both below and around her graceful surface. Creativity has thus been an essential element as I played with what was at hand and offered what I hope is a provocative interpretation. What is birthed through the contact that therapeutic analysis engenders is a new interpretation of the old symbols, myths, discourses, and new constructions of the analysand's self and her others. What I have presented back to the city after having been her ear, her addressee, her loved and hated other, her psychic chronicler and analyst is nothing more and nothing less than a convergence of images. Small intimate power points emanating from different city spaces that could come together to effect a change in her perspective.

As I commence what I hope will be the city's last session, at least for a while, I reflect upon her final, most joyful texts yet. What these texts will point to is the city's entrée into Kristeva's new discourse of maternity, which correspondingly provides a point of departure for a new discourse of *provincia* and reflections on the subjectivity of small cities in general. Below, I sketch out what I see to be Kristeva's emerging discourse and then turn to three examples in which we can observe the city connecting with her own female genius and encountering the other from full subjectivity.

Kristeva has consistently argued that in order to respond to the spectacle, the subject must find sites into which her semiotic aspect can be discharged. This would permit her to simultaneously reconnect with the symbolic even as she challenges it. This act revitalizes the system, and it also moves the subject out of her depressed silence and loveless state back to a world populated by others, thus reviving her fragile psychic life as well. These processes entail a circular voyage: the subject must first return to her origins (creative, sexual, sensorial), revisiting a chora-esque psychic space that is at once reflective and childlike, in which she can recover her abandoned semiotic, translinguistic content (the drives, the affects, and the sensory). Then, necessarily, she must move out of this space back to the symbolizing world, discharging the recovered semiotic disposition into symbolic narration. This narration may take the form of words or music, art … but it must be something communicated to others. How to catalyze this? Some scholars of Kristeva have been frustrated by Kristeva's often vague indications of how to activate this process.

In her early and highly polemic essay "Stabat Mater," for example, where she extends the symbol of the Virgin Mary as an explanatory model for abject female sexuality, Kristeva finishes her brilliant critique with a call to listen to mothers and listen to music. Not exactly a clear methodological direction! But since then, Kristeva has given us enough to work out the new discourse of maternity and femininity she finds so urgent. Several decades later, at the end of her trilogy on the feminine genius, her psychosexual model is finally laid out (a welcome relief for analysts), and in *Hatred and Forgiveness*, an extremely accessible text, she seems to bring down all of her themes (psychoanalysis, religion, women, art, writing) to more specific examples within contemporary discussions and events. In this book, Kristeva still maintains that without a secular discourse of motherhood the female subject will have a difficult time of it; however, through these two works in particular, *Colette* and *Hatred and Forgiveness*, I believe she has already offered us this new secular discourse.

Let me offer a tentative summary of what I see to be this emerging discourse before linking it to the case of the provincial city-analysand. Kristeva first elaborates her psychosexual model in *Colette*; her model coalesces around the idea that women are psychically bisexual as a result of the effort involved in switching erotic objects, as the (heterosexual) girl child separates from the mother and takes up a relationship with the father. In her understanding, this innate bisexuality foments creativity because it endows women with a certain plasticity, the ability to imagine alternatives, and the capacity to be or think multiply. Kristeva takes pains to underline that this bisexuality is declined individually, thus retaining the singularity of each female subject, just as she also locates a feminine aspect within all subjects, male or female. Singularity, as Kristeva has frequently pointed out, is an essential element of creative genius and revolt and fundamental to combating the spectacle as well, since any response to the spectacle must emerge from the body and its unique affective and sensory experiences. She then links this multiple, plastic nature to that which is Byzantine, meaning that which resists representation and frozen signification: the unrepresentable, polyvalent semiotic.

Having armed the subject with these dispositions and potentialities, Kristeva moves on to her essential argument in *Hatred and Forgiveness*: Women's bisexuality permits what she refers to as a dispassionate, yet loving experience of motherhood. This involves a particular sublimation of passion that does not deny the drives. If the mother has an innate bisexuality and a capacity for multiple amorous object relations, she will be able to release the child into the symbolic because she can then find new objects to love and release. This sublimatory and dispassionizing (versus sacrificial) experience sets up a model for relating to others. The mother can now love in a way closer to Christian *agape*, which then allows the subject to exist with others in society as individuals, instead of loving her child or others by trying to possess, change, or assimilate them. Finally, Kristeva underlines that the relationship orientation at the core of female sexuality permits transferences and displacements, which are—to complete the circle—essential to love, imagination, psychoanalysis, and interactions with the other. Rebirth, so exuberantly exemplified in the life of Colette, yet also illustrated with Hannah Arendt, among other Kristevan examples, becomes possible and permanent, as there will always be an infinite number of new objects, new representations.

Psychic life, along with the larger symbolic system in which this life is embedded, is thus endlessly renewable.

How can we understand these recent contributions in connection with Kristeva's previous work? What I see Kristeva always doing in her thinking is turning each issue to a slightly new angle, which then allows her to tell the story of the speaking subject in a slightly different way as the subject confronts a range of others. In *Powers of Horror*, Kristeva presents us with the not-yet-other, the toxic, unbearable abject that is internal-external at once and which must be expelled in order for the subject to redraw her borders. *Tales of Love* and *Black Sun* examine what happens when these processes are forestalled. In *Strangers to Ourselves*, the unbearable other is now our internal other (our unconscious) as well as our external other (the foreigner); both of them must be accepted in order to live productively. And in *Colette* and *Hatred and Forgiveness*, Kristeva spells out how the subject can achieve this: namely, through sublimatory processes. To some extent, this is what she has been saying since the 1980s. Depressed, melancholic, in love or in analysis, the subject must symbolize the internal, making it external and freeing herself from the obsessive hold these experiences can have that limit the subject's capacity to live fully. The not-yet-objects and the objects in question roll through these different positions along with the subject (from intolerable abject to the unobjectionable, unknowable inner other; to an outer other whose difference and desire are accepted).

Almond (2007) argues that *Strangers* deradicalized the Kristevan subject; while he takes his point in a different direction (that has nothing to do with female subjects), this is an apt critique because Kristeva did move away from both sublimation and the heterogeneous bodied subject. Her original speaking subject transformed herself and her symbolic order in a more revolutionary manner than in *Strangers*, whose subjects appear to rewrite legal and social practices from a more cosmopolitan discourse and who seem oddly bodiless (although, in theory, they could still be inscribed with this original radicality, of course). *Colette* and *Hatred*, on the other hand, reiterate the complex, heterogeneous, and in-process nature of the subject, and both books specifically bring the question of otherness back to the female subject or, more specifically, back to the sexed subject.

Motherhood provides a model for a constantly renewing sublimatory path, but it is not the only route. As Kristeva states emphatically (undoubtedly tired of critics who seem unable to understand metaphors), "I am emphasizing the structural experience of motherhood: I am not fundamentally pro-birth" (2007, p. 87). Analysis provides another path to sublimation, as does creativity, which is the option that my writing city will now choose and expand upon. While it is neither possible nor desirable to hold up the components mentioned here as a list against which to check the city's psychic progress, or as a series of steps to follow linearly, I do see the city moving toward a revitalized discourse of maternity/femininity through a series of sublimations via her creative work. Fundamentally, the city shows signs of a restored psychic life. To take up Kristeva's articulation of this,

> You are alive if and only if you have a psychic life. However distressing, unbearable, deadly, or exhilarating it may be, this psychic life—which combines different systems of representation that involve language—allows you access to your body and to other people. (1995, p. 6)

In other words, despite the occasionally unbearable, abject, and threatening moments in the analytical process, the city had to go through these in order to reconnect with her own semiotic resources that in turn will allow her to question the spectacle and relate to others as a co-subject with her own desire. The following texts of the city form a part of these "different systems of representations": The city is turning to art and she begins to listen to music, all the while continuing to write her way toward ever-expanding understandings of the other and his difference. In each case, the city gains this essential access to her body and to others, sublimates the passions others arouse, and relates as one subject encountering another.

DISPLACEMENTS IN THE ART GALLERY

Through art, the city opens up to transference relationships with the other and enters into productive, even amorous, displacements of the imagination. Her relationship to an exhibit from Mexico City illustrates how these displacements "unfreeze" her enchantment and show her entering into a much more mutual relationship with the urban other in the form of the nation's capital and other large cities.

The *Sin techo está pelón* art exhibition consisted of 50 works of art culled from La Colección Jumex, which is owned by Mexico's mammoth juice company, Grupo Jumex, and it was put together to inaugurate the 2010 FIC. These works of art featured a range of representations and installations depicting hyperurban dwellings, including both images and miniature 3D cities of different sorts. These "Jumex habitats," as I will refer to them, represented the city's most architectural other. They showed nothing of the colorful, textured femininity that the baroque city is accustomed to. Rather, these habitats appeared cloned, impersonal, exhaustingly ordered.

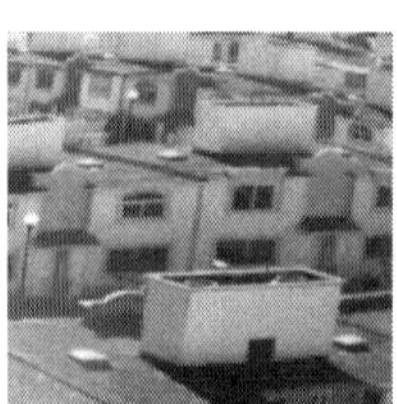

Scott Peterman, *Ecatepec*

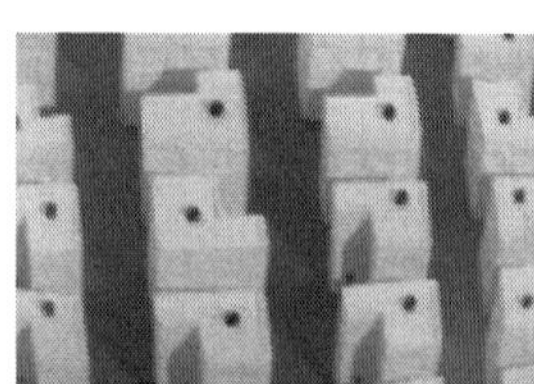

José Dávila, *Conjunto habitacional*

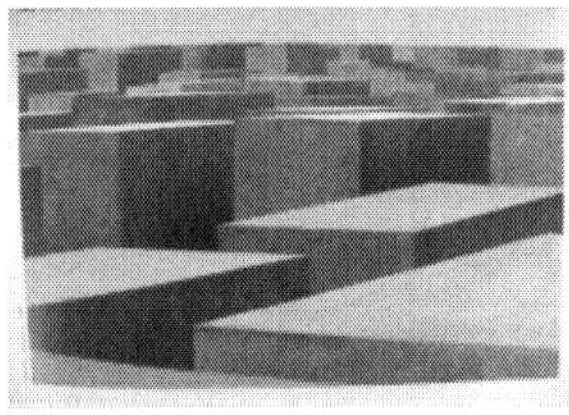

Fernando Espinoso, *Berlin, Alemania*

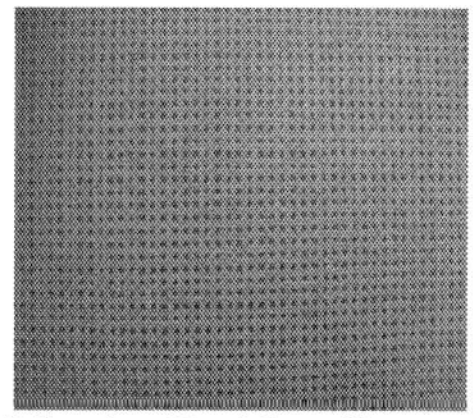

Melanie Smith, *Concrete Jungle V*

Sin techo está pelón exhibition, representative works

As representations of urbanity's most negative aspects, these überurban habitats might have been read by the city as the epitome of a threatening Santa Varvara. Indeed, it seems unlikely that the city would find a way to meet this other in any relationship short of abjection and exclusion, but something quite distinct occurs. However, the city enters into a relationship of transferences and displacements in which both she and the Jumex habitats find an addressee and gain imaginative routes out of their respective spectacles of cement urbanity and bucolic provinciality.

The city first plays her more traditional role by providing the Jumex habitats a site through which to return to their own imagination through her baroque body. The city's colonial architectural style is the polar opposite of what one observes in the megacities of the exhibition (and in the white-cube spaces of contemporary galleries). Everywhere in the city there is texture, movement, sensuality, and elaborate abundance; like a baroque painting, the baroque city can still "open up vision with hazy edges, soft focus and multiple perspectives, presenting a distinct, tactile invitation and enticing the body to travel through the illusory space" (Pallasmaa, 2005, p. 35). In other words, the city catalyzes the displacement of the tiny Jumex cities, doubly enclosed within their hopeless urbanity and within the exhibition itself, and invites them into an imaginative world.

The urban habitats of the exhibition effect a return to the maternal that *provincia* symbolizes. Within the folds of the city body, they once again belong—they can engage in the nostalgic fantasy of oneness with the maternal, assuaging their fragmentation and alienation. Architect Juhani Pallasmaa writes that "the task of art and architecture in general is to reconstruct the experience of an undifferentiated interior world, in which we are not mere spectators, but to which we inseparably belong" (2005, p. 25). The baroque-churrigueresque city offers exactly this to the exhibition. Within her maternal body, the Jumex habitats regain their wholeness and connect with their own interiority, thus alleviating their alienated fragmentation.

This provokes a crisis for the Jumex houses: Will the urban habitats fall back into the maternal body, into the past, lose their subjectivity? Will a turn inward impede future development outward/forward? Is this simply the death drive's return to a state of previous calm? This contact with the archaic maternal that is normally repressed upon entering into the social symbolic brings the Jumex subject to the edge of its subjectivity. But during this displacement, these urban habitats undergo what Kristeva terms as a "rehabilitation of the sensory" (2002, p. 5) as the provincial city lends these habitats its aura, color, sounds, and tastes. The city provides the chora, and the Jumex habitats find the seeds for revolt, reconnecting with themselves against the screen of the provincial city. Armed with renewed semiotic capacity, the Jumex homes return to the symbolic now able to reinvest their urban environments with new signification.

This is all very traditional, but now the city will renew *herself* through the exhibition. As we have been noting, the city is characterized by an intense interiority. The inexorable sameness and repetitions in a small place produce what McCarthy identifies as a "system of enclosure" in which familiarity breeds predictability, encouraging conformity and "an understanding of repetition as a return to the same familiar point" (2005, p. 117). This situation is compounded by the topography. The city's concave, bowl-shaped form exudes interiority and conjures centripetal forces, connection versus disintegration and dispersion. Equally notably, the city provides no visual egress, which can be experienced affectively as either protective or stifling, or both. Like the smallest habitats represented in the exhibition, Andrea Zittel's *A-Z Homestead Unit* (2008) and Absalon's *Cellule habitable* (1992), *Solutions* (1992), and *Proposal for a Habitat* (1991), cozy security meets frustrated entrapment and claustrophobia.

Overall, these social and architectural repetitions conspire to create "the confidence, arrogance, and illusion of unitary completeness and indivision, the spatial narcissism of introversion" (McCarthy, 2005, p. 116). And, as we have noted, this is reinforced by tourist discourse: The bombardment of tourist imagery promulgated in town coupled with the city's other repetitive and interiorizing factors reduces inhabitants' capacity to imagine, creating a brightly colored but no less deadening situation than that suffered by the city's mega-urban counterparts represented in the exhibition. If it is hard to think creative thoughts in the urban jungle, it is equally difficult to do so in *provincia*'s repetitive tranquility …

Returning to the Jumex exhibition, it would seem unlikely that the city would find an answer here—*in artwork inside a building, inside a city dominated by interiority located in the interior of the country.* However, the standard definition of interiority as "that which is contained" has been critiqued by feminist scholars from many disciplines (see, e.g., in geography, Elizabeth Grosz; in psychoanalysis, Luce Irigaray) as overly patriarchal and of limited value. These researchers advocate instead for a view of interiority as a *between-space* that links differences together. After all, interiority can only exist in relationship with what is external—one is not possible without the other, just as the interior self must have an exterior other with whom to dialogue in order to be alive. As a between-space, interiority therefore "permits the passage from one space and position to another, rather than the containment of objects and functions in which each thing finds its rightful place" (Grosz, 2001, p. 164). Borders, walls, and edges (all of which surround interiority) can thus be read as liminal zones that lead into the unknown.

Following this, while the university art galleries appear to be such closed sites, they now become a passage-space to fantasy. Beyond the huge churrigueresque-baroque door, the city finds a white space populated by her architectural fantasies and nightmares. Fantasizing, the city projects her urban fears and desires into the exhibition, and in essence, displaces herself. The tourist city becomes the spectator; the provincial city now contains global urbanity (representations of Berlin, Newark, Buenos Aires) instead of the reverse. This vertigo and feeling of being outside of oneself is furthered by the fact that many of exhibition's representations take the form of Liliputian cities—thus the small-city inhabitant ironically enters into this space only to loom over and be permanently outside of the tiny habitats within. The city exchanges interiority for exteriority and undergoes the "interpenetration of the physical and the mental" (Langan, 2000, p. 70) as she projects herself into place and takes these places into her affective experience.

These displacements break the repetitions, interrupt traditional imagery, and intervene into the symbolic. Specifically, the exhibition forces the city to confront her urban nature, that which is not contained in the symbolic language of tourist imagery. *The nightmare*: Could the provincial "best of all possible worlds," if not carefully stewarded, turn into one of these black-and-white, personality-less forms of urbanity? *The fantasy*: Such large, anonymous spaces ... This journey through displacement provokes a terrifying "incomprehensibility [that] threatens dissolution not just of place but of oneself" (Langan, 2000, p. 74). Self and other become confused as the city gazes at the exhibition: *Am I this or not this? Is this my urban home or not?* While the city projects into space, the gallery in turn "lends [the city] its aura, which entices and emancipates [the city's] perceptions and thoughts" (Langan, 2000, p. 12). In the imaginary realm of the exhibition, the city encounters her own urbanity, and choices suddenly become possible to imagine. The city can respond to the spectacle because interiority has been transcended and she can discharge her passions—her fears and desires related to urbanity—into the symbolic order.

The circle is now complete: The interiority of the city is opened up via the gallery, and the interiority of the gallery is opened up via the city. Place is kept from closing in on itself and on the psyche. The gallery thus plays an essential dialogic role for the city, permitting a reopening of what appears to be fixed and finished and creating a space into which the semiotic can be accommodated into the symbolic order—restoring the possibilities to imagine and transgress. Rather than take on the urbanite of Mexico City represented by the Jumex habitats from a position of traditional, abnegated maternity—*come tell me your urban sorrows, while I remain silent and receptive*—the city has narrated her urban anxieties and desires to another. She has released her need to possess this filial exhibit and converts the relationship into one of co-subjects: different, amorous, dispassionate. We can now understand Kristeva's injunction to "go to a museum and refashion your psychic life" (2011, p. 78). This is quite different from Don Quijote's experience in the museum![37]

THE SENSORY SELF AND THE OPERA

In a similar manner, the city also turns to music, another fertile area for psychic repair. Kristeva has long emphasized the musicality of the chora, of other languages, and of poetry. It is not surprising that the city finds a semiotic outlet here. An experience with a FIC-sponsored opera performance allows the city to reconnect with her sensory self at the very interior of the urban landscape and to respond to the spectacle from a standpoint of singularity. This leads to yet another rebirth and flowering.

When the city so violently abjected the FIC poster of the seminaked man, she was struggling to map and maintain the clean-and-proper body. As festival events moved indoors to more elite spaces, she was undergoing a stressful process of trying to control the popular sites of the body that were rapidly becoming overwhelmed with elements of the grotesque, those things that were abjected from the festival's cultured self. As we saw, despite some attempt to regulate tourist desire, she was still buying into spectacle discourse on various levels, and, increasingly, her sexual-sensorial body was being cut off from the thinking-cultured events of the FIC that she prided herself for hosting. In the 2010 FIC, however, something new happened. The opera, which is as sonically other as the Jumex habitats are architecturally other, came to the city not to be performed in any of her lovely theaters, but rather to take place in the main market, the Mercado Hidalgo.

The Mercado Hidalgo represents one of the city's most singular and intimate bodily sites. Its construction differentiates it from any other market in the nation. Built in 1910, the structure in which the market is located was originally designed to be a train station (a site of displacement!), yet it was never used as such. The entire structure sits above an underground tunnel that used to be a river—the feminine and natural diverted. Inside, the space is wide open. The main produce and cooked-food stands are on the ground floor, and tourist trinkets are sold from a second-story balcony that wraps around the edges of the market. It is, therefore, a site of cavernous interiority that is nonetheless filled up with the sensory in an abundant chaos of pleasant and unpleasant smells, tastes, sounds, and so on. While the outside may look colonial and European, the inside is decidedly Mexican.

This is also the site of the popular. The market has its own recognized subculture, traditional families, and class-based discourse. It sends out a cacophony of competing music genres that blare from pirated CDs. Tasty food is served at open stands of questionable hygienic quality. One finds live birds

[37] Indeed, after this writing, even Don Quijote emerged from the museum in the form of a series of enormous sculptures of his likeness leading from the museum (located in a pedestrian-only area) to the nearest street with normal bus and automobile transit. His partial liberation and return to public space?

at some of the basket stands and dead cow carcasses hanging eerily among the meat vendors toward the back. The bathrooms are situated behind the meat stalls. Toward the side entrances, fresh herbs, handmade tortillas, and a wildly abundant array of fruits and vegetables greet the shopper. The discarded and the served, the raw and the cooked, all intermingle in olfactory layers. The Mercado is everything a theater is not, and its vendors and patrons are not usually FIC attendees.[38]

Yet into this space, the opera arrived.[39] On what looked, smelled, and tasted like a normal weekend breakfast hour, a singer emerged from a seafood stand wired with speakers. He opened the show with an aria from the *Barber of Seville*. Over the hour that followed, the city's shoppers and breakfasters listened to music from Verdi, Donizetti, Bizet, and Puccini. One might have expected the city to reject such intrusive aural otherness. But she neither blocked out the opera by turning up her own music (which would have constituted an exclusion), nor did she turn it all off and look for wine-and-cheese appetizers or some other food we might associate with opera's sensory subjectivity to adapt herself. On the contrary—she and the opera came together in a full sensory jouissance in which two heterogeneous subjects (one of musical abundance, one of sensory abundance) met. Once again, she entered into a series of transferences and displacements, displacements that were now less about the imagination and more about love.

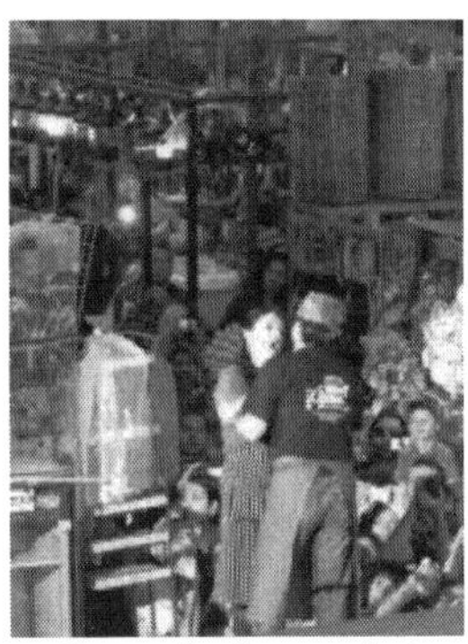

Opera in the market

The city met the opera in a place of play. As the singers performed, she too performed her bodily self; joining the music were sounds of the hammering of meat into thin steaks, the whir of the blenders serving up fresh juices, and patrons' voices asking to buy fruit, vegetables, and prepared foods.

[38] This refers to current ways of experiencing the opera. In its earlier days, those attending opera performance "were not necessarily expected to arrive on time, sit still, keep quiet, concentrate on the stage action, or stay to the end"; rather they would chat and move about during the long performances (Roselli, 1994, p. 451).

[39] The *Ópera en el Mercado*, the opera in the market, was created and directed by César Piña, who resides in Mexico City but who was born and raised in Guanajuato.

The division between the self of the market-goers and the other of the market-performers was dismantled as both entered into a realm of amorous play. At one point a little girl stood up on a stand and pretended to direct La Bohème, and at the end of the performance the singers began handing out fruit and flowers, transformed into vendors both of music and goods. In this very Kristevan-Colette flowering, words, music, bodies became one as the city discharged her sensory and semiotic content into a space shared by the symbolic other of the opera. This occurred because, in effect, the city met the opera from her own sensory, bodily singularity. As she listened to the opera arias, she breakfasted on *tacos de carnitas* in *salsa borracha* and gathered up mangos, cilantro, and *yerbabuena*. Her CDs of *duranguense* and *grupera* music continued to play, and at the end of the opera she toasted the singers with *rompope*, a Mexican eggnog-ish alcohol, in clay cups.

She also opened to risk: to a risky listening to the other. Grounded into their senses and situated in their own space, Mercado vendors and patrons opened up their ears to something new. For Kristeva, the assumption of risk is the willingness to still question and revolt, and rather uncannily the director of the opera, César Piña, used the word "risk" as well: In a televised interview afterward, he commented that listening to opera explicitly asked the market-goers (this popular aspect of the city) to take a risk. The city risked being bored or excluded from the experience and engaged in the otherness of this genre. By doing so, the city entered into full listening subjectivity and sublimated the fears and desires associated with this aural other. She did this by discharging her own sounds, textures, smells, and tastes into the spectacle … At the end of the performance, hand-painted signs were raised in the crowd, asking (in a vernacular style), "*No que no te gustaba la ópera*?" "*Cómo que no, la ópera es la ópera*." Didn't you say you didn't like the opera? Of course I do, opera is opera.

What we see here is the city encountering the opera from a heterogenic stance based on her intimate singularity, a singularity that met the opera's own unique self. The city's sensory abundance met the opera's musical complexity (a range of arias from different composers) in an encounter of love and imagination, each of which, in its own way, constitutes a transference and permits a reorganization of emotions. Listeners and performers integrated the competing "sonic signifiers" at hand with their memories, lived sensory and bodily experiences, and emotions (Nagel, 2010, p. 2008). These flights of imagination and feelings of love effectively transferred meanings to sites where there were none, namely the sites of tourist discourse. The opera allowed the city to discharge her drives, energies, and desires, a process that Kristeva notes "weaves a hypersign around and the depressive void" (1987, p. 99), thus curing the numbed spectator the city might have turned into.

By connecting with her sensory, intimate, and singular nature, the city thus rescued and recuperated both psychic and public space, which is the very definition of Kristevan transgression. And the empty nothingness of FIC discourse was transformed, made meaningful, even beautiful. The city of the narcissistic void moves toward healing, and she forgives the trauma of having been "displaced" in the negative sense from the FIC. Another connection with the body and with an aural other, which together permit a rebirth. Kristeva writes, "Let us again listen to the Stabat Mater, and the music, all the music … it swallows up the goddesses and removes their necessity" (1987, p. 263). Listening to the opera, the city's goddesses—the frozen Virgins and Don Quijotes—are no longer necessary.

ACCEPTING VULNERABILITY: DAY OF THE DEAD AND HALLOWEEN

Having embraced transference relationships and her own imagination, and having accepted her sensory and singular body, the city now accepts her fragility as a speaking subject permanently in process and in crisis. In our final encounter, she brings in a series of texts she has written about Day of the Dead and Halloween. She is anxious to show me this latest addition to her oeuvre, which will bring us to the close of this Kristevan analysis.

Her work is about Halloween, but what underwrites these texts is a prior acceptance of Day of the Dead as an ambiguous national holiday that is celebrated during the same time period. Day of the Dead, a holiday celebrated on November 1 and 2 (for dead children and dead adults, respectively), is seen as a quintessentially Mexican and, by many, as a quintessentially *indigenous* holiday. It is the moment when one's dead return from the netherworld, and they must be received with flowers, food, altars, and other traditions. However, the roots of this holiday and origins of the specific practices associated with this holiday are anything but clear. One can point to preconquest Mesoamerican practices related to death, sacrifice, and traditional mortuary practices, but Stanley Brandes (1998b) asserts, in his meticulously researched article on skull and skeleton imagery, that it is hard to draw a line from the representations characteristic of the pre-conquest past through to the present (p. 193). Scholars have also have raised questions about this supposed obsession with death, finding that the hype created around Day of the Dead in the 20th century formed part of the political and intellectual creation of *mexicanidad*, an essential national identity, rather than any historical fascination with death (p. 214).

There are also Spanish roots within Day of the Dead practice that link traditions to rural religious practices in preconquest Spain (Brandes, 1997, 1998b). But Spanish or not, the Catholic Church has never fully taken ownership of this holiday. Tellingly, there is no Day of the Dead Mass, but rather official celebrations of All Saints and All Souls days. The Church will also occasionally condemn Day of the Dead practices, especially the setting up of altars at home and in the cemetery—spaces outside of its control—as transgressions of official Catholic dogma (Brandes, 1998a).

Yet despite the fact that no one knows whether Day of the Dead is indigenous or Spanish, this matters little to the city. The city does not wake up on the Day of the Dead and obsess over the holiday's roots or worry if she is celebrating correctly. As in other sites around the country, on November 1 and

2, city residents put up altars in their homes, visit cemeteries to tend to the graves and leave offerings to the dead, and buy armfuls of *zempazochitl* flowers, candy skulls, and the ubiquitous Day of the Dead bread. The city also sponsors a unique poster contest (Cartelera de la Muerte) around this holiday, and these posters, created by local artists and art enthusiasts, are hung around the city *centro* in plazas and areas where there is much pedestrian transit. While they reinforce national subjectivity, they simultaneously manifest a local variation (the city's singularity) as, once again, identity is written out on the city body.

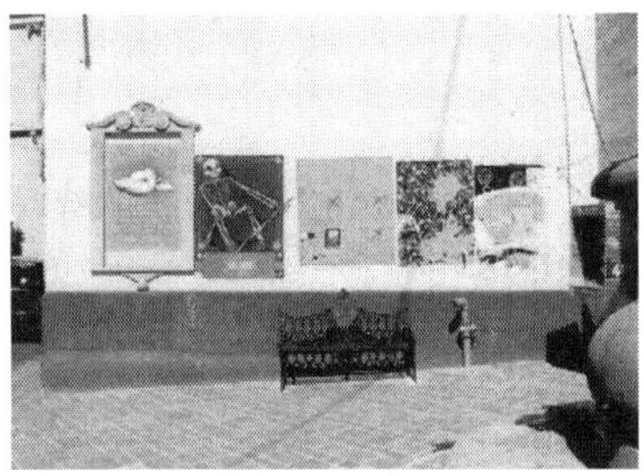

Local Day of the Dead poster contest

Day of the Dead is thus taken as a part of the self that is somewhat unknowable but still firmly of the self. The texts that result display no anxiety or crisis of subjectivity.

Into this comfortable not-knowing enters a foreign element, the American celebration of Halloween. Halloween, celebrated on October 31, is not new to Mexico, but Guanajuato has experienced the holiday more intensely in the last decade or so. Thanks to the influx of American students, tourists, media, and products, Halloween has "arrived," and the city finds herself needing to make sense of it within the Day of the Dead period and within her already overtaxed downtown space. Unlike what may occur in larger cities, here difference cannot be shuttled away to a remote foreigner neighborhood, nor can it be relegated to some other moment. What I see the city doing is working out a reconciliation of these two holidays—no matter how impure each one might be—through the act of writing. Instead of rejecting the foreign, as in the case of the FIC poster, she maintains her long-standing practices related to Day of the Dead while simultaneously opening herself to the other of Halloween, but—notably—without becoming the tourists' desire. She neither makes herself into the spectacle of Halloween nor stages an equally suspect spectacle of indigenous roots. This comes out clearly in her texts.

The first text she shares with me advertises a Noche de Disfraces, or "Costume Night." Nowhere does the word "Halloween" appear, and nowhere do references to Day of the Dead appear either. The festivity is assigned to night, which is not a temporal moment associated with Day of the Dead practice, and the images suggest only slightly scary images and fonts. The text may be read as a cautious approach to the foreign tradition, a first recognition of the other. The wavy text also says, importantly, "let your imagination fly," dress up as something else, inviting more play with subjectivity.

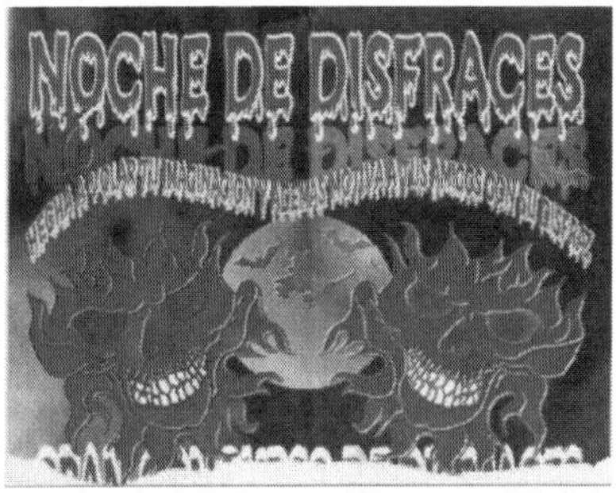

Noche de Disfraces (Costume Night)

Her second text (below) does much the same. It announces a Noche de Muertos, or "Night of the Dead." Once again, by moving the time to the night, the text invokes a separation (a reassuring of subjectivity) because it implies that daytime is for Day of the Dead, nighttime for Halloween. Space is invoked as well, albeit silently, as Day of the Dead is practiced in homes, in public plazas via large altars, and the poster contest, while Night of the Dead is encased within a bar, somewhat sectioned away from public view. However, the text does carve out a meeting point within language that relates both holidays by paralleling them through a renaming of Halloween as "Night of the Dead." This is, in effect, a sort of translation, designed to make the unfamiliar and unpronounceable into something more locally palatable. One could read this as welcoming and a slight step closer to the other than in the previous text.

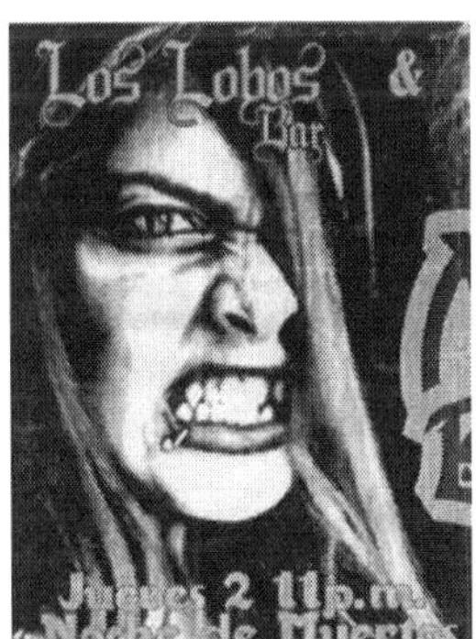

Noche de Muertos (Night of the Dead)

A subsequent text offers a Catholic, nonalcoholic Noche de Angeles, or "Night of Angels," which is odd, not only because the Catholic faith has nothing against alcohol (unlike some of the other "newer" Christian religions in town), but also because the dead are now made into angels, definitively doing away with the sort of horrific imagery that is suggestive of Halloween. It also adds in a subtle reminder from the Church that one's dead follow a Catholic path to the afterlife even if, in Mexico, they return once a year. Here, the Church, a bastion of local power and typically a proponent of the status quo, is working on its own response, which seems to constitute a dialogue with Day of the Dead, more than a rejection, and a nod toward the nighttime realm into which Halloween is inserting itself.

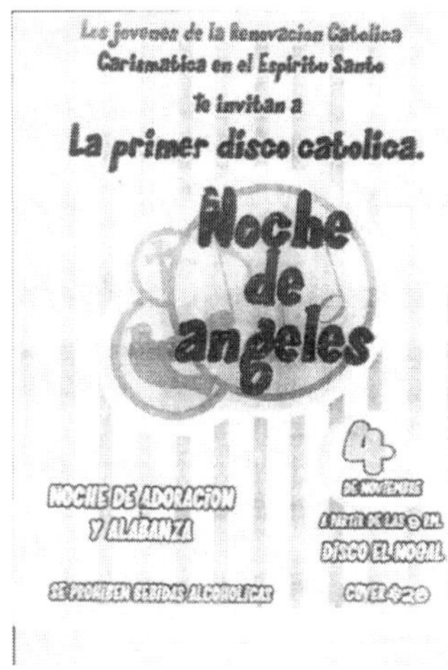

Noche de Angeles (Night of Angels)

At one point, the city writes a humorous protest against Halloween, one that ironically takes issue with the foreignness of the holiday yet employs a text-messaging style to communicate this discontent. This suggests that the city (rightly, in my opinion) conceives of opening to globalization and/or technology as something quite different than opening up to American culture, an important move given a general tendency in Mexico to confuse and conflate "American" with "global." The text translates as follows: Do you think that asking for sweets will make you happy? Did Hidalgo [the local priest-turned-insurgent and instigator of the Independence War] ask for sweets as a child? Do not accept foreign traditions."

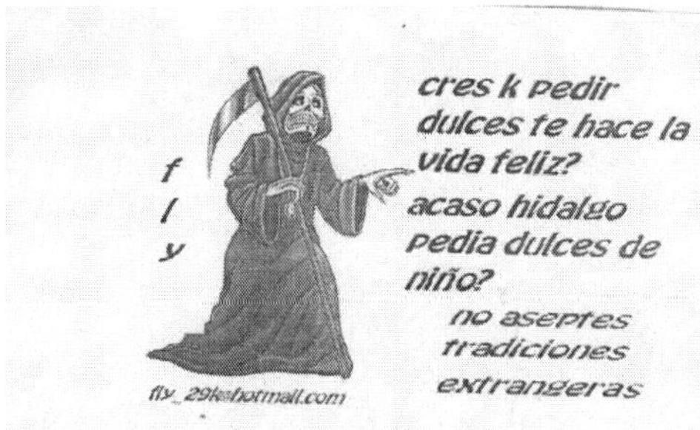

Do not accept foreign traditions …

This is open protest, creative and funny. And like everything else the city writes, nothing is black-and-white. The text employs an image of the Grim Reaper, which is more European than Mexican, and it is signed by someone using the English word "fly" in his or her email name (or perhaps the bar named Barfly), again a seeming contradiction, since it protests the foreign. Foreign language thus appears to be disassociated from foreign traditions. A simultaneous opening and closing that is difficult to take apart.

The city shows me a penultimate text in which she is able to directly address Halloween. This event is to be celebrated in a "lounge" and officiated by a DJ from Barcelona. An American holiday facilitated into Mexico by a Spanish narrator right in the center of the city? Spain explaining and facilitating the appearance of its replacement foreign other? Has the lost maternal returned to make amends? Has the city finally sublimated the separation, making the maternal Spain into "just another other" without the melancholic and narcissistic needs? The DJ is definitely Spain-as-other, Spain-as-contemporary, Spain as unfrozen from her colonial identity and deathly maternal hold on the city. This marks a long-awaited separation, and it is exceedingly different from what the city was writing in her nostalgic Don Quijote representations.

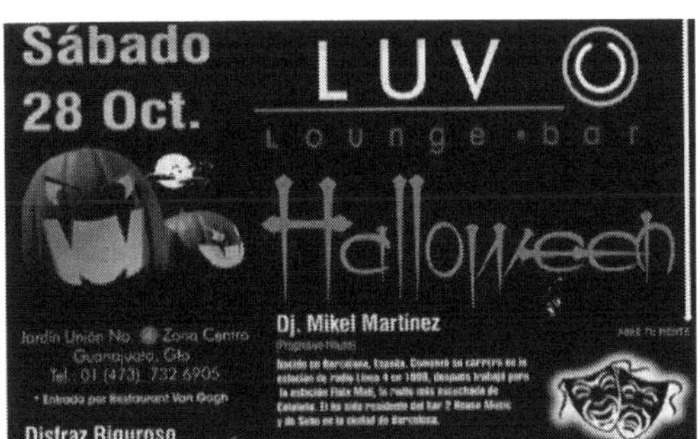

Halloween through a Barcelona DJ

As a set, the texts demonstrate that the city has begun drafting *multiple* possibilities in which the indigenous past, the Spanish present, and the American present all intermingle in the contact zone without causing any sort of nausea. This is quite an improvement from where the city began. However, it is her final text that offers the most intriguing and hopeful combination of all.

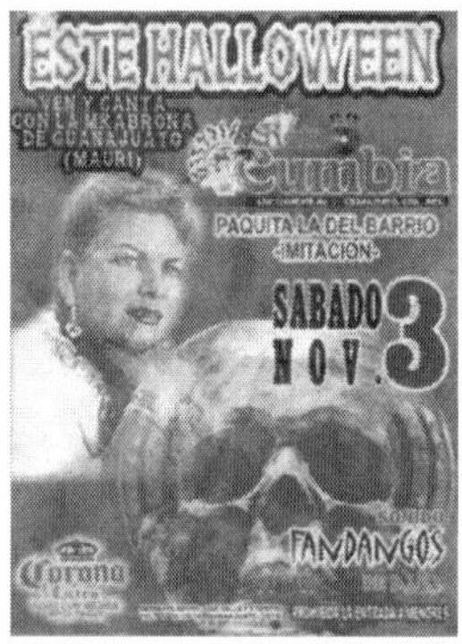

Paquita la del Barrio imitator

This flyer also addresses Halloween directly, advertising an event on November 3, a time that is past both Halloween and Day of the Dead (the future anterior?). The flyers can be seen as a tremendous parody of the spectacle, parody being one of Pratt's (1991) original "arts of the contact zone," of course. The city uses the spectacle to denounce the spectacle. At the same time, the text taken through a Kristevan lens will show that the city is also creating an in-between space, an open and heterogeneous text, a site into which she discharges her semiotic disposition (or through which she can sublimate her affects and drives into something communicable to others).

Let us first look at the many levels of in-between-ness and play that this text embodies. The text invites readers to "come and sing with the *m'kabrona*" (text-messaging version of *más cabrona*, the "most (female) son of a bitch," which in slang means "the best"). The singer is technically supposed to be Paquita la del Barrio, one of Mexico's most well-known *ranchero*-genre singers. However, the singer here is a transvestite imitator of Paquita, not the singer herself.[40] The event is being held at a *cumbia* bar: The *cumbia* is a song-dance genre of Columbian origins, and it is not a genre in which Paquita tends to sing. Next to the imitator's image glares a menacing pumpkin that looks more like a skull in some aspects (is this really Halloween

[40] Somewhat ironically, in mid-March 2010, Paquita made an openly denigrating remark about gays and adoption, which was a hot legal issue at that moment and which provoked strong reactions from the lesbian, gay, and transgender communities of both Mexico and the United States, i.e., from both the Day of the Dead and the Halloween practitioners.

or a lurking Day of the Dead symbol?). There is the Corona beer logo, which is, of course, a powerful symbol of Mexican identity. Finally, a local address is printed at the bottom.

What is authentic here? How are the self and other positions being staked out? In the text, the city has played with and confused musical genres, sexual identity, registers of language, and national identity symbols all at once—she has written something Kristeva might find Byzantine, although locally we would see this as more churrigueresque, the over-the-top baroque that permits flights of fancy. Everything in this text is exposed as polyvalent, "which unsettles naming and, by building up a plurality of connotations around the sign, affords the subject a chance to imagine the nonmeaning" (Kristeva, 1987, p. 97), to inscribe meaning where there was none, that is, to inscribe meaning into the spectacle.

The city is being multiple; she no longer needs to create exclusively perfect images of the colonial self, sealed and closed. Rather, she accepts her vulnerable heterogeneity; we find her "gay, varied and plentiful" as she moves through the Day of the Dead–Halloween texts that reach their full "flowering," as Kristeva describes Colette's work, in this final piece (2011, p. 224). No longer nauseous, she has transgressed. As Kristeva has promised, writing has become a resurrection, but within a representation that still provides room for change, just as Kristeva's texts are opaque and layered, leaving *her* room for more thinking. She states, "The end of the cure defuses passion, but by increasing the objects and discourses of passion; by doing away with a link (notably, that of transference) so as to make others possible" (p. 94). As we emerge from our transference bond and end the analytic process itself, I am convinced that the city will surely move on to find new objects, new discourses. She loves the Jumex homes, the opera, Day of the Dead and Halloween; she is loving and releasing her others in a constant cycle of renewal.

THE CITY AND KRISTEVA'S EMERGING DISCOURSE

Looking back upon all of the city's textual production considered within the intimacy of the consulting office, I see the city as having followed Kristeva's understandings of dispassionate motherhood and creativity quite closely. She moves from a narcissistic love (I am the perfect city of romance), to abjection (I cannot be grotesque, I reject the FIC poster), through mourning (I want to be/have Spain forever), to sublimated dispassion to rebirth (through Day of the Dead and Halloween and her experiments in art and music), passing through and resignifying maternal crises along the way as she creates Don Quijote images, bar flyers, and then harnesses her Virgins and T-shirt girl to move forward. Are we not seeing in the city's process simply a more vulnerable and exposed yet "normal" writing process, typical of any author? From the unspeakable, unrepresentable ideas in one's head to a first release, to extreme rejection and crisis (are these horrible drafts me or not-me?), to the difficulties of letting a piece of writing go out into public? Separating from one's work, as all writers know, brings up feelings of both loss and pleasure, but it ultimately frees up the writer for new subjects to study, new intellectual passions to work through in new sets of transference relationships. Isn't this what Kristeva ultimately hopes the traumatized Western subject will be able to do? Release his or her fixed notions of self in order to encounter the other on a much more ambivalent ground that allows both to lose and then rediscover themselves through their engagement? Sublimate passion (for a project or a person) in order to unceasingly take on new objects of love? To share and articulate our vulnerabilities for others?

My city-analysand has achieved something close to this. She is no longer divided between the different aspects of her subjectivity; she is in touch with her bodily self; she shows signs of making amends with the maternal elements; and she has located herself in the comfortable in-between of Kristeva's works, characters, and own self. By lightly moving between her passions—now literature, now art, now music—she gains a "gracious maturity and fresh vitality," avoiding both the 20th-century schizophrenia of the nation and the 21st-century fatigue so many of Kristeva's analysands complain of (Kristeva, 2011, p. 125). The city has at last accepted her own bisexual nature within the context of creativity. She is no longer the demure, asexual provincial city caught up in maternal issues and afraid of both her own body and others. She has reconnected with her body and is accepting others. From a discourse of *provincia* that emphasized interiority as stagnant, sacrificial maternity, asexuality, and closed-mindedness, we now have a *provincia* that offers its interiority as a passage to creativity, that sublimates instead of sacrifices, that embraces her body, senses, and desires, and that meets the vulnerable other from her own vulnerability. Viewed this way, the city upholds Kristeva's contention that creative work can provide a cure to our contemporary ailments and lead us out of the meaningless spectacle that now characterizes daily life:

> I would add that the more we work out/work through our signs (instead of throwing stones as in guerilla warfare, one would throw paint, as in a Pollock drip painting, or throw words out to one's analyst who would reconstruct their meaning), the more passion will be clarified without being extinguished. (2011, p. 94)

The small city would seem to agree. She has shown that the signs of self and other can be worked through and made into something extraordinary.

Nine

Conclusions

The Small City Succeeds Where the Global City Might Not

Whenever I finish a long-term treatment with an analysand, I feel a certain degree of ambivalence. On the one hand, of course, are the lingering doubts about whether we are truly finished. There is also a certain sense of mourning and loss. Like the dispassionate mother, the analyst too has to relinquish any sense of possession. I need to let this subject who was a part of me, part of my affective and intellectual life, move into her own symbolic world.

On the other hand, this analytic process has allowed me to witness a creative subject work her way out of the abyss, returning to herself and to others, which brings profound satisfaction. The city will surely lead a fuller life—a life that I will still follow in her as-yet-to-be-written future texts. Furthermore, her newfound independence is also my own in that I am pushed to new questions and new analysands . . .Before I put away these reflections upon the city's psychic voyages, however, I think about what to make of this most unusual analysand, a small but complex city.

In this book, I explored the question of how a provincial Mexican city inundated with others was working out her own subjectivity and coming to a partial and ongoing understanding of these others through text. Specifically, I wanted to know if a provincial city, othered as female within the national/Mexico City–dominated male, could speak disruptively from this position on the margin, a question that echoes Kristeva's own interrogation of women's subjectivity and the possibility of speaking disruptively within patriarchy. In order to study the city's subjectivity, I anthropomorphized her as embodied and female. I also posited her as a writer, an unusual choice, but one that afforded me a way to listen to her and to uncover some of the unconscious contents contained within (and sometimes spilling out from) her psyche.

What, then, can be said about this city I have spent time psychoanalyzing? This city whose body and writing I have explored, this city who holds me within much as I try to somehow contain her, however partially and temporarily, on paper? I offer the following tentative conclusions; like the city's infinite small plazas that constitute irregular openings in a maze of *callejón* complexity, these conclusions offer pauses in my own thinking, which are really only pauses from which to ask more questions about cities, about how to write our way to understandings of others, and about future "psycho-explorations" waiting to be undertaken …

THE CITY AS AN EAR

The city is an ear. She is listening respectfully to the others who are now embedded in both permanent and transitory ways into her own bodily center. Listening constitutes an essential prerequisite for any questioning and radical action to come. Geographer Sui notes a shift in the field away from visual understandings and metaphors toward "aurally evocative metaphors," noting that we find references now to conversation, dialogue, polyphony, dissonance, cacophony, letting data "speak," narratives, multivocality … (2000, p. 322). The city adds another voice to this claim. In my work, I thus found a city complexed with issues from the past and openly cautious about accepting too much otherness, a caution that results not only from previous experiences of others who abandoned her but also from contemporary knowledge of the harmful results that an overly touristic/otherized orientation can produce in Mexico's larger tourist destinations. She pauses, then, to listen. She listens first to her tradition, to history, and to the opinions of those who reside within. She may repress certain aspects of self that trouble her; however, she does not otherize her own self in the way that so many tourist sites tend to do. Furthermore, she listens to her bodily instincts—she listens to the collective memories written into and onto her body: the underground rivers, the tunnels, the mines, the painted colonial façades of her downtown. And unlike her megalopolis counterparts around the world, she still recognizes herself—she is not simply a collection of superficial images, but someone with flesh and blood. Someone with occasional grotesque elements that emerge next to the more idealized façade to keep her body alive and responsive. These elements surface in texts. In this sense, she is like "Colette the musician, who hears herself writing" (Kristeva, 2004, p. 204).

Uncannily, the city is also shaped like an ear. She has the same errant soft lines and wrinkles and is comprised of tunnels and channels that are at once both inside and outside the rest of the body. She is practically "made to listen," and certainly many weary urban nomads come here hoping to lean on the maternal body and whisper their fears and losses into her protecting ear. Of course, the introduction of foreign ideas and bodies into one's ear can produce vertigo. As so much otherness is drawn into the city ear, into her body, it is not surprising that she occasionally loses her balance and falters. But as Kristeva reminds us, "The ear is receptive to conflicts only if the body loses its footing" (1991, p. 17).

VIGILANT VERTIGO AS A STRATEGY

Vertigo runs through this book at many levels. I had to constantly rethink what is urban and how a place can be provincial and urban, provincial and global, at once. As the site and source of past silver wealth, is the present city really situated on the margins? How to name the unnamable spaces between center and periphery? Are the miners below or above? Black, Indian or *mestizo*? Part of the past or part of the present? And silver, is it material wealth or an ephemeral memory? Does Cervantes write Don Quijote and Sancho Panza, or do they write him? Is Spain the lost maternal or the paternal? During the vertigo of transference/countertransference processes, is the analyst the patient and the patient the analyst? Are we in Byzantium or Mexico? Is the Virgin of Guanajuato the repressed feminine or a radical figure of resistance? Is Day of the Dead indigenous or Spanish? What happens, of course, is that all of the binaries become productively confused. Everything is permanently out of place.

The city provides an argument in favor of a vigilant vertigo. Such a stance, unstable and wobbling as it may be, proclaims the advantages of entering into dialogue with the other: of listening to, writing, and loving the other even as this other shatters our sense of self and what we know. Frosh asserts,

> As long as the semiotic exists—which will be always, for the Symbolic would have no materials out of which to be constructed, were it not for the bodily drives rhythmically expressed in the semiotic register—there is a prospect for heterogeneity and disruption within every subject, male or female, and this prospect can always be glimpsed somewhere, whether in art, in language, in madness or in dreams. (1995, p. 303)

Through language in particular, the city has found a way to disrupt. Foucault, Martin, Gutman, and Hutton (1988) posit writing as a way to care for the self and to manage this vigilance, a thought echoed by Mexican feminist Sandra Lorenzano, who writes that "the blank page has the face of vertigo. There is perhaps no abyss more attractive and at the same time more terrifying" (2007, p. 371). This terrifying blank page, however, is not just the void; it is also psychic space. Once inscribed with symbolized affect, it will interrupt the spectacle. "Vertigo of identity, vertigo of words"—for the city, writing so much text both throws her off her balance and then restores a sense of self (Kristeva, 1987, p. 3). Her vertigo seems only fitting: As Kristeva commented in an interview, "I see the role of women as a sort of vigilance, a strangeness, as always to be on guard and contestatory" (Guberman, 1996, p. 45). The city is on guard, yet she permits herself to lose her footing and to be split, to not choose sides, to embrace her multiplicity. Accepting this allows for a rereading of Octavio Paz's infamous and somewhat reified notion of the "*rajada*."

RAJADA AS THE WAY TO BE

At various points in the book, I have evoked Octavio Paz's work as representative of the negative construction of Mexican femininity. Paz attributes woman's lack of subjectivity to "the misfortune of her 'open' anatomy" (1961, p. 38), which makes her weak and vulnerable. For Paz, this vulnerability is negative. He finds a solution in icons, which close off and protect women from their own opening. In the city, dominant discourses related to tourism and the UNESCO heritage status would similarly attempt to construct the virtuous provincial city as sacred and separate, by closing off and cleaning up her penetrable tunnels and plazas and by keeping the surface pristine. But like human women, the city is difficult to close off. She is multiply *rajada* (split); her mines and tunnels are open, the hills and curvy alleyways cut through her very center. Her body thus rejects any status quo attempt to preserve a smooth, sealed symbolic order.

Paz's key figure of the *rajada* woman is, of course, the traitorous La Malinche who opened herself to the other of Cortés and, perhaps, to her own desire. Mexican feminist Belausteguigoitia (2007) comments that Chicana feminists such as Norma Alarcón, Cherrie Moraga, and Ana Castillo (in *This Bridge Called My Back*) and Gloria Anzaldúa succeeded in reinventing La Malinche because migration allowed them to move into another space.[41] In response to Paz, Chicana scholars rewrote La Malinche into a feminist figure of hope and translation, a rewriting concerned less with "historical fidelity" and more with unveiling how Mexican women have been mistranslated by modernity, therefore *rajando* (cutting, disrupting) traditional imaginaries (Belausteguigoitia, 2007, pp. 206–207). Once again space emerges as central to rewriting. Belausteguigoitia notes wryly that most Mexican feminists do not embrace or understand Chicana work and that La Malinche has not been made into any sort of empowering image on this side of the border. She wonders, in a nation that silences so much, if it is necessary to leave to even attempt such rethinkings (p. 210)?[42]

[41] Key works include Alarcón's "Traddutora, traditora: A paradigmatic figure of Chicana feminism," *Cultural Critique* (Fall 1989), Moraga and Castillo's *This Bridge Called My Back* (1981), and Anzaldúa's *Borderlands/La Frontera: The New Mestiza* (1987).

[42] Jean Franco also underlines the importance of having left national space in this reconstruction of La Malinche by Chicana feminists. In her essay titled "La Malinche and the First World," she underlines the fact that La Malinche, like Oedipus, was thrown out of the kingdom, but the problem for women lies with the mother, not the father. She compares the "exogamous norm" with migration; it involves the question of separation from the maternal (2001, p. 214). Like Kristeva, she seems to be linking women and foreigners; with migration to the States, women become multiply other yet also gain the "perverse pleasure" of the foreigner and the "possibility of imagining and thinking" (Kristeva, 1991, pp. 13–14).

As this book has shown, the city has attempted rethinking within the very heart of national space, within that space constructed as most pure, feminine, sacred. Her female symbols have turned out to be anything but closed off! The Virgin of Guanajuato is the resistant female par excellence, complemented by the other figures also open to being resignified, also trying to become more human, also accepting their own desire. The Virgin of Guanajuato therefore stands in—accompanied by others; she is not "alone of her sex" (Kristeva, 1987, p. 261) — as a sign that the city can embrace her split nature and live a range of definitions of femininity. She interrupts Paz's traditional discourse about femininity and, in turn, about *provincia*.

Therefore, it is possible to answer Belausteguigoitia's question with a hopeful yes. Yes, it is possible within national space to challenge and rewrite Paz's widely accepted interpretation of La Malinche: For example, Mexican womanhood, with this local provincial potential, points to a female subjectivity that interrupts the national status quo without leaving national space. Her female body—multiple, open—enunciates a way forward via a return to the bodily self. For Paz, *rajada*—the split that he assigns to women—is rejected; being split is what men (or patriarchy-conscribed women) don't do. They are ordered not to open, not to be penetrated, not to sell out like women (and miners, and foreign companies, and tourists) who betray you. Unexpectedly, however, the city resists this. Her own ability to embrace internal otherness and to blur some of the categories of femaleness permits the suggestion that *rajada* is the way to be if one wants to stave off the Western crisis and keep representing. Furthermore, the city's posture supports the suggestion that *provincia* may be the ideal place for doing just this.

PROVINCIA AS A QUESTION—IN FAVOR OF SMALL CITIES

Provincia thus lives the split, the fold, and the vertigo that can result. Small cities now become, not an answer to a question posed by capitals and world metropolises (those global cities that so dominate scholarly analysis), but questions themselves. Small cities allow us to ask if these sites might not constitute the ideal points from which to launch semiotic and disruptive revolts in a world of alienation and spectacle. As I have attempted to show, the small city has unique experiences (psychic, bodily, and otherwise) of difference and therefore different possibilities for response than do megacities.

We know so little about small cities in theoretical terms, although many of us live in them. Bell and Jayne, editors of one of the few books specifically devoted to small cities, affirm that we don't have "wholly appropriate ways to understand what small cities are, what smallness and bigness mean, how small cities fit or don't fit into the 'new urban order,' or what their fortunes and fates might be" (2006, p. 2). Not only in Mexico, but undoubtedly in many sites around the postcolonial and even first world, small cities tend to be characterized as parochial, close-minded, slow to change, and with little of radical note. These projections may very well affect behavior, as small cities can either feel inadequate or superior, taking a "perverse pride" (as

Bell and Jayne, 2006, describe it) in being small. Certainly in the case of Latin America's *provincia*, this othering that small cities suffer comes from both the national and international levels, whether the small cities are sanctified or denigrated for their difference. Either way, they are stereotyped into rather frozen representations. But counted or discounted, taken as relevant or not, small cities are equally immersed in the Debordian spectacle, and they too constitute contemporary Western subjects prone to depression, anxiety, and the rest of Kristeva's "new maladies of the soul" alongside their global-city counterparts.

If my unique city-analysand shares some psychic aspects of smallness with other sites, she may be signaling that small cities constitute a rather perfect place from which to interrupt the spectacle. Postmodern sensibilities have told us that mega-urban cities have been reduced to worlds of surfaces, mirrors, and images so far removed from their original signifiers that they now have no connection to anything. Even though small sites are saturated with images, equally immersed in the technology that brings the images in, and subject to tourist desires and economic pressures, they are notably distinct in one important manner. Many of these images (and other-sensed texts, such as the foods, smells, and textures of a local site) are still body-specific. And small-city experiences of angst are still underwritten by a singular context of bodily, linguistic, historical, and contemporary affects that *they can still identify*. These inner resources—the bodily intimacy and knowledge of their own singularity—fortify small cities and point the way through the crises.

If all goes well, they can avoid becoming patrimony. Sjoholm reminds us that revolt is "necessarily prompted by pleasure, the enjoyment of the overcoming of sacrifice imposed by the socio-symbolic contract" (2005, p. 126). She also emphasizes that "the pleasure of the female body, defying castration, is the most radical form of subversion" (p. 90). Such a radical pleasure works to counteract the pressure the city feels to become patrimony, memory over body, a sacrifice in which the female-material becomes subjected to patriarchal regulation. In her work on silver in Guanajuato, Ferry (2005) emphasizes the key role this silver patrimony plays in local residents' source of self-esteem and economic well-being. I don't disagree; however, I wish to draw attention to the fact that, in this way of understanding and working through silver's desertion/exhaustion, the city body risks becoming transformed into words (memory) sold to tourists. By this I mean that her body could be turned into commodified space in which the nonprovincial other can return to his nostalgic maternal and salve his modern alienation. This risks making the city into Kristeva's generalized Western subject, who is

> no longer a subject but a patrimonial person, a person belonging to the patrimony, financially, genetically, and physiologically, a person barely free enough to use a remote control to choose his channel. (2002, p. 4)

McAfee expands: Kristeva's "patrimonial individual" is "so alienated from herself that she considers her body an inheritance (patrimony) that she might dispose of like any other inheritance" (2004, p. 111). This is what effectively could shut down the psychic life of this modern city-analysand. She is at risk of selling her body as if it were simply a container of material goods and tourist experiences. Commodifying her past, the city hovers at the edge of bccoming quite ironically—too modern, too global, perhaps too much a Santa Varvara.

Yet ... the city is not willing to be sacrificed and transformed into patrimony devoid of pleasure, imagination, and sensuality. Her own inner bodily myths and symbols align to whisper in the ear that she embodies small potentialities (Kristeva's "tiny revolts") for protest and rebellion. Furthermore, the very status as a UNESCO World Heritage site, shortened locally into *patrimonio cultural*, rests upon the criteria of "human creative genius."[43] This resonates directly with Kristeva's own centering of the imaginative genius in her trilogy on Klein, Arendt, and Colette. In essence, the city's bodily characteristics and symbols come together not to turn the city back to a female-maternal-nostalgic past that would essentially result in a death-wish, but rather to integrate the female and semiotic into the symbolic space of the city in a more balanced (psychically healthy) manner.

Small cities constitute intimate spaces, and they may be infinitely better positioned for the revolt Kristeva fears may be slipping from our collective Western grasp. Correspondingly, this book builds an argument in favor of the margin as an interesting and potentially powerful place from which to reexamine difference. The real question may indeed be the following: Can global urbanites remove their own need to make place into an icon, to freeze these "traditional" or "maternal" sites into something that will assuage their fears? Perhaps they would be better served to pay attention to how small cities are encountering others from a completely different position.

In short, Kristeva might find that the small city succeeds where the global city may not.

PSYCHOANALYSIS AND CITIES

Psychoanalysis has much to say about cities and, by extrapolation, about those who live in them. While this book constitutes the tiniest of efforts to bring the question of small-city subjectivity into the light, it also opens more questions than it answers. What might emerge in Kristevan analyses of other cities? What about a Lacanian or Kleinian analysis of Guanajuato? What about other marginal or provincial places with vastly different histories and geographies, both within and beyond Mexico? What about multilingual small cities? Would they have an extra skill useful for confronting otherness? What about small

[43] One of the stated UNESCO criteria for becoming part of the cultural patrimony program is that a site "represent a masterpiece of human creative genius." <http://whc.unesco.org/en/criteria> (11 Nov. 2007).

cities that might be figured as male? Gay? Buddhist or Jewish versus Catholic? How would they compare? And what about cities creating other sorts of text that might span from written texts to oral, musical, visual, and—why not?—tactile or gustatory? The psychoanalytical dimensions of studying text-producing cities working through the encounter between self and other certainly seem to call for further study. The question of how a city situates self and other within a world of complex, multiple, and mobile subjectivities is large indeed. A series of small-city studies might contribute a radically different perspective to cultural studies' existing perspectives on global cities and, perhaps, shine new light on strategies for resisting dominant discourses in a range of disciplines.

In *Murder in Byzantium*, Stephanie Delacour and Detective Rilsky find themselves in a comfortable companionship. Stephanie muses, "We were both in shock, and thus together, but differently, 'at home'" (Kristeva, 2006, p. 34). Isn't this what we are after as we search for ways to join others? Isn't this what, in *Strangers to Ourselves*, Kristeva meant by her call for "an ethics of respect for the irreconcilable" (1991, p. 182)? There is a local saying in the city that "*Todos los callejones llegan a la Plaza de la Paz* (All of the alleyways lead to the Plaza of Peace), the city's other central plaza. Do all roads return to origins, the original center? Our peaceful yet dynamic chora? Or do all roads, full of conflict as they must be, bring us to the jouissance of converging on the plaza with others involved in the same work? Studying small cities at least sets our alienated, jaded, Western selves on the path. In these twisting alleyways marked by returns, conflicts, unexpected texts, and exotic others whom we both love and hate, we must recur to language as a way to write our ways to more peaceful encounters with ourselves and our others.

THE RESEARCHER WRITES ON THE CITY

There is no closure. My city-analysand will continue to be a subject *en procès* and will wind through a never-ending pattern of quiet tension and revolt as she encounters others. And Julia Kristeva has not said her last word either.

At the end of the analytic process, I contributed text to the public city surface. In a celebration of 400 years since the Virgin of Guanajuato icon was brought to Guanajuato, my husband and I were invited along with other residents to purchase a gold disk onto which our names would be inscribed. These disks were sewed to a large shawl that was then draped over the Virgin on the occasion of her anniversary. The entire city was invited to come into the church and to walk under the shawl, which was extended from the Virgin to some structure behind her.

A final text from the analyst's notebook: As the line inches forward, we get closer to the Virgin. My name hangs on her body in a gold circle. The pious may believe that the past is once again being rewritten in a rote attempt to preserve the city's provincial identity or Catholic loyalties. But as I walk under the Virgin's blue robe inscribed with all of our names, I am tempted to wink at her. As women, as foreigners, and as writers, we both know better.

Epilogue

In the final months of editing, the violence in Mexico has reached levels previously unimaginable. As this book goes to press, the city of Guanajuato remains safe; however, it is impossible not to worry that the city's "issues" described here could suddenly be overwhelmed by the more tragically traumatic events that are affecting other cities around the country. If that were to happen, this book would quickly become a piece of nostalgia for the good old days when our greatest scandals and pleasures were defined by racy posters and unexpected opera performances. In a context where we are all increasingly and uneasily aware that everything could change, it is my strongest hope that this does not occur. This book is dedicated to all of Mexico's cities and their intense desire for peace.

About the Author

Karen Rodríguez is on the faculty in both the Visual Arts Department and the Postgraduate Program in the Arts at the Universidad de Guanajuato, Mexico. She is also the director of the CIEE Study Center in Guanajuato.

Bibliography

Aguayo-Quezada, S. (2002). *México en cifras*. Mexico City: Hechos Confiables S.A. de C.V. and Editorial Grijalba.

Aguilar Zamora, R., & Sánchez de Tagle, R. M. (2002). *De vetas, valles y veredas*. Guanajuato: Ediciones La Rana.

Ainslie, R. (2004). *Long Dark Road: Bill King and Murder in Jasper*. Austin: University of Texas Press.

Ainslie, R., & Brabeck, K. (2003). Race murder and community trauma: Psychoanalysis and ethnography in exploring the impact of the killing of James Byrd in Jasper, Texas. *Journal for the Psychoanalysis of Culture & Society*, 8, 42–50.

Alamán, L. (1849/2003). The siege of Guanajuato. In *The Mexico Reader*, G. Joseph & T. Henderson (Eds.), 171–188. Durham: Duke University Press.

Alcocer, A. (2002). *El Paseo de la Presa*. Morelia, Michoacán: Ediciones La Cañada.

Almond, I. (2007). *The New Orientalists: Postmodern Representations of Islam from Foucault to Baudrillard*. London: I. B. Tauris & Co.

Amati-Mehler, J., Argentieri, S., & Canestri, J. (1993). *The Babel of the Unconscious: Mother Tongue and Foreign Languages in the Psychoanalytic Dimension* (J. Whitelaw-Cucco, Trans.). Madison, CT: International Universities Press.

Annis, S. (1994). The museum as a symbolic staging ground. In *Museum Provision and Professionalism*, G. Kavanaugh (Ed.), 21–25. London and New York: Routledge.

Arroyo, F. (Ed.) (2006). *Ibargüengoitia a contrareloj*. Guanajuato: Congreso del Estado de Guanajuato.

Bakhtin, M. (1981). *The Dialogic Imagination*. M. Horquist (Ed.). (C. Emerson & M. Horquist, Trans.). Austin: University of Texas Press.

Bakhtin, M. (1984). *Rabelais and His World* (H. Iwolsky, Trans.). Bloomington: Indiana University Press.

Bakhtin, M. (1986). The problem of speech genres. In *Speech Genres and Other Late Essays*, M. M. Bakhtin, V. W. McGee, C. Emerson, & M. Holquist, 60–102. Austin: University of Texas Press.

Barthes, R. (1975). *The Pleasure of the Text*. New York: Hill and Wang.

Bartra, R. (1992). *The Cage of Melancholy: Identity and Metamorphosis in the Mexican Character* (C. J. Hall, Trans.). New Brunswick: Rutgers University Press. (Original work published 1987).

Bartra, R. (2002). *Anatomía del Mexicano*. Mexico City: Plaza y Janés.

Beardsworth, S. (2004). *Julia Kristeva: Psychoanalysis and Modernity*. Albany: SUNY Press.

Belau, L. (2006). Reading Kristeva and Beyond: Psychoanalysis as Textual Ethics. In *Textual Ethos Studies, or Locating Ethics,* A. Fahreaus & A. Jonsson (Eds.), 175–190. Amsterdam and New York: Rodopi.

Belausteguigoitia, M. (2007). Rajadas y alzadas: De Malinches a comandantes; Escenarios de construcción del sujeto femenino indígena. In *Miradas feministas sobre las mexicanas del siglo XX*, M. Lamas (Coord.), 191–236. Mexico City: FCE, Conacultura.

Bell, D., & Jayne, M. (2006). *Small Cities: Urban Experience Beyond the Metropolis*. Abingdon, UK, and New York: Routledge.

Berger, D. (2006). *The Development of Mexico's Tourism Industry: Pyramids by Day, Martinis by Night*. New York: Palgrave, Macmillan.
Bjelic, D. (2004). The Balkans and the "History of Shit." *Eurozine*. <http://www.eurozine.com/articles/2004-06-11-bjelic-en.html> (14 Apr. 2009).
Bjelic, D. (2008). Julia Kristeva: Exile and Geopolitics of the Balkans. *Slavic Review*, 67, 364–383.
Blanco, M. (1997). *El movimiento revolucionario en Guanajuato, 1910–1913*. Guanajuato: Ediciones La Rana.
Blanco, M., Parra, A., & Ruíz-Medrano, E. (2000). *Breve historia de Guanajuato*. Mexico City: El Colegio de México, Fideicomiso Historia de las Américas, and Fondo de Cultura Económica.
Bodin, H. (2011). Seeing Byzantium on the borders of narration, identity, space and time in Julia Kristeva's novel *Murder in Byzantium*. *Nordlit*, 24, 31–43.
Bonfil Batalla, G. (1987). *México profundo: Una civilización negada*. Mexico City: Grijalbo.
Braddock, J. (2004). Neurotic cities: Barnes in Philadelphia, *Art Journal*, 63, 46–61.
Bradley, A., & T. Hall (2006). The festival phenomena: Festivals, events and the promotion of small urban areas. In *Small Cities: Urban Experience Beyond the Metropolis*, D. Bell & M. Jayne (Eds.), 77–89. Abingdon, UK, and New York : Routledge.
Brandes, S. (1997). Sugar, colonialism, and death: On the origins of Mexico's Day of the Dead. *Comparative Studies in Society and History*, 39, 270–299.
Brandes, S. (1998a). The Day of the Dead, Halloween, and the quest for Mexican national identity. *Journal of American Folklore*, 111, 359–380.
Brandes, S. (1998b). Iconography in Mexico's Day of the Dead: Origins and meaning. *Ethnohistory*, 45, 181–218.
Britt-Arredondo, C. (2005). *Quixotism: Imaginative Denial of Spain's Loss of Empire*. Albany: SUNY Press.
Brooks, P. (1985). *Reading for Plot*. New York: Random.
Brooks, P. (1994). *Psychoanalysis and Storytelling*. Oxford, UK: Blackwell.
Broucek, F. (1991). *Shame and the Self*. New York: The Guilford Press.
Bruce-Novoa, J. (2005). Eroticism, counterculture, and Juan García Ponce. *CR: The New Centennial Review*, 5, 1–33.
Buhle, M. J. (1998). *Feminism and Its Discontents: A Century of Struggle With Psychoanalysis*. Cambridge, MA: Harvard University Press.
Butler, J. (1993). The body politics of Julia Kristeva. In *Ethics, Politics and Difference in Julia Kristeva's Writing*, K. Oliver (Ed.), 164–178. New York: Routledge.
Callard, F. (2003). The taming of psychoanalysis in geography. *Social and Cultural Geography*, 4, 295–312.
Campbell, J., & Harbord, J. (Eds.) (1998). *Psycho-politics and Cultural Desire*. London: UCL Press.
Cargill, K. (2006). Off the couch and onto the streets: Toward an ethnographic psychoanalysis. *Psychoanalysis, Culture and Society*, 11, 99–105.
Canselmo, J. A. (2003). *Terrorism and the Psychoanalytic Space: International Perspectives from Ground Zero*. New York: Pace University.
Cascardi, A. (1993). The archeology of desire in *Don Quixote*. In *Quixotic Desire: Psychoanalytic Perspectives on Cervantes*, R. El Saffar & D. de Armas Wilson (Eds.), 37–58. Ithaca and London: Cornell University Press.

Casella, R. (1999). Pedagogy as View Sequence: Popular Culture, Education, and Travel. *Anthropology and Education Quarterly*, 30, 187–209.

Chabot Davis, K. (2003). An ethnography of political identification: The Birmingham school meets psychoanalytic theory. *JPCS: Journal for the Psychoanalysis of Culture and Society*, 8, 3–11.

Cheetham, M., & Harvey, E. D. (2002). Obscure imaginings: Visual culture and the anatomy of caves. *Journal of Visual Culture*, 1, 105–126.

Chang, T. C. (2000). Theming cities, taming places: Insights from Singapore. *Geografiska Annaler*, 82, 35–54.

Cheng, A. (2001). *The Melancholy of Race: Psychoanalysis, Assimilation, and Hidden Grief*. New York and Oxford: Oxford University Press.

Coates, S. W., Rosenthal, J. L., & Schechter, D. S. (2003). *September 11: Trauma and Human Bonds*. Hillsdale, NJ: Analytic Press.

Collier, M. J. (2001). Constituting cultural difference through discourse: Current research themes of politics, perspectives, and problematics. In *Constituting Cultural Difference Through Discourse*, M. J. Collier (Ed.), 1–25. Thousand Oaks, CA: Sage.

Cornell, D. (2003). Autonomy re-imagined. *JPCS: Journal for the Psychoanalysis of Culture and Society*, 8, 144–149.

Cronin, M. (2000). *Across the Lines. Travel. Language. Translation*. Cork, Ireland: Cork University Press.

Crouch, D. (2005). Flirting with space: Tourism geography as sensuous/expressive practice. In *Seductions of Place: Geographical Perspectives on Globalization and Touristed Landscapes*, C. Cartier & A. A. Lew (Eds.), 23–25. London and New York: Routledge, 23–35.

Crouch, D., Aronsson, L., & Wahlstron, L. (2001). Tourist encounters. *Tourist Studies*, 1, 253–270.

Davis, C. (2002). Psychoanalysis, detection, and fiction: Julia Kristeva's detective novels. *French Studies and Co.*, 6, 294–306.

Davis, W. A. (2003). Death's dream kingdom: The American psyche after 9-11. *JPCS: Journal for the Psychoanalysis of Culture and Society*, 8, 128–132.

de Armas Wilson, D. (2000). *Cervantes, the Novel, and the New World*. Oxford and New York: Oxford University Press.

De Mauro, T. (1993). Introduction. In *The Babel of the Unconscious: Mother Tongue and Foreign Languages in the Psychoanalytic Dimension*, J. Amati-Mehler, S. Argentieri, & J. Canestri (J. Whitelaw-Cucco, Trans.), xv–xxviii. Madison, CT: International Universities Press.

Debord, G. (1994). *Spectacle Society* (D. Nicholson Smith, Trans.). New York: Zone Books. (Original work published 1967).

Debrix, F. (2005). Discourses of war, geographies of abjection: reading contemporary American ideologies of terror. *Third World Quarterly*, 26, 1157–1172.

Delgado-Wise, R., & Del Pozo-Mendoza, R. (2005) Mexicanization, privatization, and large mining capital in Mexico. *Latin American Perspectives*, 32, 65–86.

Denzin, N. K., & Giardina, M. D. (2007). *Contesting Empire, Globalizing Dissent: Cultural Studies After 9/11*. Boulder, CO: Paradigm Publishers.

Devisch, R. (2006). A psychoanalytic revisiting of fieldwork and intercultural borderlinking. *Social Analysis*, 50, 121–147

XVII Coloquio Cervantino Internacional. (2007). *Guanajuato en la geografía del Quijote*. Guanajuato: Gobierno del Estado de Guanajuato.

El Saffar, R., & de Armas Wilson, D. (1993). *Quixotic Desire: Psychoanalytic Perspectives on Cervantes*. Ithaca and London: Cornell University Press.

Eng, D., & Kazanjian, D. (2003). *Loss: The Politics of Mourning*. Berkeley: University of California Press.

Engle, K. (2007). Putting mourning to work: Making sense of 911. *Theory, Culture and Society*, 24, 61–88.

Ensler, E. (2001). *The Vagina Monologues*. New York: Villard.

Escosteguy, A. C. (2001). Cultural studies: A Latin-American narrative. *Media, Culture and Society*, 23, 861–873.

Farrar, M. (2000). Health and beauty in the body politic: Subjectivity and urban space. *Polity*, 33, 1–23.

Ferrer, E. (n.d.). Museo Iconográfico del Quijote. <http://museoiconografico.guanajuato.gob.mx/> (2 Feb. 2007).

Ferry, E. E. (2005). *Not Ours Alone*. New York: Columbia University Press.

Ferry, E. E. (2006). Memory as wealth, history as commerce: A changing economic landscape in Mexico. *Ethos*, 34, 297–324.

Fink, B. (2007). *Fundamentals of Psychoanalytic Technique: A Lacanian Approach for Practitioners*. New York and London: W. W. Norton.

Fink, B. (1999). *A Clinical Introduction to Lacanian Psychoanalysis*. Cambridge, MA, and London: Harvard University Press.

Forter, G., & Miller, P. A. (Eds.) (2008). *Desire of the Analysts: Psychoanalysis and Cultural Criticism*. Albany: SUNY Press.

Foucault, M. (1991). "What Is an Author?" In *Rethinking Popular Culture: Contemporary Perspectives in Cultural Studies*, C. Mukerji and M. Schudson (Eds.), 146–464. Berkeley: University of California Press.

Foucault, M. (2002). *The Order of Things* (Tavistock Publications, Trans.). London and New York: Routledge. (Original work published in 1996).

Foucault, M., Martin, L. H., Gutman, H., & Hutton, P. H. (1988). *Technologies of the Self: A Seminar with Michel Foucault*. Amherst: University of Massachusetts Press.

Franco, J. (2001). La Malinche y el primer mundo. In *La Malinche, sus padres y sus hijos*, M. Glantz (Coord.), 201–218. Mexico City: Taurus.

Frey, H. (2001). La Malinche y el desorden amoroso novohispano. In *La Malinche, sus padres y sus hijos*, M. Glantz (Coord.), 251–256. Mexico City: Taurus.

Freud, S. (1918). *Totem and Taboo: Resemblances Between the Psychic Lives of Savages and Neurotics*. New York: A. A. Brill, Moffat, Yard.

Freud, S. (1919). The uncanny. <http://www-rohan.sdsu.edu/~amtower/uncanny.html> (20 Sept. 2006).

Freud, S. (1922). Medusa's head. <http://www.cc.utah.edu/~sgs0889/laugh3.html> (2 July 2007).

Freud, S. (1927). Fetishism. In *Standard Edition of the Complete Psychological Works of Sigmund Freud, 21*, J Stachey (Ed.), 152–157. New York: W. W. Norton.

Freud, S., Strachey, J., & Gay, P. (1989). *The future of an illusion*. New York: W. W. Norton.

Fromm, E., & Maccoby, M. (1970). *Social Character in a Mexican Village: A Sociopsychoanalytic Study*. Englewood Cliffs, NJ: Prentice-Hall.

Fromm, M. G., & Smith, B. L. (Eds.). (1989). *The Facilitating Environment: Clinical Applications of Winnicott's Theory*. Madison, CT: International Universities Press.

Frosh, S. (1995). Time, space and otherness. In *Mapping the Subject: Geographies of Cultural Transformation*, S. Pile & N. J. Thrift (Eds.), 289–308. London and New York: Routledge.

Frosh, S. (1997). *For and Against Freud*. London and New York: Routledge.

Gallo, R. (2002). Can there be revolt without representation? In *Revolt, She Said*, J. Kristeva & P. Petit (Eds.), 117–133. Los Angeles: Semiotext(e).

Gallo, R. (2004). *The Mexico City Reader*. Madison: University of Wisconsin Press.

Gálvez-Jiménez, M. L. (1995). *Celaya: sus raíces africanas*. Guanajauato: Ediciones La Rana.

Gamío, M. (1916). *Forjando patria*. Mexico City: Editorial Porrúa.

Gandy, M. (1999). The Paris sewers and the rationalization of urban space. *Transactions of the Institute of British Geographers*, 24, 23–44.

Garcia Canclini, N. (1995). Mexico: Cultural globalization in a disintegrating city. *American Ethnologist*, 22, 743–755.

García Canclini, N. (1997). El malestar en los estudios culturales. *Fractal,* 2, 45–60.

Garrett-Petts, W. F. (2005). *The Small Cities Book: On the Cultural Future of Small Cities*. Vancouver: New Star Books.

Gay, P. (Ed.) (1989). *The Freud Reader*. New York: W.W. Norton.

Gee, P. (1999). *An Introduction to Discourse Analysis, Theory and Method*. London and New York: Routledge.

Giménez, G. (1999). La investigación cultural en México. *Perfiles Latinoamericanos,* 15, 119–138. <http://cenedic.ucol.mx/ccmc-construccion/recursos/6929.pdf> (17 Sept. 2006).

Gliserman, M. (1996). *Psychoanalysis, Language, and the Body of the Text*. Gainesville: University Press of Florida.

Goh, R. B. H., & Yeoh, B. S. A. (Eds.) (2003). *Theorizing the Southeast Asian City as Text:Urban Landscapes, Cultural Documents, and Interpretive Experiences*. New Jersey, London, Singapore, Hong Kong: World Scientific.

Goss, J. (2005). The souvenir and sacrifice in the tourist model of consumption. In *Seductions of Place: Geographical Perspectives on Globalization and Touristed Landscapes*, C. Cartier and A. A. Lew (Eds.), 56–71. London and New York: Routledge.

Goldstein, W. N., & Goldberg, S. T. (2004). *Using the Transference in Psychotherapy*. Lanham, MD: Jason Aronson.

Gómez, L. (2005). *The Freud Wars: An Introduction to the Philosophy of Psychoanalysis*. London and New York: Routledge.

Grant, J., & Crawley, J. (2002). *Transference and Projection: Mirrors to the Self.* Buckingham and Philadelphia: Open University Press.

Grant, M. (1997). Dressing up a Self: Fashion and Kristeva's "Subject in Process." *Melbourne Journal of Politics,* 24, 124.

Greaney, M. (2008). Violence and the sacred in the fiction of Julia Kristeva. *Theology Sexuality*, 14, 293–304.

Grinberg, L., & Rodríguez, J. F. (1993). Cervantes as cultural ancestor of Freud. In *Quixotic Desire: Psychoanalytic Perspectives on Cervantes*, R. El Saffar & D. de Armas Wilson (Eds.), 23–36. Ithaca and London: Cornell University Press.

Grolnick, S. (1993). How to do Winnicottian therapy. In *In One's Bones: The Clinical Genius of Winnicott*, D. Goldman (Ed.), 185–211. Northvale, NJ: Jason Aronson.

Grosz, E. (1998). Bodies/Cities. In *Places Through the Body*, H. Nast & S. Pile (Eds.). London: Routledge, 42–51.

Grosz, E. (2001). *Architecture from the Outside: Essays on Real and Virtual Spaces*. Cambridge, MA: MIT Press.

Gruzinski, S. (2001). *Images at War* (H. MacLean, Trans.). Durham and London: Duke University Press.

Gruzinksi, S. (2002). *The Mestizo Mind: The Intellectual Dynamics of Colonization and Globalization* (D. Dusinberre, Trans.). New York and London: Routledge.

Grzegorczyk, M. (2005). *Private Topographies: Space, Subjectivity, and Political Change in Modern Latin America*. New York: Palgrave Macmillan.

Guberman, R. M. (Ed.) (1996). *Julia Kristeva Interviews*. New York: Columbia University Press.

Guilfoyle, M. (2007). Grounding a critical psychoanalysis in frameworks of power. *Theory Psychology*, 17, 563–585.

Gutmann, M. (1996). *The Meanings of Macho: Being a Man in Mexico City*. Berkeley and Los Angeles: University of California Press.

Haigh, S. (2006). Migration and Melancholia: In Kristeva's 'Depression Nationale' to Pineau's 'Maladie de L'Exile.' *French Studies*, 60, 232–250.

Hall, J. S. (2004). *Roadblocks on the Journey of Psychotherapy*. Lanham, MD: Jason Aronson.

Hamner, G. (2002). A private happiness for all; or, How to cure national depression, hold down a career, fulfill the maternal function and still wage feminist battle with a smile. A review of Julia Kristeva, *Revolt, She Said* and Julia Kristeva and Catherine Clément, *The Feminine and the Sacred*.<http://www.jcrt.org/archives/04.1/hamner.shtml> (2 Feb. 2008).

Harari, R., & Moncayo, R. (1997). Principles of Lacanian clinical practice. *Anamorphosis*, 1, 13–28.

Hattori, T. (1998). Psycholinguistic Orientalism in criticism of *The Woman Warrior* and *Obasan*. In *Other Sisterhoods: Literary Theory and US Women of Color*, K. Stanley (Ed.), 119–138. Urbana: University of Illinois Press.

Herbert, D. T., & Thomas, C. J. (1997). *Cities in Space: Cities as Place*. London: David Fulton Publishers.

Herrera-Canales, I. (1998). *La minería mexicana de la colonia al siglo XX*. Mexico City: Instituto Mora, El Colegio de Michoacán, El Colegio de México, and Instituto de Investigaciones Históricas UNAM.

Hinshelwood, R. D. (1994). *Clinical Klein: From Theory to Practice*. New York: Basic Books.

Hind, E. (2004). *Provincia* in recent Mexican cinema, 1989–2004. *Discourse*, 26, 26–45.

Holland, N. (1990). *Psychoanalytic Psychology and Literature-and-Psychology*. New York and Oxford: Oxford University Press.

Holland, N. (1998). *The Mind and the Book: A Long Look at Psychoanalytic Literary Criticism*. Paper given at the Freud at the Millennium Conference held in connection with the opening of the Freud: Culture and Conflict exhibit at the Library of Congress, Georgetown University, Washington, DC, 15–16 Oct. <http://www.clas.ufl.edu/users/nnh/mindbook.htm> (4 Aug. 2007).

Holmes, C. (2005). *The Paradox of Countertransference: You and Me, Here and Now*. Houndsmills, Basingstoke, and Hampshire, NY: Palgrave.

Huitfeldt Midttun, B. (2006). Crossing the borders: An interview with Julia Kristeva. *Hypatia*, 21, 164–177.

Ibargüengoitia, J. (1975). *Estas ruinas que ves.* Mexico City: Editorial Joaquín Mortiz.

Ibargüengoitia, J. (1979) "Memorias de novelas." *Vuelta.* <www.letraslibras.org>.

INEGI (Instituto Nacional de Estadística y Geografía). (2004). <http://www.inegi.gob.mx/est/contenidos/espanol/rutinas/ept.asp?t=mpo> (2 Oct. 2008).

Ironstone-Catterall, P. (2005). Postcard from NYC 2004: Democracy, psychoanalysis, and trauma. *Space and Culture*, 8, 332–336.

Jardine, A. (1993). Opaque texts and transparent contexts. In *Ethics, Politics and Difference in Julia Kristeva's Writing*, K. Oliver (Ed.), 23–40. New York: Routledge.

Jaúregui de Cervantes, A. Día de la Cueva. <http://www.guanajuatocapital.com/espanol/Dcueva.htm> (4 May 2007).

Johnson, C. (1993). Cervantes and the Unconscious. In *Quixotic Desire: Psychoanalytic Perspectives on Cervantes*, R. El Saffar & D. de Armas Wilson (Eds.), 81–90. Ithaca and London: Cornell University Press.

Jucovy, M. E. (1992). Psychoanalytic contributions to Holocaust studies. *The International Journal of Psycho-analysis*, 73, 267–282.

Kristeva, J. (1977). *About Chinese Women* (A. Barrows, Trans). New York: Urizen Books. (Original work published 1974).

Kristeva, J. (1980). *Desire in Language: A Semiotic Approach to Literature and Art.* (T. Gora, A. Jardine, & L. Roudiez, Trans.). New York: Columbia University Press.

Kristeva, J. (1982). *Powers of Horror: An Essay on Abjection* (L. Roudiez, Trans.). New York: Columbia University Press. (Original work published 1980).

Kristeva, J. (1987). *Tales of Love* (L. Roudiez, Trans.). New York: Columbia University Press. (Original work published 1983).

Kristeva, J. (1989). *Black Sun: Depression and Melancholy* (L. Roudiez, Trans.). New York: Columbia University Press. (Original work published 1987).

Kristeva, J. (1991). *Strangers to Ourselves* (L. Roudiez, Trans.). New York: Columbia University Press. (Original work published 1989).

Kristeva, J. (1992). *The Samurai: A Novel* (B. Bray, Trans.). New York, Columbia University Press. (Original work published 1990).

Kristeva, J. (1994). *The Old Man and the Wolves* (B. Bray, Trans.). New York: Columbia University Press. (Original work published 1991).

Kristeva, J. (1995). *New Maladies of the Soul* (R. Guberman, Trans.). New York: Columbia University Press. (Original work published 1993).

Kristeva, J. (1998). *Possessions: A Novel* (B. Bray, Trans.). New York: Columbia University Press. (Original work published 1996).

Kristeva, J. (2000a). *The Sense and Non-Sense of Revolt* (J. Herman, Trans.). The Powers and Limits of Psychoanalysis. New York: Columbia University Press. (Original work published 1996).

Kristeva, J. (2000b). Bulgaria, my Suffering. In *Crisis of the European Subject* (S. Fairfield, Trans.), 163-183. New York: The Other Press. (Original essay published 1995).

Kristeva, J. (2001). *Hannah Arendt: Life Is a Narrative* (F. Collins, Trans.). Toronto: University of Toronto Press, 2001. (Original work published 1999).

Kristeva, J. (2002). *Intimate Revolt* (J. Herman, Trans.). New York: Columbia University Press. (Original work published 1997).

Kristeva, J. (2004). *Melanie Klein* (R. Guberman, Trans.). New York: Columbia University Press. (Original work published 2000).

Kristeva, J. (2004). *Colette* (J. M. Todd, Trans.). New York: Columbia University Press. (Original work published 2002).

Kristeva, J. (2006). *Murder in Byzantium* (C. Jon Delogu, Trans.). New York: Columbia University Press. (Original work published 2004).

Kristeva, J. (2011). *Hatred and Forgiveness* (J. Herman, Trans.). New York: Columbia University Press. (Original work published 2006).

Kristeva, J., & Malcomson, S. L. (1993). Foreign body. *Transition*, 59, 172–183.

Kristeva, J., & Petit, P. (2002). *Revolt, She Said* (B. O'Keefe, Trans.). Los Angeles: Semiotext(e). (Original work published 1998).

LaCapra, D. (1994). *Representing the Holocaust*. Ithaca: Cornell University Press.

Lamas, M., & Bissell, S. (2000). Abortion and politics in Mexico: "Context is All." *Reproductive Health Matters*, 8, 10–23.

Lamas, M. (2007). Las putas honestas, ayer y hoy. In *Miradas feministas sobre las mexicanas del siglo XX.*, M. Lamas (Coord.), 312–346. Mexico City: FCE, Conacultura.

Landry, R., & Bourhis, R. Y. (1997). Linguistic landscape and ethnolinguistic vitality: An empirical study. *Journal of Language and Social Psychology*, 16, 23–49.

Langan, R. (2000). Someplace in mind. *International Forum on Psychoanalysis*, 9, 69–75.

Leach, N. (2003). 9/11. *Diacritics*, 33, 3–4, 75–92.

Leddy Phelan, J. (1956). México y lo Mexicano. *The Hispanic American Historical Review*, 36, 309–318.

Leonard, I. A. (1992). *Books of the Brave: Being an Account of Books and of Men in the Spanish Conquest and Settlement of the Sixteenth-Century New World.* Berkeley: University of California Press.

Lomnitz, C. (2001). *Deep Mexico, Silent Mexico: An Anthropology of Nationalism.* Minneapolis and London: University of Minnesota Press.

Lorenzano, S. (2007). Hay que inventarnos: Mujer y narrativa en el siglo XX. In *Miradas feministas sobre las mexicanas del siglo XX*, M. Lamas (Coord.), 349–385. Mexico City: FCE, Conacultura.

Lowe, L. (1993). Des Chinoises: Orientalism, psychoanalysis, and feminine writing. In *Ethics, Politics and Difference in Julia Kristeva's Writing*, K. Oliver (Ed.), 150–163. New York: Routledge.

Low, S. (1996a). The anthropology of cities: Imagining and theorizing the city. *Annual Review of Anthropology*, 25, 383–409.

Lutz, C., & Collins, M. J. (1994). The photograph as an intersection of gazes: The example of national geographic. In *Visualizing Theory*, L. Taylor (Ed.), 363–384. New York: Routledge.

Maccoby, M. (1967). On Mexican national character. *Annals of the American Academy of Political and Social Science*, 370, 6–73.

MacLeod, N. E. (2006). The placeless festival: Identity and place in the post-modern festival. In *Festivals Tourism, and Social Change: Remaking Worlds*, D. Ricard & M. Robinson (Eds.), 222–237. Clevendon and Buffalo: Channel View Publications.

Margaroni, M. (2009). Julia Kristeva's chiasmatic journeys. In *Psychoanalysis, Aesthetics and Politics in the Work of Julia Kristeva*, K. Oliver (Ed.), 107–126. Albany: SUNY Press.

Marks-Tarlow, T. (1995). The fractal geometry of human nature. In *Chaos Theory in Psychology and the Life Sciences*, R. Robinson & A. Combs (Eds.), 275–284. Mahwah, NJ, and Hove, UK: Lawrence Erlbaum Associates, Inc.

Markotic, L. (2001). There where primary narcissism was, I must become: The inception of the ego in Andreas-Salomé, Lacan, and Kristeva. *American Imago*, 58, 813–836.

Maroda, K. J. (2004). *The Power of Countertransference: Innovations in Analytic Technique*. 2nd edition. Hillsdale, NJ, and London: The Analytic Press.

Marshall, K. (2000). Termination of an "infinite conversation": Reflections on the last days of an analysis. *Psychoanalytic Dialogues*, 10, 931–947.

Martín-Torres, E. (2001). *El beneficio de la plata en Guanajuato* 1686–1740. Guanajuato: Presidencia Municipal de Guanajuato.

Massey, D. B. (1994). *Space, Place, and Gender*. Minneapolis: University of Minnesota Press.

Mastrangelo Bové, C. (1984). Review: The politics of desire in Julia Kristeva. *Boundary*, 2, 217–228.

Mastrangelo Bové, C. (2006). *Language and Politics in Julia Kristeva: Literature, Art, Therapy*. Albany: SUNY Press.

McAfee, N. (2004). *Julia Kristeva*. New York and London: Routledge.

McCarthy, C. (2002). Toward a definition of interiority. *Space & Culture*, 8, 112–125.

McWilliams, N. (1994). *Psychoanalytic Diagnose: Understanding Personality Structure in the Clinical Process*. New York: Guilford Press.

McWilliams, N. (1999). *Psychoanalytic Case Formulation*. New York: Guilford Press.

McWilliams, N. (2004). *Psychoanalytic Psychotherapy: A Practitioner's Guide*. New York: Guilford Press.

Mendoza, M. L. (2007). La fermosura de Don Quijote en tierras guanajuatenses. In *XVII Coloquio Cervantino Internacional: Don Quijote en la Capital Cervantina de América*, 231-240. Guanajuato: Gobierno del Estado de Guanajuato.

Messinger Cyprus, S. (1991). *La Malinche in Mexican Literature: From History to Myth*. Austin: University of Texas Press.

Meyer Cosio, F. (1993). *El final del Porfirismo en Guanajuato*. Guanajuato: Gobierno del Estado de Guanajuato.

Molino, A. (2004). Introduction: Rethinking relations between psychoanalysis and anthropology. In *Culture, Subject, Psyche. Dialogues in Psychoanalysis and Anthropology*, A. Molino (Ed.), 20–42. Middletown: Wesleyan University Press.

Molino, A. (Ed.). (2004). *Culture, Subject, Psyche. Dialogues in Psychoanalysis and Anthropology*. Middletown: Wesleyan University Press.

Nast, H., & Pile, S. (Eds.) (1998). *Places Through the Body*. London: Routledge.

Newcomer, D. (2002). The symbolic battleground: The culture of modernization in 1940s León, Guanajuato. *Mexican Studies/Estudios Mexicanos*, 18, 61–100.

Nuñez, F., Arvizu, C., & Abonce, R. (2007). *Space and Place in the Mexican Landscape: The Evolution of a Colonial City*. College Station: Texas A & M University Press.

Nuttini, H. (2004). *The Mexican Aristocracy, 1910–2000*. Austin: University of Texas Press.

Ogden, T. (2005). *Projective Identification and Psychotherapeutic Technique*. London: Karnac.

O'Grady, K. (2002). The tower and the chalice: Julia Kristeva and the story of Santa Barbara. *Feminist Theology*, 29, 40–60.

Oliver, K. (1993a). *Reading Kristeva. Unraveling the Double-bind*. Bloomington: Indiana University Press.

Oliver, K. (Ed.) (1993b). *Ethics, Politics and Difference in Julia Kristeva's Writing*. New York: Routledge.
Palacios, L. (2006). Cuévano, una ciudad literaria. In *Ibargüengoitia a contrareloj*, F. Arroyo (Ed.), 121–140. Guanajuato: Congreso del Estado de Guanajuato.
Pallasmaa, J. (2005) *Eyes of the Skin*. Chichester: Wiley-Academy; Hoboken, NJ: John Wiley & Sons.
Paz, O. (1961). *The Labyrinth of Solitude* (L. Kemp, Trans.). New York and London: Grove Press and Evergreen Books, Ltd. (Original work published 1950).
Pile, S. (1996). *The Body and the City: Psychoanalysis, Space, and Subjectivity*. London and New York: Routledge.
Pile, S. (2005). *Real Cities: Modernity, Space and the Phantasmagorias of City Life*. London: Sage.
Pile, S., & Thrift, N. J. (1995). *Mapping the subject: geographies of cultural transformation*. London and New York: Routledge.
Pinder, D. (2005). Arts of urban exploration. *cultural geographies*, 12, 383–411.
Pratt, M. L. (1991). The arts of the contact zone. *Profession*, 91, 33–40.
Prieto, R. (2000). *Body of Writing: Figuring Desire in Spanish American Literature*. Durham and London: Duke University Press.
Quinn, B. (2000). Whose festival? Whose place? An insight into the production of cultural meanings in arts festivals as visitor attractions. In *Expressions of Culture, Identity and Meaning in Tourism*, M. Robison (Ed.), 263–273. Sunderland: Centre for Travel and Tourism in association with Business Education Publishers.
Rama, A. (1996). *The Lettered City* (J. C. Chasteen, Trans.). Durham and London: Duke University Press.
Ramos, S. (1934). *El perfil del hombre y la cultura en México*. Mexico City: Colección Austral.
Ramírez, S. (1957/1977). La organización familiar. In *El mexicano, psicología de sus motivaciones*, 119–126. Mexico City: Grijalbo.
Ramírez, S. (1961/1977). Expresiones psicológicas en la plástica de dos pintores mexicanos. In *El mexicano, psicología de sus motivaciones*, 147–168. Mexico City: Grijalbo.
Relke, D. M. A. (1993). Foremothers who cared: Paula Heimann, Margarita Little and the female tradition in psychoanalysis. *Feminism and Psychology*, 3, 89–109.
Rendell, J., Penner, B., & Borden, I. (2000). *Gender Space Architecture: An Interdisciplinary Introduction*. London: Routledge.
Renik, O., & Spillus, E. B. (2004). Intersubjectivity in psychoanalysis. *The International Journal of Psycho-analysis*, 85, 1053–1064.
Ricard, D., & Robinson, M. (Eds.). (2006). *Festivals Tourism, and Social Change: Remaking Worlds*. Clevendon and Buffalo: Channel View Publications.
Rice, A. (2002). Forgiveness: An interview. *PMLA*, 117, 278–295.
Rionda Arreguin, I. (1985). *Brevísima historia de la ciudad de Guanajuato*. Guanajuato: Centro de Investigaciones Humanísticas.
Rodríguez, K. (2009). *Dentro y fuera/Inside and Out: An Erotics of Public Space*. (B. Valdivia, Trans.). Morelia, Mexico: Azafrán y Cinabrio Press.
Rose, G. (2001). *Visual Methodologies: An Introduction to the Interpretation of Visual Materials*. London: Sage.
Rose, J. (1993). Julia Kristeva—Take two. In *Ethics, Politics and Difference in Julia Kristeva's Writing*, K. Oliver (Ed.), 41–61. New York: Routledge.

Roselli, J. (1994). Opera as a social occasion. In *The Oxford Illustrated History of Opera*, R. Parker (Ed.), 450–482. Oxford and New York: Oxford University Press.

Roudiez, L. (1980) Introduction to the translation. In *Desire in Language*, J. Kristeva, 1–20. New York: Columbia University Press.

Sánchez Valle, M. (2005). *Los minerales de Marfil y Valenciana: Guía histórica de Guanajuato*. Guanajuato: Ediciones la Rana.

Saragoza, A. (2001). The selling of Mexico: Tourism and the state, 1929–1952. In *Fragments of a Golden Age: The Politics of Culture in Mexico Since 1940*, G. Joseph, A. Rubenstein, & E. Zolov (Eds.), 91–115. Durham and London: Duke University Press.

Schultz, K. (1994). In defense of Narcissus: Lou Andreas-Salomé and Julia Kristeva. *German Quarterly*, 67, 185–196.

Segal, H. (1981). *The Work of Hanna Segal: Kleinian Approach to Clinical Practice*. New York: Jason Aronson.

Sennett, R. (1994). *Flesh and Stone: The Body and the City in Western Civilization*. New York: W. W. Norton.

Shumar, W. (2004). Shadow dialogues: on the (early) history of anthropology and psychoanalysis. In *Culture, Subject, Psyche. Dialogues in Psychoanalysis and Anthropology*, A. Molino (Ed.), 3–15. Middletown: Wesleyan University Press.

Sjoholm, C. (2005). *Kristeva and the Political*. London and New York: Routledge.

Spivak, G. C. (1981). French feminism in an international frame. *Yale French Studies*, 62, 154–184.

Stein, A. (1999). Well-tempered bagatelles: A meditation on listening in psychoanalysis and music. *American Imago*, 56, 387–416.

Stein, H. (2003). *Beneath the Crust of Culture: Psychoanalytic Anthropology and the Cultural Unconscious*. Amsterdam and New York: Rodopi.

Steinhem, G. (2001). Foreword. In *The Vagina Monologues*, E. Ensler, ix–xix. New York: Villard.

Strenger, C. (2002). *The Quest for Voice in Contemporary Psychoanalysis*. Madison, CT: International University Press.

Sui, D. Z. (2000). Visuality, aurality, and shifting metaphors of geographical thought in the late twentieth century. *Annals of the Association of American Geographers*, 90, 322–343.

Swartz, S. (2006). The third voice: Writing case-notes. *Feminism and Psychology*, 16, 427–444.

Tenorio, M. (2001). El indigenista. In *Mitos mexicanos*, E. Florescano (Coord.), 339–349. Mexico City: Taurus.

Todorov, T. (1982). *The Conquest of America: The Question of the Other* (R. Howard, Trans.). New York: Harper and Row Publishers.

Torija, J., & Olmos Fuentes, J. (1998). Leyendas y relatos de Guanajuato: Prodigios y maravillas. Reprinted in *Prodigios y maravillas de Guanajuato: Leyendas y relatos*. Guanajuato. Guanajuato: Ulyses Editorial.

Ulyses Editorial (2005). *Don Quijote en Guanajuato: Antología del Coloquio Cervantino*. IV Centenario del Quijote. Guanajuato: Gobierno del Estado de Guanajuato.

UNESCO (1987). World Heritage List. <http://whc.unesco.org/archive/advisory_body_evaluation/482.pdf> (23 Mar. 2008).

Uranga, E. (1952). *Análisis del ser mexicano*. Mexico City: Porrúa y Obregón.
Urry. J. (2002) *The Tourist Gaze*. 2nd edition. London, and Thousand Oaks, CA: Sage. (Original work published 1990).
Valdivia, B. (2006). La falsa realidad, o *Estas ruinas que ves*. In *Ibargüengoitia a contrareloj*, F. Arroyo (Ed.), 121–140. Guanajuato: Congreso del Estado de Guanajuato.
Valsiner, J. (2001). The first six Years: Culture's adventures in psychology. *Culture and Psychology*, 7, 5–48.
van Zyl, S. (2003). The creature on the couch versus the citizen on the street. *JPCS: Journal for the Psychoanalysis of Culture and Society*, 8, 88–98.
Velázquez, M. E. (2007). *La huella negra en Guanajuato: Retratos de afrodescendientes de los siglos XIX y XX.* Guanajuato: Ediciones La Rana.
Waterman, S. (1998). Carnivals for elites? The cultural politics of art festivals. *Progress in Human Geography*, 22, 54–74.
Zaldívar, M. L. L. (n.d.). Día de Dolores. <http://www.guanajuatocapital.com/espanol/Ddolores.htm> (6 Dec. 2007)
Zea, L. (1952). *Conciencia y posibilidad del mexicano*. México: Porrúa y Obregón.

Index